1 MONTH OF
FREE
READING

at

www.ForgottenBooks.com

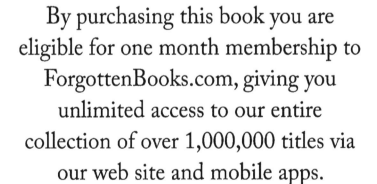

By purchasing this book you are eligible for one month membership to ForgottenBooks.com, giving you unlimited access to our entire collection of over 1,000,000 titles via our web site and mobile apps.

To claim your free month visit:

www.forgottenbooks.com/free37393

ISBN 978-0-332-69817-5
PIBN 10037393

G. Wright
160

Debary ;   IV, $\overline{II}$, 48

197 -24

197 - 98
198 - 200
200 - 06
203 - 24

TEN MORE
PLAYS OF SHAKESPEARE

BY

STOPFORD A. BROOKE

LONDON
CONSTABLE AND COMPANY LTD.
1913

TEN MORE PLAYS OF SHAKESPEARE

CONTENTS

MUCH ADO ABOUT NOTHING

Much Ado About Nothing is the first of those three enchanting comedies which, stars of the first magnitude, form in Shakespeare's sky a separate and brilliant constellation. The other two plays, in the order of their birth, are *As You Like It* and *Twelfth Night*. Two years—1599, 1600—saw their glory rise and shine.

The story of Hero and Claudio (an island of tragic sorrow circled in this play by gay and glancing tides of comedy) is taken from an Italian source, from a novel of Bandello, or from Ariosto's version of the same tale in the *Orlando Furioso*, both of which Shakespeare, if he did not read Italian, could have found, one in a French and the other in an English translation. The brightness, joyousness, and wit which, in the persons of Benedick and Beatrice, play round this sad tale, and which in the end strengthen its sadness into happiness, are Shakespeare's own invention; and so is the lower comedy of Dogberry and Verges, which, blundering through their stupidity into humour for the audience, is set into pleasant contrast with the native wit and clear intellect of Benedick and Beatrice. What is sad in the play is from Italy: what is gay is from Shakespeare.

Nevertheless Benedick and Beatrice, though invented in England, are Italian in nature rather than English. The Prince (though he be Spanish), Claudio, Antonio, Leonato, Hero, and her maids, breathe the air of Italy, and are steeped in that Italian life with which Shake-

A

speare was so well acquainted. No one, even now, can continuously read the host of tales from Boccaccio onwards, in which the novel-writers of Italy recorded the life of Italy, without a more profound knowledge of that life than history will ever teach him; or without being so permeated with its spirit that to live in it would seem to him easy, and to write of it (if he had a touch of genius) equally easy. Shakespeare had done this. Like all those who read at all in London, he had read a host of translated Italian tales, and their Italian spirit is in all the characters of *Much Ado About Nothing*. In sentiment, in morals, in evil and good passions, in its high honour and villainy, in its scenery, pageantry, and love of war, the play is Italian. When, then, Shakespeare, penetrated with this Italian atmosphere, created Benedick and Beatrice, they also became, in his moulding hands, as Italian as the rest, even more Italian. They have the Italian wit, wit for its own sake, rejoicing in itself—Tuscan wit rather than Sicilian—with here and there a Fescennine touch. A seriousness emerging now and then in the midst of its brilliancy, and characteristically Italian, divides it from French wit; and when the events of the play turn towards tragedy, this seriousness gains the upper hand with both Beatrice and Benedick. Those deep sources of grave feeling (which in the Italian nature underlie its easy gaiety) rise to the surface in the dark and sorrowful hours of the play, and rule and dignify the action of Beatrice and Benedick. The dazzling lightness of their wit slips away from them for the time. With serious, with almost sombre steadfastness, they meet the heavy trial which tests their insight and their strength. Moreover, it is when these solemn passions rise in Benedick and Beatrice, that their love, at first so lightly felt, is changed. In the atmosphere of the high emotions of pity and indignation which they feel for the fate of Hero, their love grows into a deep and weighty passion. For the noble emotions, felt and acting for the sake of others, lift the more personal emotions up to their own loftier level.

These then are Italian; but Dogberry, Verges, and the watch are English; true but comic sketches of Shakespeare's London. Their jokes are English, their self-conceit is English, their ponderous incapacity is that of the·English small tradesman, their names, like that of neighbour Seacole, are English. Verges sounds odd, but it comes from verjuice, and is the name of a usurer in an ancient manuscript, 'Father Verges.' Dogberry might be now found in Whitechapel. Yet, English as they are, they fit in very well with the rest, so great was the amalgamating force of Shakespeare. No shock tells us that they are not of the same race as Leonato and Antonio, or that they are strangers and foreigners in the streets of Messina.

Considered as a drama, this play has scarcely any plot; but it is none the worse for that. Elaborate plots are mostly wearisome in serious comedy. An elaborate plot entangles its action, which ought to be simple; and encroaches on the characterisation, which ought to be manifold, subtle, and complex. In this play the plot is so simple that it could be detailed in three minutes, but the characterisation is extraordinarily minute, intertwined, vivid, incessantly varied, delicately felt along every fibre, and alive with thought. It is on this, and not on plot, that the interest of the drama depends. What the characters think and feel, not the story, is the play. A number of little events, scarcely recognised as we read, push on the action, and call from moment to moment on the intellectual eye to follow them. They are only a background for the characters as they grow up into a firmer and closer reality.

The scenery is less marked than it is in *Twelfth Night* or in *As You Like It*. It is of a palazzo and a garden, with pleached alleys, arbours, and an orchard; and the rest is placed in a church and the streets of Messina.

Of late, it has been (like many other Shakespeare plays) made into a most spectacular affair, and this is a great mistake. When dances and elaborate pageantry and fanciful additions are crowded into it, the spectacle devours the drama; the soul of Shakespeare seems to fly out of the words, the inter-play of the characters tends to be swamped, their thought and passion to be overlaid; and we say to · ourselves—'How much better it were could I but read this play at home in a pleasant twilight.'

Again, if we miss in this play, as some do, the involutions of such a plot as we have in the *Merchant of Venice*, we are more than dramatically satisfied by its vivid presentation of human life. Characters of many kinds (each delightfully varied) open hour by hour before us; they move in and out of one another as swiftly, as interchangingly, as trout in a stream. Their thoughts are quicker than their changes. They are thrilling with youth and gaiety, with the serious passions of love, wrath, envy, indignation, sorrow, patience, friendship, audacious hope, excelling joy—even with the passion of death.

In a quick succession of scenes, by day, by night, in the castle, the villa, and the streets of the city, in the masquerade, in the church, we are borne, in vital agitation, along the stream of human life. Not even in *Twelfth Night* or in *As You Like It* is the livingness of life more living; not even in these is Shakespeare's power of creation greater. And Beatrice and Benedick are the quintessence, the centre of this life. They receive it; reflect it brighter than they received it; but they radiate more of it than either they receive or reflect.

One dark character is the blackness which sets off the

brightness of the play. Don John, the bastard brother of
the Prince, has no redeeming quality. When Shakespeare
made a bad man, he generally was stern enough to make
him villainously bad. He knew that evil, when it was
nourished, gave birth to more and more of evil, till it consumed itself. The fate of evil is to be done to death by
its own venom, perhaps by its own children, so naturally
moral is the Universe. Don John, soured by his bastardry,
has cherished envy as his sweetheart, and the snake that
lives in it has so poisoned his soul, that he belies an innocent girl only because he wishes to feed the snake he loves.
He has sinned against the Prince, his brother, and is now
forgiven and favoured by him. He hates his brother, and
Claudio his brother's friend, because of their kindness and
forgiveness.

> I had rather be a canker in a hedge, than a rose in his grace ; . . .
> I am a plain-dealing villain. I am trusted with a muzzle, and en-
> franchised with a clog ; therefore I have decreed not to sing in my cage.
> If I had my mouth I would bite.

When he hears of the marriage of Claudio, he hopes it will
enable him to hurt those his envy hates.

> Will it serve for any model to build mischief on ? . . . That young
> start-up hath all the glory of my overthrow : if I can cross him any
> way, I bless myself every way. . . . Let us to the great supper. . . .
> Would the cook were of my mind !

> Any bar, any cross, any impediment [he is speaking of the marriage]
> will be medicinable to me : I am sick in displeasure to him ; and what-
> soever comes athwart his affection ranges evenly with mine.

And he devises with his bravo Borachio that the Prince
and Claudio shall hear Margaret, in the shape of Hero, talk
with Borachio out of a window as if she were his mistress.
So the treacherous dog slays, for all he knows, an innocent
sweet girl—a very flower of youth and beauty. What is
the use of him ? some say. Why, to make the story out
of which the play is woven; to make the little plot which

is to be happily ended. He comes in just to do that; and when the mischievous knot he has tied is undone, he slips away to Naples, and no one ever thinks of him again till the last two lines of the play. Shakespeare does not like the villain to escape, as the villain so often does in real life. He does, on the whole, make a point of poetic justice. And Don John is seized and punished when the fun is over.

What too, say others, is the use of Dogberry and Verges? They are an excrescence on the play. No, indeed; they are the means whereby the evil is unravelled, whereby tragedy is turned into comedy, and sorrow into joy. And if Shakespeare chose to untie the trouble by a fantastic means which enabled him to make us happy with laughter, and yet to like the old fools who cause our laughter, why should he not? He is no less but more the dramatist for that. And the world has been all the pleasanter.

The characters are, for the most part, disposed in twos —Antonio and Leonato, the Prince and Claudio, Dogberry and Verges, Hero and Ursula, Borachio and Conrad, Benedick and Beatrice. Each of these doublets represents a single type, and the type (being set forth in two forms with individual differences) is all the more fully represented. The Prince and Claudio image the young nobles of the time. War is their business and pleasure, love their relaxation, incessant chaff their conversation. They are never serious except on the point of honour. On that they are as sensitive and fretful as a porcupine. They are capable of real friendship and, when in arms, of brotherhood. The one point where Benedick touches their type closely is in this strength of friendship. When Beatrice cries 'Kill Claudio,' he answers, 'Not for the wide world.' Their type is clear, and Shakespeare knew a hundred examples of it.

Leonato and Antonio represent the typical old men of

whom Shakespeare made so many studies. Here, the men are both weak from senility, but retain the hot temper of their youth. They differ only as two apples differ; but Antonio is a more decayed apple than Leonato. Their old age makes a good contrast to the youth of the Prince and Claudio. This contrast is admirably wrought out in the scene where they challenge Claudio for a villain. Each of them does it differently. Shakespeare, though he keeps the sameness of the type, differentiates the individuality of the men. Dramatic change, dramatic work for the actor—he never fails in both !

Even Borachio and Conrad, types of the mercenary bravos who attended on the fine gentlemen of the time for what plunder they could get—even these, while their type is identical, are differentiated. Each has his own character—and each, for the actor, a different part to play. So have Dogberry and Verges, though they belong to the same type, and to the same class. Verges is Dogberry's echo, but he is also something more, and this ought to be made clear on the stage. The custom is to make Verges very old, and Dogberry a middle-aged man. Were I to stage the play, I would make them of the same age. One would feel then (more strongly than one does when Verges is made a doddering old man) the difference between the two men, and yet the sameness of their type. Dogberry's masterfulness would then be more prominent, and so would his conceit and his ignorance. The contrast then would be not of age and middle-age, but of character and character.

As to Hero and Ursula, they have been brought up together in the same conventional circle of social life. They think and feel the same way, and look on life through the same eyes. The only difference between them is made by the difference in rank, and by the maid observing that difference in relation to her mistress. But their minds have grown together into harmony. And the likeness is so great, that Shakespeare felt it necessary to represent in another character the type of the waiting-maid which Ursula ceased to present clearly when she grew into Hero's likeness. Therefore he placed along with this couple who had become one, Margaret, the gamesome lady's-maid, who is risquée in her talk with her mistress, and has Borachio as a lover—so anxious is Shakespeare for variety of character and of life.

Quite different from these conventional types are Benedick and Beatrice. There were, in any society of the time, a host of men like Claudio or Leonato, a multitude of women like Hero. But there were not half à dozen men like Benedick, or women like Beatrice. By dint of originality, of intellect, of a high sense of honour, and of a nobler passionateness than the rest, they stand alone in the midst of the action which seems to whirl round and round them, to touch only the outside of them. They take their part in their world, but there is a region in their soul into which that world cannot enter, which it does not understand. No one can class Benedick with the Prince or Claudio, or Beatrice with Hero and Ursula. Yet these two, like the other doublets, are of a similar type of character. Their difference is only that made by the difference of sex. They are both fully conscious of their originality, of the cleverness, even afterwards of the depth of character, which separate them from the rest. They own no master, no influence, save their own self-mastery, self-influence. Their wit is of a similar kind, and both of them rejoice in it, cherish it, are vain of it, and excite it to battle. When they love, their passion runs on similar lines; and alike in seriousness when it grows deep, is also alike, when the serious matter is past, in its power to spring into gaiety in a moment and to laugh at itself. Their last battle of wits, before they marry, is an excellent example of this. Then their brightness of speech, their audacious pleasure in life, out of which grows their excellent good sense and their power to handle affairs, are also similar. If a star danced when Beatrice was born, another star danced close at hand when Benedick was born. All this similarity is differentiated by the difference of sex, and Shakespeare marks that at every point. The type is the same, but the woman presents it one way, the man in another.

The isolation of these two from the rest, and their similarity, inevitably draw them together. Yet, at the beginning, they are sharply in opposition. Each of them, proud (the one of his wit, the other of her wit), plays for conquest, and neither of them sees that it is because they are so like one another that they are antagonistic. They touch and sparks fly, but the more they touch the closer they grow ; and the sparks have a natural affinity. Their original disharmony arises out of a real harmony of character, and when the Prince's trick is played upon them, it reveals to them their mutual sympathy. Therefore they love one another easily. Therefore they think and feel together on affairs outside of themselves. Of all the characters, the friar excepted, they alone believe in Hero's innocence.

Were they in love before the play opens? That question has been put. I answer that they were only interested in one another. Beatrice says she will have nothing to do with a man, Benedick that he will have nothing to do with a woman. This is wonderfully foolish if they wish to be apart. Their statement, common to both, forces them to think of one another. The misanthropist and the misogynist when they meet must interest one another. They are fated, I may say, to love one another in order that Nature may be avenged on their violation of her first command. Benedick admires the beauty of Beatrice, but hates her tongue. She increases his abhorrence of women. That is fatal; there is often nothing so near love as the ignorant aversion which forces a man to think of a woman, and to isolate her in his imagination—but then, it is not love yet. Beatrice asks after him at once, and pounces on him the moment he appears. So far it is plain she is interested in him. But she likes him now only as a stalking-horse for her wit. Of course, she gets the better of him. Not only is her wit brighter and quicker, though less intelligent, than his, but she has the advantage of knowing that courtesy will not allow the man to be as sharp as she is. Benedick is a gentleman, and his answers are restrained by that. Beatrice takes this advantage, and, since the advantage is unfair, she is often carried away beyond good manners, over-excited by her own wit. When he is silent through courtesy, she lays on her whip more vigorously. There is no love in that; and Benedick, revolted at last, flies when he hears her in the distance. That also is not love, but, for the moment, actual distaste. Nor is the talk of Beatrice concerning Benedick with the Prince and Leonato, or that of Benedick concerning Beatrice with the Prince and Claudio, such talk as latent lovers would use. It is nothing but mockery, not one touch of underlying sentiment. Moreover, their general conversation is uninterrupted brilliancy —flash after flash of cold-cut jewellery. When they are really in love, their talk is altogether different. Shakespeare marks the change so plainly that the theory that they are in love at the beginning of the play falls to pieces. After the scene in the garden, their wit is traversed by silent moods, by dreaming, by a pretence of not being well. Until the very last scene, they have no pleasure in fencing with one another. Love has sheathed their swords.

Once more, had their interest in one another at the beginning even a touch of love in it, it were not necessary for Hero or the Prince to lay on so very thick, in the garden scene, the painting of the love of Beatrice for Benedick, of Benedick for Beatrice. No; conceive them as interested in one another, and no more, when the play begins.

There is one more remark to make upon this play as a whole. Less of the passion of love exists in it than in any other of Shakespeare's comedies. Claudio's love for Hero is plainly of a flimsy character, the light love of a soldier for a gentle girl—light enough to suffer that the Prince should take her away from him, to make him prefer to his love of Hero the favour of the Prince. Hero has no intense affection (like Rosalind or Viola) for Claudio. She marries Claudio because her people wish it. Benedick and Beatrice do not become deeply in love till the scene in the church is over, when they see into the strength of character they both possess.

In accord with this, there is less of the lovelier elements of poetry in this play than in the other comedies. In a pure comedy, it is love which makes the poetry beautiful and impassioned; and Shakespeare, having shut out of this subject any intensely felt love, has also shut out of it those beautiful passages which he has sown broadcast over *As You Like It* and *Twelfth Night*. It is natural this should be so. He is always within the limits of Nature when he had attained, as in these comedies, to his matured power.

In the first scene the matter of the play is introduced and prepared; the characters which events are to develop are clearly sketched, and isolated, each in his own individuality. Beatrice and Benedick take at once their prominent place. The contest of their wits begins. They

both declare their horror of marriage, and we are prepared for the amusing conversion which is to follow.
That sketch is made.

Then Claudio professes his love for Hero; we see his
heart, and the Prince declares he will help him to Hero.
It is not much of a heart, but his love-speech is pretty
enough. It is that of a young noble of the time to whom
war and glory and adventure were more than love :—

> O, my lord,
> When you went onward on this ended action,
> I look'd upon her with a soldier's eye,
> That liked, but had a rougher task in hand
> Than to drive liking to the name of love :
> But now I am return'd, and that war-thoughts
> Have left their places vacant, in their rooms
> Come thronging soft and delicate desires,
> All prompting me how fair young Hero is,
> Saying, I liked her ere I went to wars.

That sketch is made.

Then in the second scene with Don John and his
bravos the treason which is to trouble all this pleasant
life is also sketched. And the outline of the whole play
is before us when the Act closes. All is clear for the
evolution of the drama.

The beginning of the second Act is the Masquerade.
In it all the characters are expanded. Benedick and
Beatrice are set into still sharper antagonism in order to
heighten the fun of the stratagem which is to bring them
together. She gets the better of him again, and the
natural vanity of a man, especially of one who feels that
he is superior to the crowd, is so much hurt that his
relief in finding afterwards (as he thinks) that Beatrice
has been all the time in love with him, makes him love
her all the more. To have a sore place healed by the
person who made it sore is a great incentive to affection.
But now, he frets and fumes, and, alone with the men,

lets loose his hurt vanity on Beatrice, with so much wit
that half the bitterness is done away with. We laugh
with him, but we do not laugh at Beatrice. He lets it be
seen that she has been victorious; and Beatrice herself,
conscious of that pleasing element in his speech, would
have felt flattered rather than hurt.

> O she misused me past the endurance of a block! an oak but with
> one green leaf on it would have answered her; my very visor began
> to assume life, and scold with her. . . . She speaks poniards, and every
> word stabs: if her breath were as terrible as her terminations, there
> were no living near her: she would infect to the north star. I would
> not marry her though she were endowed with all that Adam had left
> him before he transgressed: she would have made Hercules have turned
> spit; yea, and have cleft his club to make the fire too . . . all
> disquiet, horror, and perturbation follow her.

So much then is added to his character—a little fret of
vanity dwells with his wit. It is not an unpleasant
vanity. He can laugh at it himself, and he does. He is
not one inch less a man for it, nor does it interfere with
his honesty of purpose or with his good sense. And now
another trait is added to his character. He hears that
the Prince, who has promised to help Claudio to Hero,
now woos her for himself. At this, his sense of honour,
which is deep, is offended; and he tells Claudio what he
has heard. Claudio, to whom the favour of the Prince is
more than Hero's love, takes this betrayal too easily for
a lover. But Benedick does not; he lets the Prince know
plainly that his conduct has been dishonest to friendship and to his word, and is heartily glad when he finds
he has been mistaken. In this way, the serious element
in Benedick's gay character is made by Shakespeare to
emerge. We begin to see what he will be when trial and
trouble come, when Beatrice needs a solid man on whom
to lean.

Beatrice also develops into something higher. She
comes in with Hero and Claudio, and is delighted with her

cousin's happiness. We have only met her, as yet, as a
sharp-tongued lady. Now we see her affectionate heart.
She does not betray one touch of sarcasm in this scene.
She is only gay and loving. 'Cousins, God give you joy,'
she cries out of a full heart, and we forget her biting
speech. The central waters of her life are merry, but not
shallow. 'In faith, lady,' says the Prince, 'you have a
merry heart.' And her light talk with him, when she
refuses to marry him, is as pleasant from its good sense
as it is from its quickness of wit. 'No, my lord,' she
says, 'I will not have you, unless I had another for
working days: your Grace is too costly to wear every
day.' She leaves the scene, but leaves the atmosphere of
her affectionate gaiety behind her. It has quickened the
wits of the Prince, and he proposes the merry labour of
bringing Signor Benedick and the Lady Beatrice into 'a
mountain of affection the one for the other.' She were
'an excellent wife for Benedick, and he is of a noble
strain of approved valour and of confirmed honesty.'

With this commendation, which raises Benedick into a
higher place in our thoughts, and with a new and better
opinion of the character of Beatrice, the scene closes. How
slowly, how carefully Shakespeare builds up his fine
characters!

Every one knows the double scene in the garden when
Benedick and Beatrice are befooled into the seriousness of
love. Surely, along with the befooling of Malvolio in such
another garden of pleached alleys, arbours, and orchards
(the gardens so resemble each other that I fancy Shakespeare drew them from one he knew), there is no finer or
more delightful piece of comedy, so gay, with a touch of
seriousness behind it; so good-natured, so graceful, and
with so right an end in view. In order to make it more
dramatic Benedick is seen at first alone, and declares in a
soliloquy that freedom of his from the snares and love of

women, which the next quarter of an hour is to enslave for ever. He protests so much that I wonder if Shakespeare did not mean us to think that Beatrice had now crept into his imagination. For the first time he seems to think marriage a possibility.

I do much wonder that one man, seeing how much another man is a fool when he dedicates his behaviours to love, will, after he hath laughed at such shallow follies in others, become the argument of his own scorn by falling in love : and such a man is Claudio. I have known when there was no music with him but the drum and fife ; and now had he rather hear the tabor and the pipe : I have known when he would have walked ten mile afoot to see a good armour ; and now will he lie ten nights awake, carving the fashion of a new doublet. He was wont to speak plain and to the purpose, like an honest man and a soldier ; and now is he turned orthography ; his words are a very fantastical banquet,—just so many strange dishes. May I be so converted, and see with these eyes ? I cannot tell ; I think not : I will not be sworn but love may transform me to an oyster ; but I 'll take my oath on it, till he have made an oyster of me, he shall never make me such a fool. One woman is fair ; yet I am well : another is wise ; yet I am well : another virtuous ; yet I am well : but till all graces be in one woman one woman shall not come in my grace. Rich she shall be, that 's certain ; wise, or I 'll none ; virtuous, or I 'll never cheapen her ; fair, or I 'll never look on her ; mild, or come not near me ; noble, or not I for an angel ; of good discourse, an excellent musician, and her hair shall be of what colour it please God. Ha ! the Prince and Monsieur Love ! I will hide me in the arbour.

Then—he hears of the terrible depth and passion of Beatrice's love for him, and it does not occur to him (since the white-bearded fellow speaks it) that the story is incredible. It is his natural vanity which deceives him so very easily, and perhaps his wonder—of which indeed we have heard—that Beatrice, alone of women, should not like him. His phrase

Is 't possible ?   Sits the wind in that corner ?

is delicious. The over-stating of Beatrice's love—her weeping, sobbing, beating her heart, tearing her hair, praying, cursing—

O sweet Benedick ! God give me patience,

makes the scene more amusing. That Beatrice should do this is incredible; that Benedick should believe it (were not vanity unfathomable) seems still more incredible. His speech, when it is all over, especially the naïve vanity of the beginning, is quite enchanting. Then, his vanity, which is only on the surface of this honest-hearted man, is forgotten in the rising of his love. He discounts all the mockery which will be lavished on him. What is it to him if he loves the woman and the woman loves him? I am I, and let the world go hang. It is a delightful soliloquy. Here is the beginning of it—

> This can be no trick: the conference was sadly borne. They have the truth of this from Hero. They seem to pity the lady: it seems her affections have their full bent. Love me! why, it must be requited. I hear how I am censured: they say I will bear myself proudly, if I perceive the love come from her: they say too, that she will rather die than give any sign of affection. . . .

The same net is set for Beatrice, and the result is similar. But what a difference between her speech and that of Benedick! There is no vanity in her words, no thought such as Benedick's of what others will say when she changes, but only repentance for her past pride and scorn; none of that self-consideration of which Benedick is so full; it is complete, frank giving up of herself. Shakespeare, having made her a little sharper, at the beginning of the play, than becomes a woman in the eyes of men, now spreads the softness which comes of loving over the whole of her nature, and lifts her on to a higher level (by the absence in her of his vanity and self-thinking) than that on which he has placed Benedick. But the softness does not weaken her character. On the contrary, in defence of Hero, in wrath against Claudio, she is stronger than she was before. The softness has to do with herself alone. It casts out her self-assertiveness—an immense step towards nobility of character. Other changes in her are made by Shakespeare, now that he has given her love. She has lost all her wit most curiously. She is almost too humble, almost out of character. Love has lowered her plumes. But then she has been greatly moved by finding out how gravely Hero and Ursula blame her pride and hard-heartedness, how much they think that she has sacrificed loving-kindness on the altar of her wit. Hero has drawn her sharply—

> But Nature never framed a woman's heart
> Of prouder stuff than that of Beatrice :
> Disdain and scorn ride sparkling in her eyes,
> Misprising what they look on ; and her wit
> Values itself so highly, that to her
> All matter else seems weak : she cannot love,
> Nor take no shape nor project of affection,
> She is so self-endear'd.

Of course, Hero is exaggerating a little in this—for her purpose. Beatrice is far better than that. It is her dancing gaiety of youth which has carried her away, and the pleasure of using her rapier of speech. But now that the centre of her is touched, we see how full and deep are the waters of loving-kindness there ; and we are not surprised when they surge upwards into a splendid passion of indignation when Hero is belied. Beatrice, like Benedick, but more fully than Benedick, is slowly and nobly expanded by Shakespeare in this scene.

This is the first scene in which we begin to have a closer acquaintance with the 'gentle Hero.' Once before, in the masquerade, and emboldened by her mask, she interchanges a few words with Don Pedro. They are touched with her cousin's sharpness and wit, and I do not believe that, unmasked, she could have said them—

D. PEDRO. Lady, will you walk about with your friend ?
HERO. So you walk softly, and look sweetly, and say nothing, I am yours for the walk ; and especially when I walk away.
D. PEDRO. With me in your company ?
HERO. I may say so, when I please.

D. Pedro. And when please you to say so ?

Hero. When I like your favour : for God defend the lute should
be like the case !

Gaiety, it is plain, is also in her gentle soul, which, for the
most part, is silent. When she comes in with Claudio
and her father, and Beatrice talks of her betrothal, she
does not say one word—a quiet maiden on the edge of
womanhood. But here in the garden with Ursula, her
servant and friend, she speaks at her ease with confidence
and freedom. She is clever: her sketch of the way
Beatrice handles men could scarcely be better done. But
she is more than clever. Had she not loved the birds,
she had never known how the lapwing runs, nor yet compared Beatrice to the wild hawks that haunt the cliffs—

> I know her spirits are as coy and wild
> As haggards of the rock.

She feels what is beautiful, and makes her little
thoughtful analogies between the nature she loves and
the human life she knows. ‘Go,’ she says to Ursula, ‘and
bid Beatrice

> steal into the pleached bower,
> Where honeysuckles, ripen’d by the sun,
> Forbid the sun to enter ; like favourites,
> Made proud by princes, that advance their pride
> Against that power that bred it.’

> .   .   .   .

> Now begin ;
> For look where Beatrice, like a lapwing, runs
> Close by the ground, to hear our conference.

And Ursula, her echo, caps her mistress's simile drawn
from nature with another of the fish that ‘cut with her
golden oars the silver stream.’

These two have lived and thought together. The only
other touch of Hero's character, before the painful scene
in the church, is given when, dressing for her marriage,
she says with regard to her dress—

> God give me joy to wear it ! for my heart is exceeding heavy !

Her silent, sensitive nature feels, especially as she is not really in love, the presentiment of the coming sorrow. It was Shakespeare's mystic way to make characters he meant to be sensitive (like Romeo, Juliet, and the Queen in *Richard II.*), tremble for a moment in the shadows of the future. When we next meet her, trouble has come.

Meanwhile Beatrice and Benedick have both carried away Cupid's arrow in their gizzard, and it infects all their ways and speech. They flash in wit no more; they are silent, dreaming, seeking solitude. The change is so marked that much wit is broken upon them, and they themselves are so conscious of the change that they try to explain it by saying they are ill. 'Gallants,' says Benedick, 'I am not as I have been.' Then he explains that he has the toothache, and, mocked for that, is pettish with the mockers.

> Well, every one can master a grief, but he that has it.

Beatrice is just as foolish. Her voice is so odd that Hero cries out—

> Why, how now! do you speak in the sick tune?

'I am out of all other tune, methinks,' answers Beatrice, very sentimentally. She is as pettish as Benedick, and more sensitive. Even Margaret conquers her in wit. She cannot endure a joke about Benedick. She hurries every one. She too is out of sorts.

> 'Tis almost five o'clock, cousin; 'tis time you were ready. By my troth, I am exceeding ill: heigh-ho!

All this double and amusing change should be made the most of by the actors, because it is an introduction to a change in the play.

This new gravity and seriousness in the two principal characters, which now replaces their previous gaiety and brilliancy, changes the whole atmosphere of the play, and

prepares us for the deep shadow which will soon darken
its movement. What that shadow is we know. Don
John has blackened the honour of Hero. Borachio, his
bravo, talks to Margaret at her window and calls her
Hero, and the Prince and Claudio listen and are convinced
that Hero is a wanton. 'They will,' they cry, 'denounce
her publickly in the church.' This is the tragic element,
and it is black enough. But Shakespeare was not now,
when he was writing the three comedies of which this
was the first, in the humour to be too severely tragic.
Therefore, it is into the very centre of the tragic part of
the drama that he brings his audacious fun, and shoots
on to the streets of Messina all the lumbering stupidities
and self-conceits of the English watchmen of his time.
He invents with parlous joy Dogberry and Verges, and
their band of constables. He invents them with as much
care as the rest. He gives them a whole scene to themselves. He brings their boundless vanity and incapacity
into contact with Leonato, Claudio, and the Prince, when
these are as empty of common sense and as incapable of
seeing the truth as the foolish constables. He brings
their low life face to face with the 'high life' of Messina;
and whatever it may think of them, Dogberry at least,
self-idealised by his happy vanity, thinks himself as good
as any man of Messina. Their foolery intermingles excellently with the tragedy, and in the end is used to change
the tragic event into happiness.

There are few parts in Shakespeare more difficult to
act well than those of Dogberry and Verges, because the
humour is more forced than is usual with Shakespeare.
The miscalling of words seems carried too far, and is a
little wearisome. The boundless stupidity of Dogberry
is only made humorous by his boundless vanity. He is
absolutely convinced of his intellectual greatness, of his
capacity to handle affairs of every kind—and perfectly.

There is no question put before him by the watch which
he does not answer with a chuckle of self-satisfaction.
And when he is called an ass, he thinks the world is
falling into ruin.   It is, he thinks, far the most important
event which has occurred in Messina for years, and he
cannot get away from it.   The part ought to be acted
very well—for it is exceedingly difficult.

Now comes the Event, the scene in the church at the
beginning of the fourth Act—the denunciation of Hero.
In it all the characters will be tried in the fire.   It is a
repulsive scene.   The public denunciation of a woman by
the man who comes to marry her, exposing her shame to
the whole world, instead of a private repudiation to save,
at least, the honour of her family, would be in our eyes a
disgraceful act, wholly unworthy of two gentlemen like
the Prince and Claudio.   The shame it gives us to hear
it is only saved by our knowledge of Hero's innocence,
and by the pity which we feel for her.   Our pity changes
into indignation, and is voiced by Beatrice.   But we
never recover any admiration for the Prince and Claudio.
It is true they saw Hero, as they thought, talking to a
man out of a window; but if they had ever looked at
Hero, they should have disbelieved their eyes.   At least,
they should have inquired before they condemned.   Nor
do I understand how Leonato believes in his daughter's
guilt so easily.   Fathers, it is true, do not see clearly what
girls of sixteen are, but still—Leonato is more than
ordinarily foolish.   Beatrice is not so blind.   She laughs
the accusation to scorn, and she carries Benedick with
her.   These two emerge pure gold out of the testing.

One has never thought much of Claudio; he is a boy,
with a boy's courage, weakness, fine fashion and vanity,
quite ready to give up Hero in order to curry favour with
the Prince.   His high and mighty conduct in the church
is the vengeance of hurt vanity.— He thinks of no one

but himself. Only his extreme youth excuses him, yet, even with that excuse, he earns our complete disgust; and the Prince, clothed in the same shame, may walk away with him. The Prince was Leonato's guest; he had been received with honour and rich entertainment. Leonato was an old man, worthy of character and rank, Governor of the city—yet the Prince allows his favourite to stain with nameless shame, before the whole town, the daughter of his host. He is in the same ugly box with Claudio. His conduct is even worse, for his vanity has not been hurt.

I think the ugliness of the conduct of the two men under this central test, and not only the ugliness but their unnatural discourtesy, got on Shakespeare's literary nerves, and caused him in this scene not to write so well as usual. When the subject, as in this scene, is wrongly or inadequately conceived, the execution is sure to be inadequately or wrongly done. The artist often does not know that his conception of the thing is wrong till the inadequate execution of his work tells him that something has gone astray. He has been unconscious till this moment of revelation that his original arrangement of the subject was out of truth. Now, he knows, but it is too late to alter the thing done. It must stand; and here I think it stands. Neither Claudio, Leonato, nor Hero speak those words which cannot be changed, which contain a hundredfold more than they seem to contain. Leonato's immediate belief (on the hearsay evidence of Claudio and the Prince) in his daughter's vile impurity is apart from nature. All he says about it is foolish or violent. He seems to have passed, almost in a moment, from a sensible man into senile weakness. This is more Shakespeare's fault—if I may put what I mean in that way—than Leonato's. The conception of the scene is ill-shaped and the execution of it is also ill-done. Then, again, Claudio's accusation, while the girl stands before him, clad in her modesty, looking, as he says, 'as chaste as is the bud ere it be blown,' is odiously immodest. Its savagery can only be accounted for by his hurt vanity. Yet, as the child looks on him, he seems, at the end, to half-repent, washes his words with tears—the wretched fool—and swears that for her sake he will love no more. The Prince backs him up, and Don John scoffs in the distance. This villain doubles his villainy. He knows Hero is innocent, but sacrifices the child only to gratify his spite against the Prince and Claudio. He ought to be torn asunder. I am glad he is taken at the last. Few things in Shakespeare are wickeder than his speech about Hero's wanton ways—

> Fie, fie ! they are not to be named, my lord,
> Not to be spoken of ;
> There is not chastity enough in language,
> Without offence, to utter them.   Thus, pretty lady,
> I am sorry for thy much misgovernment.

What Hero says so quietly on the accusation is in her character, but not quite so vitally true to her nature as I should have expected from Shakespeare. She seems to come to the verge of saying the absolutely right thing, but not quite to say it. Of course, she is utterly confounded by the infinite distance between herself and the accusation, and all she says marks her maiden amazement, her maiden ignorance.

'Is my lord well, that he doth speak so wide ?' she whispers when she is charged with sensuality. 'This looks not like a nuptial,' Benedick says. 'True, O God !' cries Hero ; and the cry is good, but might be better invented. Better, however, is her cry, when her father joins the catechism instead of defending her : personal indignation begins to thrill through it—

> HERO.   O, God defend me ! how am I beset !
>   What kind of catechising call you this ?
> CLAUD.   To make you answer truly to your name.

HERO. Is it not Hero ? Who can blot that name
   With any just reproach ?
CLAUD.   Marry, that can Hero ;
   Hero herself can blot out Hero's virtue.
   What man was he talk'd with you yesternight
   Out at your window, betwixt twelve and one ?
   Now, if you are a maid, answer to this.
HERO. I talk'd with no man at that hour, my lord.

And then, this delicate child, too gentle for these storms, too innocent to bear these stains, stretched suddenly on the very rack of shame, when she is as white as the curdled snow, hears her father believe in her guilt—

   Hath no man's dagger here a point for me ?

It is the last blow. Her natural defender has abandoned her, and she swoons away. It is the best thing she could do. The Prince, Claudio, and Don John leave the church, and Benedick, Beatrice, Leonato, and the Friar are left on the ground.

Since he is old, and weak through passionate grief for himself, for his daughter, and his shame, we may partly excuse the senile outburst with which Leonato repudiates his daughter, and trusts the evidence of Claudio and the Prince more than that of his daughter's eyes. He comes forth from the testing event as poorly as possible. He sees his daughter recover from her swoon, and look upon him with her innocent eyes. ' Dost thou look up ? ' he cries in a rage of contempt. ' Yea; wherefore should she not ? ' answers that excellent Friar. He is, in Shakespeare's thought (who is almost always kind to Friars), a man of the world as well as a just churchman. He has seen too much of men and women in hours of trouble, when innocence was hurt, when guilt was suddenly revealed, not to know at once that Hero is without stain ; that there has been a shameful mistake. He comes nobly out of the test—wise, affectionate, tolerant—the master of the situation. He has noted the lady, and marked

> A thousand blushing apparitions
> To start into her face ; a thousand innocent shames
> In angel whiteness beat away those blushes ;
> And in her eye there hath appear'd a fire,
> To burn the errors that these princes hold
> Against her maiden truth.

Pity her father could not see with those eyes! He re-iterates his accusation, blinded by selfish thoughts of his own dishonour. Not till Benedick suggests that Don John may have tooled this treachery, does his fatherhood, still blustering, rise above his selfishness, and swear to vindicate his daughter. Then the Friar proposes that Hero should die till her honour is cleared. Dead, she will be regretted, even were the accusation true. Claudio will repent with all his heart—and the lines he tells of this are too lovely and too wise not to quote—

> When he shall hear she died upon his words,
> The idea of her life shall sweetly creep
> Into his study of imagination ;
> And every lovely organ of her life
> Shall come apparell'd in more precious habit,
> More moving-delicate, and full of life,
> Into the eye and prospect of his soul,
> Than when she lived indeed.

So, his advice is taken. Hero, Leonato, and the Friar leave, and Benedick and Beatrice are left alone. These two, in the day of trial, are equal to it, and above it. Shakespeare lifts them, in this hour of passion, to the highest point of their characters, above all that others knew of them, above all they knew of themselves. They had not been deceived into belief in Hero's shame. Benedick, though he loves the Prince and Claudio, does not join himself to them. He is at first silent—a grave man when the affair is grave. Then he speaks his astonishment.

> For my part, I am so attir'd in wonder
> I know not what to say.

He supports the Friar, but yet is faithful to friendship;

not quick to change, a man to be trusted! And then he pledges his honour to deal justly with the whole matter. Beatrice is lucky; she has found a man.

> Signior Leonato, let the Friar advise you:
> And though you know my inwardness and love
> Is very much unto the Prince and Claudio,
> Yet, by mine honour, I will deal in this
> As secretly and justly as your soul
> Should with your body.

Now comes that delightful dialogue between these two who have not yet revealed their mutual love. It is a mingled strain of love and of indignation. In Benedick the love is greatest, in Beatrice the indignation, and Beatrice (as swift in wrath as she was in wit) makes the avenging of Hero the price of her love. All the deep affection of her nature has been stirred; we have got down to the central depth of the woman—to an infinite pity, to wrath for another's wrong, and fire of love. And this, which is for Hero, creates in her an atmosphere of passion in which her love for Benedick, which has, as yet, only been requital of his, rises into personal passion for him; and that, in its turn, swells her indignation into a fury of righteous wrath. This beating to and fro of two passions, each increasing the power of the other, and the transference of the intensity of both to Benedick who has been already thrilled by the air of passion which breathes from Beatrice, is a noble piece of drama. Their talk is like the alternate strokes on the anvil of two fierce hammers plied at lightning speed. The dialogue dwells first on Hero's wrong, then on love, then on what a man who loved might do for the woman he loved.

> BENE. Come, bid me do anything for thee.
> BEAT. Kill Claudio.

They are not intelligent who say that is unwomanly. It is of a woman's very essence. It is the outbreak of a

thousand sorrows, feelings, wraths, tears, agonies of indignation, which have surged and collected within Beatrice
since Claudio denounced her cousin. How, the moment
she had sympathy, could she have avoided it! It was the
inmost wrath of her womanhood, and once it began to
move, it went on, completing its indignant circle. Benedick saw thus to the fiery heart of the woman, and it was
well for him. Great reverence and honour must have
been added to his love. Nor was he unworthy of it. His
answer to her cry ' Kill Claudio,' shows how strong the
man was. His friendship is not mastered by his love, till
he is securely convinced that Claudio has wronged Hero.
' Kill Claudio,' she cries—

BENE. Ha! not for the wide world.
BEAT. You kill me to deny it. Farewell.
BENE. Tarry, sweet Beatrice.
BEAT. I am gone, though I am here : there is no love in you : nay,
I pray you, let me go.
BENE. Beatrice,—
BEAT. In faith, I will go.
BENE. We 'll be friends first.
BEAT. You dare easier be friends with me than fight with mine
enemy.
BENE. Is Claudio thine enemy ?
BEAT. Is he not approved in the height a villain, that hath slan-
dered, scorned, dishonoured my kinswoman ? O that I were a man !
What, bear her in hand until they come to take hands ; and then, with
public accusation, uncovered slander, unmitigated rancour,—O God, that
I were a man ! I would eat his heart in the market-place.

The last phrase is as fierce as fierceness itself. All
that she says afterwards is weaker, and might well have
been omitted. It lowers the pitch. The phrase itself
seems too terrible for a woman to use. But Beatrice was
of that type of woman who, at the top of indignation not
for her own but for another's wrong, and in the thrilling
atmosphere of love, would say anything to express and
expand her heart. Of course, she would not have done
it. It may be spoken, not accomplished.

Some have even said it would be impossible even for a
man.   But that is not so when men are maddened, in
days of terror and vengeance.   I wonder where Shakespeare found the thought.   He uses it again in another
way when Aufidius declares his hatred to Coriolanus:

> Where I find him, were it
> At home, upon my brother's guard, even there,
> Against the hospitable canon, would I
> Wash my fierce hand in 's heart.

Did he know of such a deed? I have heard the story told.
In the French Revolution, during the days of the
September massacres, a tall man, holding his left hand in
his breast, entered a cabaret and called for a large cup of
wine.   He drew his hand out of his blouse, and in it was
a heart dropping blood.   Holding it high, he squeezed it
till the blood streamed into the wine-cup.   And with a
cry he drank.   It was the heart of his enemy, his
daughter's ravisher.

It is terrible to hear of it.   It must have been terrible
for Benedick to hear it spoken by the woman he loved.
It is no wonder that he grew serious and spoke with a
man's gravity.   He too, like Beatrice, in these grave
affairs, shows the steadfast centre of his soul.

BENE.   Think you in your soul the Count Claudio hath wronged
Hero?
BEAT.   Yea, as sure as I have a thought or a soul.
BENE.   Enough!   I am engaged: I will challenge him.   I will kiss
your hand, and so leave you.   By this hand, Claudio shall render me
a dear account.   As you hear of me, so think of me.   Go, comfort your
cousin: I must say she is dead: and so, farewell.

When he meets the Prince and Claudio, he goes straight
to the point.   They joke with him about Leonato's anger.
'There's no true valour,' he answers well, 'in a false
quarrel.'   He tells Claudio he is a villain who has killed
a sweet lady.   He tells the Prince that he must dis-
continue his company.   He too has been guilty of Hero's

death, and he leaves them confounded with his earnestness. He, except the Friar, is the only worthy man of the whole lot, and he, like Beatrice, comes out of the crisis pure gold.

No one acted this noble character better than he whose loss we all deplore; better than Sir Henry Irving. It suited his genius exactly. It suited his figure, his face, his natural manner, and his nature. Benedick and he were one, and it was a great delight to see him play his part with Ellen Terry, whose grace, intelligence, and passion made her Beatrice the very image in mind and body of Shakespeare's heroine. Irving was always nearer to the seventeenth century than the nineteenth. He was Italian in that the courtier and the soldier of that time were combined in him. He had the manner also of that time. And in his chivalric sense of honour, in a certain restraint of passion, in his lovableness, in the swiftness of rush into deep feeling, in his courtly carriage towards men, and much more to women, in his intellectual power (for even when one did not agree with his reading of a character, one was conscious of the intellectual power with which he had studied and conceived it), in all these points and in more also—points of noble character, happily inherent in his own nature, and also inherent in Benedick— he was the best Benedick on the modern stage. I do not think at any time the part could have been better acted. He was what Shakespeare meant.

And now these two fine creatures, having discovered one another in this tempest of fateful sorrow, having seen the serious foundation of their characters, and having passed beyond the trouble better than they entered into it, return to their brightness and gaiety; take up again the weapons of their wit, play with the world and with one another, and admire, because they love, each the other's cleverness. The closing scene, where they both pretend not to care for one another, is excellent comedy. Both are delighted with life, and in full enjoyment of all things. And Benedick has become through love so young, so happy, so inspired by honest pleasure, that he will not allow anything in the world to interfere with his dancing out his joy—not supper, not even the punishment of Don John. And he sweeps round, with gay audacity, upon the Prince who attempts to mock him.

D. PEDRO. How dost thou, Benedick, the married man?

BENE. I'll tell thee what, Prince; a college of wit-crackers cannot flout me out of my humour. Dost thou think I care for a satire, or an epigram? No; if a man will be beaten with brains, he shall wear nothing handsome about him. In brief, since I do purpose to marry, I will think nothing to any purpose that the world can say against it; and therefore never flout at me for what I have said against it; for man is a giddy thing, and this is my conclusion. . . .

Prince, thou art sad; get thee a wife, get thee a wife. . . . Strike up, pipers!

There is no need to speak further of the fifth Act. The discovery of the villainy of Don John is made by Dogberry. What cunning envy has tied, stupidity unties. The universe is on the side of innocence in this play. When Shakespeare drew Cordelia, Desdemona, Ophelia, the universe did not take that side. What a pity, what a serious thing it is, that we do not know why it changes so!

II

TWELFTH NIGHT ; OR, WHAT YOU WILL

Twelfth Night, or *What. You Will* (acted by Shakespeare's company before the Court, about Christmastide in 1601-2), probably owed its first name to the fact of its being acted as the Twelfth Night performance of that year. Moreover, John Manningham, a member of the Middle Temple from 1601 to 1603, records in his diary, February 2, 1601-2, that he saw it acted on that day in the Hall of the Middle Temple. We may then fairly date its composition, 1601. Then also the allusion in the third Act to the new map, with the augmentation of the Indies, enables us to say that it must have been written after 1599 or 1600, for that map was first issued in Hakluyt's *Voyages,* published in one or other of those years.

Its second title, *What You Will,* is a piece of Shakespeare's gaiety; and all I have said about the title *As You Like It* may apply to this title. The play is a varied picture of human nature, ranging from the highest to the lowest in rank, from the wisest to the most foolish—a delightful, broken landscape of the world of men and women, full of love and laughter, fancy and imagination. We may take out of it what we will, leave aside what we will, wander in it where we will. Shakespeare made it for his own pleasure in humanity, and for our pleasure. When he had finished it he was pleased. He had fulfilled his will. Then he smiled to himself and said, 'It is mine no longer. I give it to the audience; let them have their will with it.' And its readers and the playgoers of the world have always willed to have it. It has kept the stage for three hundred years, and it is as fresh and as delightful to-day as it was of old. Viola, Malvolio, the Duke, Sir Toby Belch, Maria, have been the favourite parts of excellent actors and actresses. Even in the inferior parts a reputation can be made. ·Shakespeare, who felt with actors, took wonderful pains to give plenty of attractive work to all the members of his company, to give to the smallest acting-part points to be made which should draw the attention and the praise of the audience —a different view of his duty from that which prevails among the dramatists who write chiefly for the Stars and neglect the minor personages.

This play was written about the same time as *Julius Cæsar*, perhaps at the same time. It is not improbable that Shakespeare, like many a great artist in music or painting, had two subjects of a different spirit and conception on hand at the same time. And when he was tired of the graver or the gayer subject, he sought that which was opposite to that on which he had been at work. He changed the climate of his imagination, and so kept it in health.

It illustrates not only the range of his genius, but also the easy power with which it worked, that he could pass in a moment from the atmosphere of *Twelfth Night* to that of *Julius Cæsar*, from the pleasure-loving Duke to the Stoic Brutus, from the delicate pain of Viola to the restless sorrow of Portia. As I think of it, it seems quite wonderful. We change from a world full of graceful gaiety and fantastic mirth, of broad and honest humour, of love at play, of music and song, to weighty State affairs, to a world where two universal ideas of government are in a death-grapple. We pass from the fleeting court of a provincial Duke, and the palace of a lady of fashion in a far-off corner of Illyria, to the Forum and the Capitol of 'great and glorious Rome.' Yet Shakespeare's mastery over this small, secluded circle of events is as finished as his mastery over the huge events which transformed the government of the known world.

No play is more exclusively, more fantastically gay. Were it not for a few passages in which the depths of human nature are sounded, it would seem to be the out-breaking of a young man's fancy and jollity. It touches alike the most delicate fantasies of love, and the most honest breadth of jovial humour. Not a trace of tragedy, of the deep sorrows of the world, is to be found in it. And this is curious, for it is the last of the early comedies, the last in which for many years the rooted happiness and brightness of Shakespeare's soul appeared.

Some speak of its 'romantic pathos,' of its sadness, as relieved by the broad comedy of the lower characters. I can trace no real sadness in it at all. It is like a dance on some festal day in an old Italian garden. The ladies and the courtly wooers move in stately, graceful measures on the grass; where now and then, to vary the pleasurable day, their retainers, masked like nymphs, satyrs, fauns, jesters, singers (and one whom they mock), might dance with delight an interlude, while the statelier company look on. And the sun shines, and the air is clear.

The play goes trippingly from the beginning to the end. It is romantic enough, not the real romantic; a sort of Renaissance-romantic like the introduction to the *Decameron*. When it touches sadness, it is not sad seriously. The sadness of the Duke is the same kind of sadness which Romeo had when he was in love with Rosa-line, a sadness which is happiness; it is joy in the attire of mourning, youth dramatising the slight monotony of its radiant life by inventing sorrow which is not sorrow, but a fresh way of feeling life. Had his love-sadness been real, he had never changed so easily from Olivia to Viola. He thinks it real, of course; every young man does.. Did he not think it real, it would give him no pleasure, and it is the pleasure of it that he likes. It is a game of his youth, a dance of graceful feelings in a rose-garden of his soul.

Viola is no more sad than the Duke. She cherishes, like many a young girl, her hours when she clothes the world and life in dainty grey—sweet imaginings of sorrow on the edge of joy, aromatic pains, momentary despairs, uprushings of passion which, while they flush her being, live on the fine edge which divides pleasure from pain. In one of these she speaks herself to the man she loves, and yet, being garmented like a man, does not betray herself. A great consolation to give her passing sorrow words, and not offend her womanhood! Once she has spoken, her flying sadness vanishes away. And indeed she had no right to be sad. She was having a most enchanting time. She was in love, and at her age even what seem its miseries are more delightful than maturer pleasures. And the flying miseries were well compensated by the joys of her life. She was always with the man she loved. He disclosed his whole heart to her. She was his most trusted companion. She learnt to know his nature and character to their recesses. She knew him as a man knows a man, and as a woman knows a man—a parlous knowledge. That he was in love with Olivia was of course disagreeable. But I do not think she was ever afraid of that love reaching its end. She loved so well herself that she must have detected the root-unreality in the Duke's love. Then she knew Olivia did not care for him, and before long she knew this with certainty, because Olivia fell in love with her. When that took place, she was sure that victory was in her hands. And she (as we well see from all her talks with Olivia, in which she plays every kind of game with the circumstances) enjoyed with the ardent coquetry of youth the amusement of the situation. She was not at all sad, nor had she any right to be sad.

Olivia is not sad either. She has her own will and way completely. When is a woman sad under these circumstances? As to the others, Sir Andrew and Toby Belch, Feste, Maria, Fabian,—they are on the top of mirth and jollity. Even Malvolio, till he is made a gull of, is quite happy in his self-conceit; and if he loses his happiness, he is the cause, in its loss, of vast amusement to others. Sebastian reaches the peak of joy; and though Antonio and the Captain, who are the most unselfish of all the characters, suffer for it, yet we know at the end that they emerge into peace and pleasure.

No; the play is brimming over with the delight of youth, with mirth of every kind, with stately pleasure, with the prankfulness of love, with effervescent life. The whole spirit of it is in this verse:

> What is love? 'tis not hereafter :
> Present mirth hath present laughter ;
>   What's to come is still unsure :
> In delay there lies no plenty ;
> Then come kiss me, sweet and twenty,
>   Youth's a stuff will not endure.

This spirit was deliberately wrought into the whole play by Shakespeare. He might have made a more serious comedy out of the story which was the original of the play—the *History of Apolonius and Silla*—a story half sad; romantically sad. But he did not choose to do that, but to make it mirthful and joyful. And the proof of that is, that he invented Malvolio, Sir Toby and Sir Andrew, Maria, Fabian, and the Clown, not one of whom appears in the original novel by Bandello from which *The History of Apolonius and Silla* was derived. He poured (out of his own desire to laugh and be happy) a flood of gay and jovial humour into the story. Sir Toby Belch is like a resuscitation of Falstaff, with a tenth of Falstaff's intelligence and wit, and none of his heart. He and Maria seem to live for nothing but fun, and for making fun of fools. Aguecheek is even more their butt than Malvolio. He is their continual entertainment, and, in his infinite conceit of himself, he is his own entertainment. Malvolio is made a fountain of fun. The whole underaction is of a reckless gaiety.

When we think of the plays that followed, this is very curious. This play is the last of the joyous comedies— like a farewell to mirth. Never again is Shakespeare the same. And it is an abrupt farewell: *Twelfth Night* is followed immediately by *Julius Cæsar*, within the year— a play dealing with great political issues, with tragic workings of the soul. But such work was not unknown before to Shakespeare. *Richard III.* and *Richard II.* are as tragic, though the issues were not, as those of Cæsar, world-wide. By itself *Julius Cæsar* does not prove that the temper of Shakespeare's soul had changed. In the old days it might have been followed by some lively comedy of youth and love. Now it is different. It is followed by a series of solemn, weighty, terrible, unrelieved tragedies in which (with matured and awful power of thought, imagination, and execution) he goes down into the incommunicable deeps of sin and sorrow and sacred passion. The temper of his soul has changed, but why, we may conjecture, but we cannot tell. It is enough to say that *Twelfth Night* is a dividing line in Shakespeare's development both as an artist and a man. The sunlight of this play shines no more for years; storm and darkness follow, horror and pain.

The scenery of the play is less defined than it is in other plays. It is of a city in Illyria, close to the sea-coast, with woods and hills towards the inland among which the Duke hunted. The city is large, with suburbs where the hostels chiefly are; the streets, where some of the scenes take place, are wide; and the secluded villas, with full gardens, have gates which open into the streets and into the woods in their rear. The town has been long established. It is full of 'memorials and famous things' which adorn it and are visited by travellers.

Two places are chiefly occupied by scenes in the play—the Duke's palace among sweet beds of flowers and woods, and Olivia's house and garden. Olivia's house is large. It lodges many retainers; and Malvolio, its steward, has much to do. The garden has wide walks and box-tree alleys, and at the bottom of it there is a large orchard, where the duel is to take place between Viola and Sir Andrew. Two other slight scenes are laid on the neighbouring sea-coast after a violent storm in which Sebastian and Viola are shipwrecked. The waves are still seen thundering on the beach. This is the scenery of the piece.

The plot is very slight and the subject thin. In order to make it into a larger and more various representation of human life, Shakespeare invented an underplot, also a slight one, which might be called *The Mocking of Malvolio*. This fills up all the previously uninhabited portions of the main subject, and fills them with as un-sentimental an assemblage of folk as the folk in the upper plot are sentimental. The sentimental elements and the unsentimental make a livelier, more dramatic impression from their contrast; and the contrast itself makes the dancing life of the play more interesting to an audience. It affords great opportunities for that variety of act and incident which, when a dramatist gives it us, delights us most. Each hearer finds something to yield him pleasure. There is plenty in the play to interest men and women of a refined and idle society, and plenty more to amuse men and women of a coarser type; and as for the idealist and the dreaming lover—they have food enough and to spare. Music and love and high courtesies interchanged in courtly gardens, are interlaced with drinking and jollity and practical jokes and a riot of laughter.

Yet, though there are these two sides of life in the play, there is really only one class of society represented. This is the rich, aristocratic class, who have nothing to do but hunt and sing, dress and make love, and now and then to go to war; who have an agreeable surface cultivation, a pleasure in music and poetry and beautiful things; and who (for it is Shakespeare who writes) have good manners, honest and honourable souls, and the habit of yielding to impulse. This is the class who have retainers and flatterers, and persons who live upon them. These also have nothing to do but to amuse themselves; and they use their patrons for that purpose—folk like Sir Toby Belch, Fabian, Feste, Maria, even Malvolio. However different these are from the upper class, they form a necessary outskirt of the same society. The society of the play is then one society; and Shakespeare must have seen plenty of it in the houses of his friends— Southampton, Pembroke, Essex, and the rest. The Duke, with his musical and literary tastes, and his high sense of honour, may well have been the image of one of the young nobles of the time. Olivia, too, is drawn from the life; so, probably, is Malvolio.

The play opens with the Duke among his lords and musicians, and full of his love for Olivia, who refuses to see him. For seven years she will encloister herself—so very resolute does the boredom of the Duke's wooing make this young woman, who, in a fortnight or so, is wildly in love with Cesario. This is enough to make us understand that the drama is to be one of those in which Love is the prank-player of the world. And, indeed, the first speech of the Duke strikes this dominant note of the play. The spirit of Love in him calls for music to feed his passion:

> If music be the food of love, play on ;

but the roving imaginations of his love soon exhaust that food, and he asks for more of another kind. For Love is greater than its means, devours them all, and calls for impossible satisfaction. This is Cupid in his cruelty, as Shakespeare often represents him, as Spenser drew him—Cupid in his freakishness, half a child, half a god, who makes his victims in this play—victims who love the game yet suffer in it—now kind, now cruel, hoping, despairing, accepting, refusing, yielding, repelling, fanciful, and serious; who plays, as with toys, with Olivia, Sebastian, Viola, the Duke, even Malvolio; who turns upside down the best-assorted plans, just as his lordship for the moment wills—

> So full of shapes is fancy,
> That it alone is high fantastical.

The Duke is like Sir Philip Sidney, or one of that Elizabethan type. His youth, we are told, is 'fresh and stainless, free, learned and valiant.' He is a great lover of music, and of the best kind; of old, antique and simple melodies, not the

> light airs, and recollected terms
> Of these most brisk and giddy-paced times :

> O, fellow, come, the song we had last night.
> Mark it, Cesario, it is old and plain :
> The spinsters and the knitters in the sun
> And the free maids that weave their thread with bones
> Do use to chant it : it is silly sooth,
> And dallies with the innocence of love,
> Like the old age.

This is a delightful person, who loved the right things, and for the right reasons. Then he is careless of self-interest, loves Olivia not for her money, but because she 'attracts his soul'; that is, he is in love with his own ideal of a woman which he has embodied in her. He knows nothing really of Olivia. Hence, at the close of the play, it is so easy for him to love Viola, whom he has known through and through in long companionship.

In all the imaginations of an imagined love, he is just like Romeo in love with Rosaline before he met Juliet. It is a fantasy of passion that he feels, not passion itself. Like Romeo, he seeks solitude—

> I myself am best, when least in company.

Like Romeo, he unlades his heart in words to Curio, even in the hearing of his court. When Viola joins him, he 'unclasps to her,' whom he thinks a youth, 'the book even of his secret soul.'

The deeper passions are not like this. They are surface-smooth and still, like profound waters. Music, to which the Duke, with his love of beauty, is always flying for solace, does not relieve the greater passions, but disturbs them into storm.

The Duke's love is love in idleness; and he is always discussing it, and holding it in different lights, feeling it in different ways and surroundings, and seems always as if he were at play with it. Once, however (Sc. IV. Act 2), he is in his love-talk more serious than elsewhere. He compares the love of men and women; but first, with a dim consciousness that he has talked and acted too fancifully for real love, he defends himself—

> For such as I am all true lovers are,
> Unstaid and skittish in all motions else,
> Save in the constant image of the creature
> That is beloved.

After this, he grows more and more serious. Let the woman take, he says, a husband elder than herself; for men's fancies are more giddy and unfirm, more longing, wavering, sooner lost and worn than women's are. Let the man have passed by the changing times of youth, lest,

when a woman has given all and is constant, she find the
man weary. Such is his grave view when he looks beyond
himself. When his own love is in question, he takes
a directly opposite view, quite forgetting, and this is in
harmony with his character as a young man, his previous view. A man, like himself, is embodied constancy,
big with immortal love. As to women, whom he has
just praised for giving all and not wearying, 'they lack
retention—their love may be called appetite that suffers
cloying, surfeit and revolt.'

> Make no compare
> Between that love a woman can bear me
> And that I owe Olivia.
> VIO.   Ay, but I know,—
> DUKE.   What dost thou know?
> VIO.   Too well what love women to men may owe:
> In faith, they are as true of heart as we.

That is, as men. All this (though the Duke does fly
from side to side of opinion) is quite serious in him, much
more so than elsewhere. And I think that Shakespeare,
in the piercing of his genius, makes the Duke feel unconsciously more grave, and be higher in feeling, because at
the moment he is wrapt in the atmosphere of Viola's
profound passion. The song he asks for is not light or
gay, but serious as death itself—

> Come away, come away, death.

The Duke's liking for this black-edged kind of thing is
also quite in character. It belongs to sentimental youth,
when thwarted in love, to exaggerate the fanciful sorrow
and imagine itself in the arms of death; to put all Nature
into mourning, and in dainty grief to linger round the
grave it has, in melancholy imaginations, dug for itself.
But all the time he knows that there is not the remotest
chance that his youth will ever occupy it. A young man
has far too much pleasure in thinking about the grave, to
induce him to destroy the pleasure of thinking of it by a

death which will quench all thinking. And the Duke, having indulged in the emotion of the song, passes on to another phase of feeling. It is otherwise with Viola. The song or the tune of it, falling into Viola's heart, which is filled to the very brim with the waters of true love, makes on her a profound impression.

> How dost thou like this tune?

asks the Duke; and Viola answers—

> It gives a very echo to the seat
> Where love is throned.

And the note of true passion in her voice surprises the Duke. 'Thou dost speak masterly,' he says. In all his fine speeches he has not reached that thrilling tone.

Thus is built up by Shakespeare this delightful young man, who having nothing to do, falls into a phantasy of love. He is a much more worthy person than we should imagine him from this sentimental dallying with love. We remember the Captain's character of him and of Olivia. And at the end of the play, when he finds that his love for Olivia is put to confusion, he behaves admirably, like an honourable gentleman who rules himself, and is fit to rule others.

Over against his half-imagined love is set the real love of Viola—over against the youth who is scarcely yet a man, Viola, whom love has lifted in a few days out of girlhood into womanhood. She has all the wisdom which is learnt not from outward experience which for the most part darkens wisdom, but from the waters of the soul being moved to their unfathomable bed and throughout every atom of them, by the pervasive spirit of true love. In the extremely difficult position she is in towards the Duke and Olivia, she never makes a mistake. All she says is not only to the point of the moment, but is also a help for her in the future. She does not calculate this, but does it unconsciously; and her boldness in confession of love, which might by some be thought unwomanly, is excused by her being disguised as a man. There is indeed a frankness in her love, even when she is known as a woman, which becomes her well; and which arises not only from the truthfulness of her nature, but also from the fulness of her passion. Almost every young woman in Shakespeare's work has this frankness, this open, unmincing confession of love, when love has touched them home. They are not ashamed of it; it is their glory and their joy. Why, they think, if love is the root, the fountain, the all-present fire of their life, should they not confess it? Why not, indeed? No one, no man at least, thinks Juliet, or Miranda, or Viola, or Rosalind, or Portia, or Hermia immodest. On the very contrary! Their confession sounds the depths of modesty; and all the enchantment of modesty is let loose by it.

In this play, then, which is concerned, like others, with different forms of love, Viola is the image of deep, true, and imaginative love—love as a passion, not only of the senses, but of the intellect and the soul. When we meet her first, she is not in love; but her native tenderness, so full afterwards when she is in love, appears when she speaks of her brother whom she believes to be drowned in the storm from which she has escaped. And in her little tender phrase there is hidden the imagination which makes hereafter her words so full of grace. I cannot explain why there is so much of her and of her lovely turn of thought in these first few words—but so it is—

> This is Illyria, lady,

says the Captain.

> Vio. And what should I do in Illyria?
> My brother he is in Elysium.

Tenderness, loneliness, imagination, meet in the words; and as her tenderness increases afterwards, so also does her imagination expand with it. Whenever love moves her deeply, as when she speaks of herself as of a sister who never told her love, every little phrase is full of the imagination which pierces to the heart of the subject on which she dwells. And this is constant in her character.

Then, having given two lines to mark these elements in her, Shakespeare opens to us her clear common-sense, her quick intelligence, choosing, after inquiry into all the circumstances, the best thing to do. No one can be more practical, an element in character which is, more often than foolish persons think, the active comrade of the pure imagination. This practical intelligence in her, its quickness and insight, makes her just the person to manage the two difficult positions in which she is after-wards placed—her position with regard to the Duke, and also to Olivia. And admirably she manages both. Moreover, in this first talk with the Captain, we touch a vein of sententious thought in her, as if she had reflected much on life and men—

> There is a fair behaviour in thee, captain ; ·
> And though that nature with a beauteous wall
> Doth oft close in pollution, yet of thee
> I will believe thou hast a mind that suits
> With this thy fair and outward character.

The same kind of sententiousness—side thoughts on life, records of contemplation—appears at least twice after-wards; once, when she finds out that Olivia loves her as if she were a man,

> Disguise, I see, thou art a wickedness,
> Wherein the pregnant enemy does much.

again, when she says of Antonio,

> Methinks his words do from such passion fly,
> That he believes himself :

and again, full of experienced thoughtfulness, strange in

a young girl, when she broods over the conversation she has had with the fool:

> This fellow is wise enough to play the fool ;
> And to do that well craves a kind of wit :
> He must observe their mood on whom he jests,
> The quality of persons, and the time,
> And, like the haggard, check at every feather
> That comes before his eye.   This is a practice
> As full of labour as a wise man's art :
> For folly that he wisely shows is fit ;
> But wise men, folly-fall'n, quite taint their wit.

Jaques could not have put the whole matter more concisely or truly in one of his soliloquies than this slender girl has done.

When we meet Viola next, she is established at the court as the Duke's page, dressed as a man, and in love with the Duke who is in love with Olivia, and who sends Viola to be his ambassador to Olivia—a situation as amusing to an audience as it is puzzling and troublesome to Viola.

The situation is contained in the first thing she says. She wants to know from Valentine if the Duke is inconstant.   She hopes he is not of an inconstant nature (at least, so I think Shakespeare read her thoughts), for she would have his love, yet she must also hope that he will not be constant, for she would have him out of love with Olivia.   This is a troublous riddle for her to solve.   The riddle is doubled when she finds out that Olivia is in love with herself, with a woman. It is no wonder Viola, with her good sense, refuses to worry about it all, and throws the solution into the hands of time.

> O time ! thou must untangle this, not I ;
> It is too hard a knot for me to untie !

That first conversation with Olivia, how clever, how elusive, how leading and misleading it is, and how mockingly it begins.   Moreover, it is full of gaiety, of Viola's

enjoyment with her task, and with the situation. As I
said, it is quite a mistake to think that Shakespeare did
not mean Viola to have all the natural liveliness of her
youth.   In spite of her love, and the cross circumstances
of her position, she cannot help playing with the oddness
of the affair.   She feels all its humour.

> I am the man : if it be so, as 'tis,
> Poor lady, she were better love a dream.
>
> .   .   .   .   . ;
> What thriftless sighs shall poor Olivia breathe !

And I am sure she laughed.   Yet, when her love, or
anything which has to do with true love, is touched, the
seriousness of her passion speaks.   One little phrase
marks this. ' Are you a comedian ? ' asks Olivia. ' No, my
profound heart,' answers Viola in a kind of aside. The
phrase is almost torn out of her by the passion underneath. Then she gaily answers the question. Then,
again in this talk, her love leaps out unconsciously.

> My lord and master loves you : O, such love
> Could be but recompensed, though you were crown'd
> The nonpareil of beauty !

There is no sense in your denial of his love.   I could not,
were I the Duke, understand it.

' Why, what would you do ? ' cries Olivia, who by this
time has caught the infection of love from Viola.   Then
Viola's imagination breaks into speech, her secret love
impassioning her words : I would

> Make me a willow cabin at your gate,
> And call upon my soul within the house ;
> Write loyal cantons of contemned love
> And sing them loud even in the dead of night ;
> Halloo your name to the reverberate hills,
> And make the babbling gossip of the air
> Cry out, ' Olivia ! ' O, you should not rest
> Between the elements of air and earth,
> But you should pity me !

It is no wonder that the passion in the words, fired by

her own love for the Duke, finishes Olivia. She is swept in a moment into love. 'You might do much,' she answers.

The atmosphere of love is round all that Viola is; and it creates love in whomsoever it touches. It infects Olivia. It has already infected the Duke. He loves Cesario; he needs only one touch of circumstance to love Viola. 'With an invisible and noble stealth,' she creeps into the study of his imagination, even while he woos Olivia. Then comes that charming, delicate, graceful conversation with the Duke, as delightful as dramatic to the audience, who know that Viola is talking of herself, while he thinks she is of his own sex; in which Viola, while disclosing her love in every word, is of an exquisite tenderness and modesty—one of the quite lovely visions which Shakespeare had of a woman's heart. Every moment Viola is on the edge of forgetting she is a man. When the Duke says—

> For women are as roses, whose fair flower
> Being once display'd, doth fall that very hour.

the woman in Viola leaps forth—

> And so they are : alas, that they are so ;
> To die, even when they to perfection grow !

It must have been only his preoccupation with Olivia which, when he heard that, shut the Duke's eyes to the fact that his page was a woman. He orders her now to go to Olivia, but Viola, at the point of intensity to which she has been brought by the music, by the hour, by the intimacy of the conversation, cannot bear to be sent to Olivia; delays her going, describes herself and her love in veiled images, hoping perhaps that he might see the truth. This is the well-known passage—

> A blank, my lord. She never told her love.

But the Duke is blind; Viola can bear his blindness no more; better than this, it is to go to Olivia !

Sir, shall I to this lady?

the very thing she has been trying to avoid. Quite inimitable is all this to-and-fro of dramatic feeling.

And to Olivia she goes; and again, in a gay reaction, plays with the situation. Olivia declares her love, and Viola, whom the touch of love always thrills into her own passion, thinks of the Duke, and cries out the intensity, the singleness of her affection—

> By innocence I swear, and by my youth,
> I have one heart, one bosom and one truth,
> And that no woman has ; nor never none
> Shall mistress be of it, save I alone.

She leaves Olivia, and is egged on to a duel with Ague-cheek by that practical joker, Sir Toby. Few scenes are more charming on the stage than Viola's pretty cowardice in which her womanhood revolts from the sword she wears; than her final resolution to carry through the duel; her rescue by Antonio, who mistakes her for Sebas-tian; and her solitary joy in the thought that her brother, after all, may be alive. For the moment she forgets the Duke, and the tenderness of her natural piety as a sister is on her lips, and in her sweet imagination.

> Prove true, imagination, O prove true,
> That I, dear brother, be now ta'en for you !
> .   .   .   .   .   .
> O, if it prove,
> Tempests are kind and salt waves fresh in love.

Olivia, to whom I turn, is another instance of that freakishness of the God of Love, with which Shakespeare so often pleased himself. He has drawn one kind of love in the Duke, another kind in Viola. He draws still another kind in Olivia—the quick-flaming love which is more of the senses than the soul, born in a moment of impulse, unable to restrain itself, confessing its weakness, increasing its heat the more it is repulsed, proud of its passion, and hastening, like a torrent, to its satisfaction.

Yet, in the circumstances, there is some excuse. She has been wooed incessantly; everything has been laid at her feet by the Duke, and incessancy, flattery, and subservience have bored this fine lady. For the first time in her life, she meets in Cesario with a man, as she thinks, whose whole talk is a delicate mockery of her; who, it is plain, does not care a pin for her beauty and her wealth; who woos her for another, and who is clearly glad to get away from her. And this, being strange and new, takes her fancy, and when she sees that Cesario is a most beautiful young man, with, moreover, the gift of eloquence, and witty withal, her fancy slips in an instant, and with all the sudden impulsiveness of a wilful and idle woman, into love; which, being checked and repelled, runs at once into passion. She is herself astonished by this—

> Not too fast : soft, soft l
> Unless the master were the man. How now !
> Even so quickly may one catch the plague ?   .
> Methinks I feel this youth's perfections
> With an invisible and subtle stealth
> To creep in at mine eyes. *Well, let it be.*

And with that little phrase, instinct with the recklessness of a woman who has always followed, and is able to follow, her own will, she accepts the situation—and her resolve to see no man, and to mourn her brother in a seven years' solitude, is as if it had never been. And yet she has some sense of the strangeness of her conduct, and she declares it is the fault of Fate, not of her will—

> Fate, show thy force: ourselves we do not owe ;
> What is decreed must be, and be this so l

An interesting woman—interesting as an example of some of her own class who have nothing to do and plenty of wealth and will to do it with; but not interesting in any other fashion. At the last, she is frankness itself. She flings her confession of love into Cesario's

face. Nor wit nor reason can her passion hide. Then, by
an immense good fortune, she finds Sebastian, the very
image and mirror of Cesario, and her most jealous and
too doubtful soul can now live in peace. With the same
sudden speed with which she loved at first, she hurries on
her marriage. Olivia would be a little vulgar were she not
so reckless. She is rough, even ill-mannered, to the Duke.
But then, the Duke would go on wooing her till she was
bored. And a woman's boredom includes death to the
man who bores her, complicated with protracted torture
to avenge what she has suffered. Some praise her for the
conduct of her house, but it seems to me she let it drift;
and I trust Sebastian got Sir Toby Belch into some decent
order. Yet, I need not wish that, for he married Maria;
and I am sure that clever girl reorganised, with enough
sympathy, the old toper. Sebastian, of course, thinks
that Olivia manages her house perfectly. It would be
odd if he did not. But, afterwards, when he broke Sir
Toby's head, and drove Sir Andrew back to his country
house, it looks as if he had changed his mind. Olivia
does not really trouble about these disorders. She is too
great a lady. She tells Maria to tell the drunkards not to
make so much noise. She hands matters over to Malvolio
to look after. When Malvolio comes in smiling and
cross-gartered, thinking she is in love with him, she is
scarcely aware of his existence; and when he presses it
upon her, she is only sorry that he has lost his senses.
In the last scene she is just to him, but he is not of her
class; and she dismisses even the thought of his being
abused with one word, half pity, half scorn—

Alas, poor fool, how have they baffled thee!

Olivia is Shakespeare's study of a 'great lady in her youth,'
whose will is her only law. Sebastian, with his courage,
his high sense of honour, his loving gratitude to Antonio,

his noble blood on which the Duke dwells, his youthful delight in his good luck, and his joy in Olivia's love, will get on very well with her if he follows her moods. But he is scarcely in the play.

Below all this high level of fine society is the underplot carried on by the retainers of Olivia's household and a friend from the country. It might be called, I said, *The Mocking of Malvolio.* The characters are Sir Toby Belch, Sir Andrew Aguecheek, names invented to suggest the men; Fabian, the Clown or rather the paid Jester, Maria, Olivia's waiting-maid, and ·Malvolio. Malvolio is the steward and the rest are hangers-on to the rich house. Malvolio excepted (he is their enemy and their foil), they are as reckless, wild, and ill-behaved as folk who, having nothing to do, to earn, or to pay, are likely to be. I dare say there were hundreds of such folk about the houses of the Elizabethan nobles.

Olivia did not rule them; and Sir Toby, being her uncle, presumed on her indifference. But it was not likely that any of the retainers of the great houses of the time were in the midst of their quaffing and eating, singing and roaring, half so witty, amusing, dramatic, as these pleasant folk are in the hands of the magician who created them. They carouse night and day, and have no respect, since Sir Toby leads them, of place, persons, or time. Yet they sing no lewd ditties, but one of the most graceful songs in the world. And in spite of their material grossness, there is no such vile grossness in their talk as Shakespeare's contemporary dramatists would surely have inserted. Their conversation is as clean as the moon.[1] Moreover it is most excellent fooling, inimitably fitted for the stage. Their wit almost excuses their excesses ; every

[1] It is remarkable that when the darkness fell on Shakespeare, his lower characters sometimes use a grossness in thought and speech, which was not so before.

one bubbles up with humour. Even Sir Andrew, who is silly, is humorously silly, and is the fruitful cause of humour in others. He is such a fool that Sir Toby thinks he reaches the ideal, the archetype of silliness. Sir Toby has been compared with Falstaff, but, as I have said, foolishly. He is a drunkard, and has a drunkard's ideality at times; but, sober, he is a nonentity compared with Falstaff, who is, with all his love of sack, never drunk; and is wittiest and wisest not only when he is playing with men and circumstances, but when he is quite alone and musing upon the world. Sir Toby is the jovial toper, with a turn for fun, and an ear, like every one else in the play, for good music. It is his creed that, where there is no jollity, there is no life; and he makes everything that is against his jollity into an excuse for it.

> What a plague means my niece, to take the death of her brother thus? I am sure care's an enemy to life.

'Every night,' scolds Maria, 'Sir Andrew is drunk in your company'—

> With drinking healths to my niece : I 'll drink to her as long as there is a passage in my throat and drink in Illyria.

There is the man. He deserves a good study, and so does Sir Andrew Aguecheek, but there is no time for this. They are admirably set together; and it is worth while to compare the natural silliness of Sir Andrew with the self-endued silliness of the Clown. The one thinks himself wise and witty and is neither; the other pretends to be a fool, but has the low and cunning wisdom of his calling.

Maria is the wittiest of them all. She keeps with prudence her place with Olivia; lures Sir Toby into marrying her; manages these drunkards into some quiet; invents the practical joke they all play on Malvolio, and, to her credit, enjoys the result more than any of them.

She is the queen of this lower world. 'Good-night, Penthesilea,' cries Sir Toby. 'Wilt thou set thy foot o' my neck,' he says again, enchanted with her cleverness. He marries her for her wit. Follow me, she cries. To the gates of Tartar, answers Sir Toby, thou most excellent devil of wit. This ideality in marriage reconciles me altogether to Sir Toby. And Maria deserved to become Olivia's aunt by marriage—a very amusing situation—and no doubt to be pensioned off; for her deceiving letter, which makes of Malvolio a gull, is a very miracle of cleverness. Almost as clever is her description of Malvolio, where her hearty dislike of the man pierces to the falsehood in him. Hate has good eyes for bad things.

> The devil a Puritan that he is, or anything constantly, but a time-pleaser ; an affectioned ass, that cons state without book and utters it by great swaths : the best persuaded of himself, so crammed, as he thinks, with excellencies, that it is his grounds of faith that all that look on him love him ; and on that vice in him will my revenge find notable cause to work.

Olivia also sees through the pretension of this man, and more clearly than Maria. She has no hate of him to obscure any part of her judgment; and she sketches him to himself in one of the few wise things she says. Malvolio has been girding at the fool's folly, as if it were a most shocking thing—

> O, you are sick of self-love, Malvolio, and taste with a distempered appetite. To be generous, guiltless, and of free disposition, is to take those things for bird-bolts that you deem cannon-bullets.

Live and let live, she thinks; even the fool has his place in the world, just as Lafeu thinks of Parolles. And folly which has no self-love is better than worldly wisdom which has it. It is better that the world of men should be 'mostly fools' than mostly Carlyles. This world of ours which self-love makes so troublesome is none the worse for all the folly which does not think of itself.

Malvolio is not a pleasant person. I dare say Shakespeare —though this would be unlike his custom—did represent in him a certain disagreeable element in Elizabethan Puritanism. The Puritans seem to have been on his mind. He mentions the Brownists in this play. But I do not think he meant to satirise Puritanism itself in Malvolio, or the honest Puritans, of whom he must have known and honoured many. What he made a fool of in Malvolio was the Puritanism which opposed all mirth and jollity as sin. 'Dost thou think,' cries Sir Toby to him (and the phrase hits a universal folly in this extreme type), 'dost thou think, because thou art virtuous, there shall be no more cakes and ale?' What he satirised was the Puritan who used his grim morality as a ladder to self-advancement. His wide humanity would dislike the first, his deep sense of honour would despise the second. But Malvolio is worse than any rigid Puritan. His will is evil because he is up to the throat in self-love. Every one who is noticed by the Countess stands in his way. He hates them all for this, and they hate him. And when self-love begets self-admiration, its vanity grows with speed to a monstrous size. When we are half through the play Malvolio believes (before Maria's letter) that Olivia is in love with him, and that he is lord of her household. Of course, he tumbles into the snare laid for him, and becomes a greater and a greater fool, till (like Olivia, who, seizing her own way, says that Fate has done it) he declares that Jove himself has taken his matters in hand. 'Well,' he says, 'Jove, not I, is the doer of this, and he is to be thanked.'

Nothing better could have happened to him than his imprisonment as a madman. It gave him the chance of finding out that self-love was much more wicked than all the drunkenness of Sir Toby, or the reckless life of the household. And, indeed, it seems to have done him some good, or Shakespeare wished to touch the noble as well as the ignoble fibre of Puritanism. For, when he is asked what he thinks of the opinion of Pythagoras—'That the soul of our grandam might haply inhabit a bird,' he answers—and the answer contains the strength of Puritanism—'I think nobly of the soul, and in no way approve his opinion.' But the vanities of self-love return when he is loosed, and are all alive again. He still believes that Olivia has loved him, *then* that she has done him wrong—Olivia! who scarcely recognised his existence!—so hard it is to break down the building self-love has architectured. At last, when he finds out that he has been notoriously abused by the sportful malice of a waiting-maid, a drunkard, a silly knight and a fool; when all the building of conceit falls into laughable ruin, the central vice of the man breaks into fury, and he flings them all his savage farewell—

I 'll be revenged on the whole pack of you.

And now I finish this lecture with things that taste sweeter in the mouth. In the fifth Act the personages are brought together, and all that they say not only harmonises with, but enhances, their several characters. Olivia is still Olivia; Viola is Viola with her passion deepened. The Duke, while retaining his sentiment, is developed into a man and a master of affairs. Sebastian is himself, and has broken Sir Toby's head, and made havoc of Sir Andrew; and Sir Toby, knocked out of his humour by pain, and made truthful by drink, settles the character of Sir Andrew who offers to help him to a surgeon—

Will *you* help? An ass-head and a coxcomb and a knave, a thin-faced knave, and a gull !

When Olivia, thinking Viola to be her husband Sebastian, claims him before the Duke, Viola, in this crisis, throws all concealment of her love aside. She turns to the

Duke, who has threatened her with death to spite Olivia,
and cries—

> And I, most jocund, apt and willingly,
> To do you rest, a thousand deaths would die.
>
> OLI.   Where goes Cesario?
> VIO.   After him I love
> More than I love these eyes, more than my life,
> More, by all mores, than e'er I shall love wife.

No hesitation; full, frank assertion of undying love. Given
the moment, nothing can be more natural to Viola's
character. She who once said she never told her love,
now, angry with Olivia's claim, and wrought to the height
of passionate feeling, breaks into open and intense expression of her love; and is most true to her character
when she seems to contradict its past. She is following
the Duke, when Olivia calls her 'husband'! Then the high
honour of a gentleman shines in the Duke. He checks
his departure, and demands the proof. It is apparently
given, and though he turns in wrath on Viola—

> O thou dissembling cub! What wilt thou be
> When time hath sow'd a grizzle on thy case?

he says no more; he threatens no more. He remembers
that he is a gentleman—

> Farewell, and take her; but direct thy feet
> Where thou and I henceforth may never meet.

To relieve this intense moment, Sir Andrew enters with
his head broken, and declares that Viola has done it.
Then, and most dramatically, Sebastian enters, and all
the knot is disentangled. The discovery of Viola by
Sebastian, of Sebastian by Viola, while the rest look on in
wonder, is most delicate and lovely—

> SEB.   Do I stand there? I never had a brother;
> Nor can there be that deity in my nature,
> Of here and everywhere. I had a sister,
> Whom the blind waves and surges have devour'd.
> [To VIOLA]. Of charity, what kin are you to me?
> What countryman? What name? What parentage?

VIO.   Of Messaline : Sebastian was my father ;
        Such a Sebastian was my brother too,
        So went he suited to his watery tomb':
        If spirits can assume both form and suit,
        You come to fright us.
SEB.   A spirit I am, indeed
        But am in that dimension grossly clad
        Which from the womb I did participate
        Were you a woman, as the rest goes even,
        I should my tears let fall upon your cheek,
        And say—Thrice welcome, drowned Viola !

With that, all the trouble is past.   Viola, reverting to the practical side of her character, explains the matter with brief clearness; and then, turning to the Duke, her eyes alit with love, passes into her world of imaginative passion—

DUKE.   Boy, thou hast said to me a thousand times
        Thou never shouldst love woman like to me.
VIO.   And all those sayings will I over-swear ;
        And all those swearings keep as true in soul
        As doth that orbed continent the fire
        That severs day from night.

Now all the pretty play is over.   It has been part of the great world.   Wherever it is played or read, it is part again of the great world of man.   And perhaps the last verse of the song, with which the Clown closes it, means to tell that truth.   If it does not, 'tis no matter—

      A great while ago the world begun,
        With hey, ho, the wind and the rain,
      But that's all one, our play is done,
        And we'll strive to please you every day.

III

JULIUS CÆSAR

THE play of *Julius Cœsar* is the form into which Shakespeare cast the materials he had collected out of *Plutarch's Lives* of Cæsar, Antony, and Brutus. The subject was a common one. Polonius says in *Hamlet*: In the university 'I did enact Julius Cæsar: I was killed in the Capitol: Brutus killed me.' Every one knows how much life Plutarch gave to his characters, but the life which Shakespeare gave them was more full, various, and feeling than Plutarch's power could paint. A multitude of stories interesting as history, a host of philosophic remarks interesting as Plutarch's, illuminate but sometimes overwhelm the presentation of these three men by Plutarch. In Shakespeare's play, the men themselves are the first interest; and only those events and passions are chosen out of the history, which develop the characters, urge on the action of the play, or enliven the scenes into a vivid reality. The political philosophy, of which there is a fair sprinkling in the play, does not seem to proceed from Shakespeare, but from the very nature of each of the characters he has separately individualised. Even when Brutus, Cassius, Casca lay down identical theories, the expression of them is different on the lips and in the mind of each. In all that Plutarch writes of his men we are in touch with Plutarch, but in this play we do not touch Shakespeare, but Brutus, Cassius, Antony, Casca, Cicero, or Cæsar. And in this contrast is contained the eternal distinction between the man of talent and the man of genius, between the describer and the creator, between the intellectual man and the poet.

Then, again, a creative genius, having collected his materials, feels his mastery over them, and uses them as he pleases. He is going to make a greater matter than that which actually happened; something that will endure when the historical events have become dreams. Therefore Shakespeare makes what changes he will in the history of Plutarch. He makes Cæsar's triumph occur on the same date as the Lupercalia. It really took place six months previously. He brings the murder of Cæsar, the funeral speeches, and the arrival of Octavius in Rome, into the circle of one day instead of many. He combines into one the two battles of Philippi, quietly setting aside the interval of twenty days between them. This is the imagination dealing as it pleases with facts. It is possible historians may dislike it, but what talk we of historians when there is such a man as Shakespeare.

Nor does he less show his sense of mastery over his materials when he takes from Plutarch, whenever he thinks them good enough for his purposes, the very words that Plutarch uses or invents. It is true they were in the noble English of North's translation—contemporary English with which Shakespeare was in sympathy—but all the more one would think that he would avoid transcribing whole sentences, almost word for word, out of North's prose into blank verse. Not at all. Genius takes all it wants, and is confident of its right to do this. 'I have power to adopt what is good,' Genius would say if he were questioned, 'because it is better where I place it than it was in its original surroundings.'

The play appeared in 1601. Weever's *Mirror of Martyrs*, printed in 1601, refers to Antony's speech in this play, for which there is no original in Plutarch. Hence we know that *Julius Cæsar* preceded Weever's book, and probably was written ,in 1600. It was acted at the beginning of 1601.

The subject-matter of the play was of great interest at this time. Perhaps in 1562, certainly before 1579, and again in 1588, there were plays on the fate of Cæsar. In 1589 a play with the title *Julius Cæsar* was known, and was acted by Shakespeare's company in 1594. Then, after Shakespeare's play, that is, after 1601, a number of plays represented various portions and views of the same subject. Indeed, the matter has always engaged the thoughts of men, their passion and their genius. It is a political interest;—the natural war which has existed since the beginning of the world between the idea of Liberty and the force of Autocracy; and this play, where the two powers clash, where they are impersonated in Cæsar and Brutus, has been, on many a stage, the means of giving expression to the anger and pity of those who, among a people degraded by the gratuities and coaxing of Imperialism, lived and died for the rugged liberties they could not win.

That interest has been seen and felt in this play. What has not been seen and felt in it—at least not to my knowledge—is that it puts, indirectly, into artistic form the two reasons why revolutions which are in the right do not always succeed against forms of government which are in the wrong: that is, why a struggle for freedom fails against a tyranny, or, if it should succeed for a time, as in the French Revolution, why it finally falls again under the power of a despotism.

The first of these reasons is—that the single idea which belongs to all the revolutionists is not kept apart, in each of them, from personal motives. Each man adds to it his own interest or his own passion; and these several interests or passions divide the men from one another. Then unity is lost, and with the loss of unity, force is dispersed. Of all the conspirators, only Brutus had a single aim uninjured by any personal motive. Shakespeare makes that plain. His Cassius, Casca, Cinna, and the rest, had each his own axe to grind, or his own personal envy of Cæsar. Not one of them is ever able to conceive the impersonal, the unselfish attitude of Brutus. Brutus—and this is the deep tragedy of the play —far apart from the rest in his own ideal world, thinks, stands, lives, and dies alone. His is a position which has been repeated again and again in the history of revolutions. It was, to give one example from our own time, the position of Délécluze in the story of the Commune. The other conspirators have little bond of union except the desire to slay Cæsar; no uniting ideal aim in which their individual selfishnesses are absorbed. Where that is the case, as often it has been in the story of the struggle of Ireland, and, as yet, of the working classes in England and abroad, failure is certain.[1] Even if, for the moment, they act together, as in the slaughter of Cæsar, they fall asunder, each to his own interest, when the act is accomplished; and their want of union for one collective, ideal aim ruins their cause. The only thing which binds the conspirators together after the death of Cæsar is that they are all proscribed, and have to fight for their lives. It is astonishing how clearly this comes out in *Julius Cæsar.* It dominates the play till the death of Cæsar. It is not neglected afterwards. Even the great and vital friendship between Brutus and Cassius is imperilled by the personal aims of Cassius. On the eve of the battle which will decide their fate, these two friends all but split usunder.

[1] There have been many men like Brutus whose aims were pure of self in the struggle of Ireland and in that of the working class, but there have been only too many who played the part of Cassius, Casca, and the rest.

Again, a still more important reason why revolutions against Imperialism fail, is that their leaders have no settled form of government ready to replace that which they have overthrown; and no men, trained in official work, to use as means for carrying on a government. The consequence is, that after the outburst everything is at sixes and sevens; the various parties devour one another; and in the confusion the mere mob of the violent, unthinking, drifting people get the upper hand. Anarchy, then, makes every kind of human life and effort, and all property, uncertain; and then the steady body of the whole State, sick of disturbance, illegality, change, uncertainty, welcomes despotism again, because it governs. This was the career of the French Revolution.

Shakespeare makes the lesson clear in this play. The pure political idealist, like Brutus, is absolutely at sea the moment he has destroyed the government of Cæsar. And Cassius, Casca, Cinna, like Brutus, have nothing ready with which to replace it. They are all left, in ridiculous failure and confusion, face to face with the mob whom the embryo imperialism of Cæsar has weakened and degraded by amusements and gratuities. Nothing can be better put than this is by Shakespeare in the blind, futile, inconsequent, disintegrated talk of the conspirators after they have slain Cæsar. Brutus, their noblest comrade, is at this crisis the most amazingly foolish of them all. He loses his head. He shouts like an Anarchist. He thinks all Rome is on his side. He is absolutely ignorant of the people he has only conceived in his study. He thinks Rome will govern itself. He takes no measures to set any government on foot. He believes in Antony! He acts like a man in a dream. He makes a speech to the people, hands them over to Antony's seductive tongue, and walks home, as if he had done nothing and had nothing more to do, to talk the matter over with Portia. The inevitable follows; and he flies for his life with Cassius through the gates of the city he has, by his action, handed over to a more organised despotism than Cæsar ever exercised.

Imperialism has won, Republicanism has failed, and Shakespeare, in the quiet apartness of the Creator, marks out, through the dramatic action and speech of his characters, what are the main points of the event. He records things as they are, and in the quarrel seems to take no side. This is the proper position of a great dramatist. Yet, as in *Coriolanus*, where Shakespeare's sympathy seems, on the whole, to be on the side of the tribunes, so here, and more probably here than in any other play, the personal sympathy of Shakespeare seems to emerge on the side of Republicanism. He has, as always, his 'good-humoured contempt of the mob.' But there is a heightening of his phrasing, an intensity of the soul he puts into his words when he speaks of Brutus or makes him speak, which draws me into the imagination that his sympathy was with the thoughts of Brutus, the republican. There is not enough on which to base any definite conclusion, but there is enough on which to base a suggestion. And this suggestion of his personal sympathy with the Republicanism of Brutus is perhaps buttressed by the strange and half-contemptuous sketch he makes of Cæsar, the great imperialist. It is unlike any other image I know of Cæsar. He is represented as subject to superstitions, as wavering to and fro, as led by the nose by his enemies, as vain even to insolence, as having lost his intellectual powers in self-sufficiency, as one who thinks himself separated altogether from his fellow-men. His speeches are almost the speeches of a fool. Shakespeare seems to have gone out of his way to make this representation, this *dénigrante* representation; and it is very curious when we contrast it with the

lofty, dignified, and beautiful representation he makes of
the man who embodies Republicanism.   I do not say that
Shakespeare was a republican; that would be absurd.
Nobody knows what he was; and he was not likely to
openly sympathise with Republicanism, even of the kind
then conceived, under the rule of Elizabeth.   But he was
likely to be opposed to despotism, to maintain the freedom
which England had already won.   And it is worth saying
that when this play was written in 1601, Elizabeth had
tried to enforce the Tudor despotism, to impose her
own will on Parliament; and was successfully met and
defeated by Parliament quietly insisting on its ancient
liberties.   She yielded with a good grace; but no
Londoner, and least of all one of Shakespeare's vast
intelligence, could be unaware of this struggle.   A great
contention of this kind steals into the thoughts and
imagination of men, and consciously or unconsciously
influences their work, even though the work have nothing
to do with the struggle itself.   I think it possible, then,
that the representation of the contrasted political ideas
of Brutus and Cæsar, which Shakespeare (to the advantage of Brutus) makes so plain, was indirectly coloured
by the struggle between Elizabeth and the Parliament—
between the despotic will of the Queen and the ancient
liberties of England.

But all this is scarcely an argument, much less an assertion.   The common thing to say is that Shakespeare, on
debatable matters, such as politics and religion, took no
side himself.   And one proof of this impersonal attitude
is, that even if he sympathised with the political ideas of
Brutus, he as plainly did not sympathise with his weakness in action, with his inability to govern or to manage
men.   His representation of Brutus both before and after
the death of Cæsar, is of a man totally unfit to handle
events or to direct a State.   Shakespeare may have thought

it right to oppose despotism, but even despotism was
better than anarchy. Brutus was a better man than
Cæsar or Octavius. But Brutus could not govern, Octavius
could.

The play is a political play, and of a kind different from
that of any other in his works, even from that of *Coriolanus*. It is concerned with affairs of State throughout,
and when the ordinary passions of human life enter into
it, they come as episodes. The domestic and personal life
of Coriolanus is more important for that play than the
affairs of the State. But in *Julius Cæsar*, on the contrary, the relation between Portia and Brutus, the friendship between Brutus and Cassius, are extraneous; do not
affect the dramatic conduct of the drama, or the catastrophe. They are relieving interludes of great charm, and
made more charming still not only by the invention of
Lucius, who in his happy youth has nothing to do with
the storm of events around him, but also by the gentle
and gracious relations between the boy and his master
Brutus. But none of these things interfere with the main
action—with the contest between Cæsarism and the old
Republicanism of Rome, between a worn-out Past and a
living Present. Brutus is defeated; Cæsar conquers; and
the play is rightly named *Julius Cæsar*.

Some have said it ought to be named by Brutus's name,
and that he is the true hero of the drama. But great as
Brutus is in the drama, and apparent master of its action,
Cæsar is in reality the cause of all the action and its
centre. His spirit dominates the whole. But in the first
part it is not the Cæsar of the play who dominates, it is
the Cæsar who *has been*; the life, the doings, the spirit of
the Man who in the past has bestrid 'the world like a
Colossus.' What Shakespeare has made of the existing
Cæsar is what a man becomes who having been great,
thinks his will divine, even the master of Fate; and fall-

ing into that temper which the Greeks called Insolence, becomes the fool of Vanity and the scorn of the gods who leave him to relentless Destiny. Shakespeare's picture of Cæsar resembles the picture drawn by the Greek tragedians of the chiefs who, isolating themselves from their fellow-men, equalised themselves to the gods in their self-opinion, and placed themselves—as the gods did not—above eternal Law. But his present folly does not lessen Cæsar's past greatness; and Shakespeare takes pains to show how great he was, and how great he still is in the minds of men. The play opens with his triumph over Pompey. Brutus loves him, while he hates his idea of Empire. Cassius, Casca, while they cry him down, exalt his image in our eyes. When they slay him, they are like men who have murdered a world. Even the starry powers, in Shakespeare's imagination, emphasise his greatness. The whole heaven, when Cæsar comes to die, is racked with storm; lions roam the streets, the dead rise from their graves. And when he is dead, all his vanity and folly are forgotten instantly. Rome rises to drive out his assassins. His spirit broods over the rest of the play in executive power. It is Cæsar who wins the battle of Philippi, who plants the sword in the heart of Cassius and of Brutus. The theory of government, because of which he died, defeats the theory Brutus held; the new world he initiated disperses to all the winds the old world that Brutus, in vain, tried to reanimate. Cæsar is lord of the play; Brutus is in the second place.

Being thus a Drama concerned with Statesmen and State affairs, there is but little in it of human passion at its height. The note of the play is low in sound. There is the passion for liberty in Brutus, but it is the passion of the student, not of the man of action. The same high passion is supposed to be in the other conspirators, but it is really the mean passion of envy which influences them.

There is neither loftiness of motive nor depth of wrath for freedom in anything they say or do.

Then, with regard to Brutus, his Stoic nature forbids in him deep emotion; and his personal love for Cæsar prevents him from feeling any intensity of indignation against Cæsar. His love for Cæsar depresses into a still sadness his eagerness for liberty. Moreover, he is not angry with anything Cæsar has as yet done. He slays Cæsar lest he should do wrong to liberty in the future. This doubt as to whether Cæsar will become a tyrant or not (the slaughter of Cæsar being only to prevent a possibility) would naturally take all passion out of his thought and act. Scepticism—save vaguely with regard to itself—is naturally unimpassioned, except in a young man like Hamlet. Brutus was a mature man and a Stoic. Sad and earnest then, in quiet Stoicism, without any passion, his mind works, and his hand strikes. His sense of what he thinks himself compelled to do depresses rather than excites him. Therefore, with regard to the passion for liberty, the dramatic note is low and still.

Then, again, the human relations of this play do not reach the high levels of the great emotions. They are chiefly the relations of friend to friend. Antony is Cæsar's friend, but his friendship is mixed with his political selfishness. His various speeches over Cæsar's body rise now and then into a semblance of passion, but they are calculated. He sees himself rising into power on Cæsar's death. He is as cool as an iceberg when he talks with Octavius and Lepidus.

Again, the friendship of Brutus and Cassius is a true friendship but not an equal one. An unequal friendship does not stir into movement the deeper waters of feeling. The stronger nature of Brutus has another world in which to live where Cassius cannot come. One feels this apartness again and again in the famous dialogue between

them. Even in the reconciliation there is that conde-
scension on the part of Brutus which is incompatible
with an impassioned friendship.

Only in the relation between Portia and Brutus is there
any deep emotion in the play, and the scenes between
him and her scarcely belong to the movement of the
drama. Shakespeare knew how noble, when it was good,
was the type of the Roman woman as mother, wife, and
friend; and Portia claims from Brutus all that a man
owes to one who has become bone of his bone, flesh of
his flesh. She must also be spirit of his spirit, thought
of his thought. 'Tell me all,' she cries,

> by that great vow
> Which did incorporate and make us one,
>
> .   .   .   .   .   .
>
> Am I yourself
> But, as it were, in sort or limitation,
> To keep with you at meals, comfort your bed,
> And talk to you sometimes? Dwell I but in the suburbs
> Of your good pleasure? If it be no more,
> Portia is Brutus' harlot, not his wife.

Then, to that impassioned voice, answers that cry of high
emotion, so rare on the lips of the Stoic:

> You are my true and honourable wife,
> As dear to me as are the ruddy drops
> That visit my sad heart.

As to Portia, she is compact of love. When he is with
her, she sees everything he does. All his restlessness
is open to her, and reflected by her. Till his heart is
fully disclosed to her, she has no peace. When he goes
away from her to slay Cæsar, her soul goes with him.
She sends the boy to the Senate-house, but forgets to tell
him what to do in her excitement. She can scarcely
keep her passion silent, calls on a mountain to press down
her tongue; sees, as if she were present, what is being
done in the Capitol; hears the noise of the fray; half

betrays to the Soothsayer her knowledge of the conspiracy—

Why, knowest thou any harm 's intended towards him ?

At last, she can bear the weight of her passion no more.

> I must go in. Ay me, how weak a thing
> The heart of woman is ! O Brutus,
> The heavens speed thee in thine enterprise !
> Sure, the boy heard me. Brutus hath a suit
> That Cæsar will not grant. O, I grow faint.

That is of feeling quite intense; and the last news of her confirms its intensity. The woman in her cannot bear the strain of the danger Brutus is in from Octavius. She falls into distraction and swallows fire. This is the one presentation of deep passion in the play, and it is isolated from the rest of the action.

Though the image of Cæsar dominates the play, and Cæsarism conquers in it, yet its main subject is the working out of the fate of Brutus as the last hero of Roman liberty; and the fall of Republicanism in his death is the true catastrophe of the Drama. The representation of this might have been made more impassioned. But, even in this, passion was excluded, because Brutus, being a Stoic, his law of life excluded passion. Shakespeare was forced then to keep his representation of Brutus quiet. And nowhere is his careful work as an artist more remarkable, more close to his conception of a Stoic student pushed into the storm of great affairs, than in his slow, restrained, temperate development of the character of Brutus. Again and again we expect a high outburst of poetry. The events seem to call for it from Brutus. But Shakespeare does not choose him to rise above the level of his Stoicism; he does not even permit the tide of his own emotion, as he writes, to erase the stern lines of the character he has conceived. Twice only (after Cæsar's slaughter, and during the battle), Brutus is swept out of his self-restraint.

Nevertheless the position of Brutus, though it is marked by this self-quietude, is a noble subject for dramatic poetry. It is the struggle of the hero who belongs to a past world against the victorious pull of the present world. And since Brutus is high-hearted, and his idea morally right, and the world he fought with ignoble and unmoral, his overthrow does not lower him in our eyes. He is conquered by circumstance, but his soul is unconquered. He becomes more fit for lofty tragic poetry when, as the play moves on, he stands alone in his nobleness, apart not only from his enemies, but in the purity of his motives from his friends. And the tragic in him is lifted into splendour of subject when we see clearly that which he did not see till he came to die: that the death of Cæsar—the means, that is, which he took in order to bring back to Rome the freedom that he loved—was the very event which riveted on Rome the Imperialism which he hated. Few situations are more poetic. The ghost of Old Rome stands on the threshold of Imperial Rome, and fades before its worldly splendour. But as the phantom fades away, we follow it with praise and honour. It will rise into life again when Imperial Rome shall have fallen into the helpless ruin it deserved. The spirit of Brutus can never die.

In the very first scene (in Shakespeare's preparing fashion), two main elements of the drama are represented. There is, first, the mindless mob, spoilt by the bread and games successive leaders have given to it; which has no care for liberty or any policy, only for entertainment. The second is the division of Rome into violent parties. We see the partisans of Pompey and Cæsar, hot with anger; then, in another class, all those

who, like the tribunes, hold some office, and are enraged
with Cæsar who threatens to take all offices into himself.
These two elements become as it were two *leit-motifs*,
which occur again and again throughout the play. We
hear in the first Scene the growl of the popular storm
which threatens Cæsar. In the next we are in the thick
of it. Cæsar enters in triumph. A short dialogue, quick
and crisp, sketches the pride, the superstition, the inso-
lentia of Cæsar—the temper of one whom the gods have
doomed; the flattery which has brought him to this point
of foolishness; the pride which could not conceive that
misfortune or death could touch him. When the Soothsayer bids him beware, he cries—

> He is a dreamer ; let us leave him : pass.

The pageant then passes on, and Cassius and Brutus are
left alone. We hear that Brutus has been brooding of
late, apart from his friends, in silence. No one knows, not
even Cassius, what turn his thoughts have taken on the
politics of Rome. Has he even discovered himself what
he thinks? There are thoughts in us which we need to
hear shaped by another person or by some event before
we are conscious that we have had them for a long time;
and Brutus is in this condition when Cassius probes him
about Cæsar—

> Bru. Into what dangers would you lead me, Cassius,
> That you would have me seek into myself
> For that which is not in me ?

Then the event finishes what Cassius had begun. A
shout at a distance forces out of Brutus the dominant and
concealed thoughts within him, and crystallises them
into expression—

> What means this shouting? I do fear, the people
> Choose Cæsar for their King.

On that Cassius works to win Brutus to his side against
Cæsar; and at every point of the dialogue the character

of Cassius is dramatically divided from the character of Brutus. Brutus only cares for the public weal, for his republican ideal. Cassius is consumed with envy of Cæsar; and the bitter hatred of envy appears in the stories he tells of Cæsar's physical weakness—anything to degrade the image of the man he hates—as if Cæsar's not being able to swim well, or his trembling in a fever, proved that he was not a better man than Cassius or Brutus. This has no effect on Brutus, who is incapable of envy. Brutus scarcely hears him. He is listening for a renewal of the shouts. Then Cassius, seeing that the chord of jealousy and envy does not answer to his touch, changes his attack, and changes its motive three times in the course of his speech until at last he strikes the note which is answered in the soul of Brutus. First, it is discontent with Fate that he touches—'Why should we be underlings and he half a god?' That note does not touch Brutus. Then he tries ambition—'Why, Brutus, should you not be as great as Cæsar?' That also does not affect him either. At last he sounds the note of the ancient liberty of Rome—

> There was a Brutus once that would have brook'd
> The eternal devil to keep his state in Rome
> As easily as a king.

That echoes in the soul of Brutus; and to develop it further into act, Cæsar enters in all his pomp. Shakespeare's pictorial imagination strikes out, as it were in flashes, the outward appearance and the characteristics of the passers-by—

> Look you, Cassius,
> The angry spot doth glow on Cæsar's brow,
> And all the rest look like a chidden train :
> Calpurnia's cheek is pale, and Cicero
> Looks with such ferret and such fiery eyes
> As we have seen him in the Capitol,
> Being cross'd in conference by some senators.

It might be made a picture of. Then Cæsar (in the one

speech he makes which is worthy of his intelligence),
sketches Cassius so vividly that he is immortalised; and
then Antony with one slight touch—full of flying power—

> Yond Cassius has a lean and hungry look ;
> He thinks too much ; such men are dangerous.
>
>   .   .   "   "   .   .   .
>
> He is a great observer, and he looks
> Quite through the deeds of men ; he loves no plays,
> As thou dost, Antony ; he hears no music :
> Seldom he smiles, and smiles in such a sort
> As if he mock'd himself, and scorn'd his spirit
> That could be moved to smile at anything.
> Such men as he be never at heart's ease,
> Whiles they behold a greater than themselves,
> And therefore are they very dangerous.

Here and here alone Cæsar speaks up to the level of his
former self. When he has passed by, Casca takes up the
presentation, and we see, as if we were on the spot,
the scene when the crown is offered to Cæsar, and the
mob, and the women, and Casca's own bitter envy. Then
in a single phrase Cicero is painted; the cultivated
literary man who is isolated from the common herd in
dainty pride of culture.

> Cas.   Did Cicero say anything ?
> Casca.   Ay, he spoke Greek.

Every blunt word of Casca lays bare his embittered and
jealous heart, and we can almost see the 'quick metal'
in his face. Even more vividly is the heart of Brutus
disclosed to us in this masterly dialogue. The desperate
thought which has been born in him—that Cæsar must be
silenced—grows steadily while he listens to Cassius and
questions Casca. He is thinking of what Cæsar has done,
and of that alone. He questions, questions, that he may
be sure that Cæsar is trying for the crown, that he may
set his mind at rest. Though he says little, it is enough
to enable us to follow his soul in doubt. Must I slay
Cæsar whom I love ? Is there no way out of it ? I must

have time to think. To-morrow, Cassius, come to me, or I will come to you. His mind runs round the circumference of his thought, but never quite enters the circle; hesitating, this way and that dividing his dread, his impulse, and his duty. And so, in this slow progress of his thought to its shaping, we leave him for a time. He leaves Cassius alone, who comments on his character: 'Noble, yet so simple that he may be wrought into my conspiracy.'

The night falls then, and the third Scene opens amid a great tempest, full of terror and portents. The meaning of it in the play is put afterwards on Calpurnia's lips:

The heavens themselves blaze forth the death of Princes.

We have seen how often Shakespeare used the common belief that Nature mixed herself up with those great human events which, striking at chief men, struck at humanity. Nay, more, he made Nature reflect the passions of men when they reached intensity. He writes as if he believed that a spiritual power in Nature was in touch with the deep things in man and in his history. We remember the storm which accompanies the murder of Duncan; the fury of the elements which reflects and heightens the agony of Lear. And here, to develop this thought of his, and at the same time to dramatise it, he represents at length what each of his characters thinks of the storm. And it affects them all in a different way. This suppression of his own idea, and this out-creation of it in other lives than his own, other thoughts than his own, is most masterly in this scene, and most effective on the stage.

Casca, the envious scoffer, who respects nothing, is like many of his tribe, smitten by the storm into superstitious terror. With his sword drawn, breathless and staring, thinking the world is ending, he meets Cicero; and the little sketch of Cicero is delightful. He is perfectly unmoved by the terror of the night; as quiet as if all the stars were shining in a peaceful sky—only astonished by the state of mind in which Casca presents himself. Hear how placid are his sentences—

> Good even, Casca : brought you Cæsar home ?
> Why are you breathless ? and why stare you so ?

And to Casca's relation of the awful sights—a lion met near the Capitol, a man with a burning hand, men all on fire walking the streets, the owl shrieking at noonday, and the skies dropping fire—he replies in a philosophic strain as if he were in his study; and then asks about the news of the day, as if he were at his club—

> Indeed, it is a strange-disposed time :
> But men may construe things after their fashion,
> Clean from the purpose of the things themselves.
> Comes Cæsar to the Capitol to-morrow ?

This is the educated, cultivated man to whom, absorbed in literary and political interests, the wild games of Nature (who to his mind pursues her natural course even in storm) are of no importance. Just so might Burke or Darwin have looked on the elemental war.

Neither does Cassius care a straw for the raging of the tempest, but not for Cicero's reason. The fury of hate in his heart is greater than the fury of the storm. The lightning and the elemental roar express his soul, and he walked in them with joy. He sees in the dreadful prodigies of the night the warning of Cæsar's end— Heaven itself is speaking its wrath with Cæsar. Then, as the tyrannic hate within him seeks fresh forms of expression, he says no longer that the storm is the message of divine wrath. It is itself the image of Cæsar. It is he who is the dreadful night of Rome; it is he that thunders, lightens, opens graves, and roars like the lion in the Capitol. He is our fear and destruction.

Finally the hate and envy of Cassius break out into that impassioned speech by which he bursts open the heart of Casca, and claims him as a brother in his envy—and in his conspiracy.

> And why should Cæsar be a tyrant then ?
> Poor man ! I know he would not be a wolf
> But that he sees the Romans are but sheep :
> He were no lion, were not Romans hinds.
> Those that with haste will make a mighty fire
> Begin it with weak straws : what trash is Rome,
> What rubbish and what offal, when it serves
> For the base matter to illuminate
> So vile a thing as Cæsar !   But, O grief !
> Where hast thou led me ?   I perhaps speak this
> Before a willing bondman ; then I know
> My answer must be made.   But I am arm'd,
> And dangers are to me indifferent.

He ends by saying to Casca that 'three parts of Brutus is ours already,'

> and the man entire
> Upon the next encounter yields him ours.

This phrase, while it marks the slowness in the growth of Brutus's resolution, which Shakespeare has so carefully wrought out, introduces us to the next scene in which Brutus at last makes up his mind.   The storm still goes on—'the exhalations whizzing in the air' give light enough to read by—but the rain has ceased.   Brutus is walking in his orchard, and the dawn is near at hand. He too has cared nothing for the storm.   His soul is stormier, with its dreadful purpose, than are the heavens. Shakespeare lays bare this soul, restlessly ranging over motives, possibilities, casuistries, and settling finally into the resolve to slay for the general good the man he loves; not because Cæsar has done anything as yet against liberty, but because he may—and, 'lest he may, I will prevent him.'   What Cæsar is, he says, if given greater power,

> Would run to these and these extremities :
> And therefore think him as a serpent's egg
> Which, hatch'd, would as his kind grow mischievous,
> And kill him in the shell.

'Tis a mean argument; and only a philosopher would use it and think it good. Once, during the soliloquy, the unphilosophic side of Brutus contradicts it—

> To speak truth of Cæsar,
> I have not known when his affections sway'd
> More than his reason.

Then he gets back to his mere philosophy, changing and shifting.

Some say that in this soliloquy Brutus is unlike his previous character. But Shakespeare is representing a mind travelling over a host of arguments for and against the deed it considers. The disordered spirit of Brutus is tossed to and fro; even now he cannot come to certainty. It needs to settle him down into full resolve, that Rome should call on him for help. And the sealed papers flung in at his window, crying to him to 'awake, and strike and redress, in the name of his great ancestor who drove out the Tarquin,' finally secure his resolution. Then he looks back on the long struggle, and in his loneliness paints the tempest of thought through which he has passed— marvellous words they are—half of the philosopher, half of the man who has loved Cæsar, and not one line of a man of the world.

> Since Cassius first did whet me against Cæsar
> I have not slept.
> Between the acting of a dreadful thing
> And the first motion, all the interim is
> Like a phantasma or a hideous dream :
> The Genius and the mortal instruments
> Are then in council, and the state of man,
> Like to a little kingdom, suffers then
> The nature of an insurrection.

Now, when at last the mind of Brutus is free from doubt, the conspirators arrive. They are in the garden, the storm is dying away; and the presentation to the eye of the whole scene is rendered more vivid by the little dialogue (while Brutus and Cassius talk apart) of Casca and Cinna about the part of the heaven where the sun arises. They talk of 'where the east is' while they wait to arrange how the foremost man of all the world is to die. This is Shakespeare's way, as it is the way of human life, of mingling the common with the uncommon, the great with the small, the deeds which shake the world with a brawl at an inn in Eastcheap.

Then Brutus, developing still more the high-mindedness of his character, will have no oath taken. No need for that if they are Romans who know they have an unselfish cause to maintain; every drop of whose blood is guilty if they break their promise. This is far too lofty a strain for the conspirators, whom other motives drive. They do not even answer him. Such words as

> The even virtue of our enterprise

must have struck cold on the passions of envious Casca and jealous Cassius. The loneliness of Brutus comes home to us.

Then emerges also his folly as a politician. It is the retired student, engaged only in ideas, who speaks when it is proposed to slay Antony as well as Cæsar. Our course, he says, would be too bloody then. Would we could kill Cæsar's spirit, and not Cæsar. Mark Antony is nothing without Cæsar.

This is too childish-foolish for this world. Brutus has no eye for men, or for affairs. He never even thinks of Octavius. He has not measured the latent power of Antony, nor does he measure him justly after the murder. He hands the whole of Rome over to him when he lets him speak over Cæsar's body. His position as a politician is ridiculous; his position as a noble thinker is honourable. Cæsar dead, Antony was not only Antony, but Cæsar as well; and Cæsar is nowhere more alive than when he sways the hearts of the Roman people in the speech of Antony. The only way the conspiracy could have succeeded was, once Cæsar was slain, by the slaughter of those that loved Cæsar. Napoleon understood that; so did Antony and Octavius. The tender-heartedness and the personal morality of Brutus were, in the circumstances, fatal to his cause. All this is the careful drawing of Shakespeare, who did not work (as I have often said) with the careless indifference which some think an attribute of genius.

Yet when we turn from the futile politician, and the philosopher ignorant of the world, to the man, with what charm does his tender-heartedness arrive! The conspirators depart; Brutus is left alone. He calls his attendant, Lucius. The boy is fast asleep. And Brutus, looking at him, loves his youth, and will not disturb him—

> Boy! Lucius! Fast asleep! It is no matter;
> Enjoy the honey-heavy dew of slumber:
> Thou hast no figures nor no fantasies,
> Which busy care draws in the brains of men;
> Therefore thou sleep'st so sound.

And this interlude of the tenderness which lay beneath the stoicism of Brutus is continued by the scene with Portia which instantly follows, and on which I have already commented.

The morning comes, and we are placed in Cæsar's house. The storm has not quite passed away, and the doomed man enters, to be met by his wife who urges him to stay from the Capitol. There is that which is terrible in the insolent pride Cæsar shows throughout this scene. There is that which is pitiable in the weakness with which he yields to his wife, and then, when his pride is appealed to, to the conspirators. This kind of pride is the very top of weakness. All the evil omens are in vain. His pompous and inflated speeches, intolerable when he is speaking in the third person, seem to challenge the gods, and to despise all men but himself. Shakespeare, like a Greek dramatist, meant them to contain his fate and the cause of it. They partly explain the hatred and envy of Cassius and the rest; and it is a fine piece of art which thus modifies our horror of his murder by our natural dislike to this tone of haughty defiance. And in the death scene this is continued. His insolence becomes so great that it seems to claim the dagger. He says he will spurn 'like a cur' the man who would alter his will. 'Hence!' he cries, as the conspirators press their suit upon him—'Hence! Wilt thou lift up Olympus?' Again Decius claims his friend's return from exile. Cæsar answers,

> Doth not Brutus bootless kneel?

This motives the last blow, and brings us up to it without too great a shock.

Then follows the confusion of the conspirators, who do not know what to do; the dispersal of the people, and the conspirators left alone with their dead master. It is a wonderful scene; at first they do nothing but shout—

> Liberty! Freedom!—Tyranny is dead!
> Run hence, proclaim, cry it about the streets.

It is almost like the shout of Caliban—as foolish at least as his. Brutus bids the Senators not to be affrighted. Casca tells Brutus to speak to the people. 'Where's Antony, where's Publius?' cry others. This is all these foolish persons think of doing after their momentous act. No prevision, nothing arranged, no measures for government,—and the whole world upturned!

Then they begin to talk, half-philosophic talk about life and death, and how their deed will be acted over on a future stage, as if they thought they were playing a tragedy, and had done nothing in reality. And Brutus, shaken to the centre of his stoicism, falls into melodrama quite outside his character; bids them bathe their arms in Cæsar's blood, wash them up to the elbows, smear their swords, and, waving their red weapons in the market-place, cry 'Peace, freedom, and liberty.'

At first all this seems, in the bloody circumstance, unnatural. But, in reality, nothing can be better done than Shakespeare has here done. The inner agitation of the conspirators shows itself in these absurdities. They begin to feel that they have shaken the world. They have let loose forces they cannot manage, and terror and confusion seize on their heart and brain. They dare not give voice to the overwhelming dread. And they take refuge in this surface-talk, in these inane boastings; even Brutus is shocked into melodrama. It is like Hamlet bursting into fantastic phrase after he has seen the ghost. It is almost a comfort when Antony—who is contending for his life, who knows what will follow on this deed, who sees the overthrow of Brutus and his own success, if only he can for a few hours secure his life from the conspirators' daggers—comes upon the scene. He is politic enough. He persuades Brutus that he will act with him. Cassius suspects him; but Brutus imputes his own single-eyed love of liberty to Antony, and consents, like an idiot, to Antony's speaking at Cæsar's funeral. Antony is nobly managed. Were he only the hypocrite, we should despise him. Shakespeare does not leave it so. Even though his life is on the card, he cannot help breaking out into pity and praise when he sees his master dead, but he manages to pass this off as an offering to friendship, while he agrees in principle with what has been done. In him, and in Brutus, craft and simplicity stand face to face, and both men are true to the character Shakespeare has made for them. As a politician Antony is wise and Brutus a fool. As a man Brutus is noble and Antony ignoble—and yet not quite ignoble. His personal love and wrath for his

F

friend, arising continually through his deceiving speeches, redeem him in our eyes. At last, he is left alone with the dead, and the long repressed rage bursts forth in that impassioned address to the pierced body of Cæsar, wherein, in the last words, we see beforehand what is coming, when

> Cæsar's spirit ranging for revenge,
> With Atè by his side come hot from hell,
> Shall in these confines with a monarch's voice
> Cry 'Havoc,' and let slip the dogs of war.

One catastrophe has been—the death of Cæsar; but out of death Cæsar rises again, an avenging spirit. Another catastrophe, the death of Brutus, is at hand. It is the true catastrophe of the play—the overthrow of the Republican, the triumph of the Imperial, form of government. Cæsar, *in* Antony, does this, and Cæsar's true revenge is the victory of his idea.

The second scene closes the third Act. It is the scene of the speeches in the Forum. The speech of Brutus is entirely in character, doctrinaire, sententious; convinced, even to a touch of vanity, of his rightness; so convinced that he does not doubt the people being of his opinion (imputing his own thoughts to every man in the crowd); so convinced that he begs them, for his sake, to hear Antony. In every phrase Shakespeare writes down the folly of the man, his unimaginable unfitness to lead, to convince, or to understand a mob of citizens whom an imperialistic policy had debauched with gifts. Nevertheless, they cheer Brutus when he has done! Then Shakespeare, with one imaginative touch, makes it clear that they have completely misunderstood the action and the speech of Brutus.

ALL.   Live, Brutus! live, live!
1 CIT.   Bring him with triumph home unto his house.
2 CIT.   Give him a statue with his ancestors.
3 CIT.   *Let him be Cæsar.*

Listen to that; the people wish to make him that which he hopes he has destroyed. He has slain Cæsar that there may be no more Cæsars. 'Let him be Cæsar,' is the answer of the mob. Alone, alone, Brutus goes away, the fool of fancy, self-deceived.

Then Antony begins the speech that every schoolboy knows. It is charged with contempt of the mob. He plays on them as a musician on an instrument. The subtle changes of his speech, from praise of the con- spirators—harmonising himself with the impression Brutus has made on the crowd—to praise of Cæsar, dropping the first as he feels his listeners coming into sympathy with the second; his personal grief for Cæsar breaking forth into tears that win him the sympathy of the people, and finally impassionate them into love of Cæsar; his careful, reiterated appeal to their curiosity by his reserve with regard to Cæsar's will till he has lashed them into insatiable eagerness; his final appeal to their hatred of ingratitude, the vice the people have always hated most; his exhibition of the dead body to their eyes: 'Look, look and pity'—are one and all most masterly, and, as we read, it is finally the mighty intelligence of Shakespeare that impresses us more than even the mighty events of the history. The last appeal, with its fascin- ating touch of narrative—with its linking of each separate wound to the name of a conspirator—is full of a splendid knowledge of the way to excite a people :—

> If you have tears, prepare to shed them now.

Then comes that astonishing scene, in which Antony lashes the excitement of the mob into fury, in which we seem to see and hear the tumult growing, swelling, raging, till the Forum roars; till all Rome is so filled with mad- ness of wrath that the mob slays Cinna the poet because he bears the name of Cinna the conspirator;—and Antony, left alone, while the mob rush forth to burn and slay, caps it all with triumphant cynicism—

> Now, let it work. Mischief, thou art afoot,
> Take thou what course thou wilt.

The rest, the fourth and fifth Acts of the play, are concerned with the fall of Brutus and the conspirators. The interest lessens slowly but steadily, till it dies away almost altogether in the fifth Act. It is only the interest of a death-bed; of the last and convulsive effort of Roman Republicanism, wounded to the death by the slaying of Cæsar, to live again.

It is a pity, I think, that the story of this slow departure was extended over two Acts. They had to be spun out by needless interludes, such as the intrusion of the poet, and the interview of the opponents before the battle; and the last Act might well, by some condensation of the suicides of the conspirators, have been brought into the fourth Act. But I am too bold in saying this.

There are, however, two great sources of interest in both the Acts. One is the overbrooding of Cæsar's spirit—the master, though dead, of all the events and of all the characters. He still overstrides the world. This is marked out by Shakespeare in different ways.

In that remarkable first scene of the fourth Act, where Lepidus and Octavius are sketched (waiting for their full conception and finish in *Antony and Cleopatra*), the world that Cæsar ruled alone is divided into three.

'Did not great Julius bleed for justice' sake?' Brutus cries in the midst of his quarrel with Cassius.

'When Cæsar lived,' cries Cassius, 'he durst not thus have moved me.' 'Strike as thou didst at Cæsar,' he cries again, when he bares his breast to Brutus. The dead man is an overshadowing third in that interview.

Again, before the end, to Brutus alone in his tent, the

ghost of Cæsar enters, and the iron soul of Brutus is dis-
tempered. His hair stares and his blood is cold. The
spirit is the fierce presentation to his eyes of that which
always fills his mind. Were not an atmosphere created
by the besetting thought, the ghost of Cæsar could not
have appeared.

In the parley between the chiefs, Antony drives home
the murder of Cæsar to their souls with bitter words.

As Cassius dies, he calls on Cæsar—'Cæsar, thou art
revenged.'

When Brutus is resolved to die, Cæsar is with him—

> The ghost of Cæsar hath appear'd to me
> Two several times by night : at Sardis once,
> And this last night here in Philippi fields :
> I know my hour is come.

And as he runs upon his sword, his last cry is—

> Cæsar, now be still :
> I kill'd not thee with half so good a will.

The second interest is the further development of the
characters of Brutus and Cassius. The unfitness of
Brutus for public affairs is now, in these last acts, fully
expanded. Even in the midst of the storm of events,
Shakespeare with careful finish paints Brutus as still the
reader of books, the philosopher of the study. When the
Council of War is over he resumes the book he has been
reading; he carries it in the pocket of his gown—

> Let me see, let me see : is not the leaf turn'd down
> Where I left reading? Here it is, I think.

Then, having made us think of Brutus as a student, he
develops further his unfitness, as such, for public affairs.
Brutus claims to be a better captain, a better soldier than
Cassius—which he is not. He gives the wrong advice
before the battle. He loses the battle itself by his
hasty action. Because he is absolutely convinced of his

moral rightness he thinks that he is also certain to be
right in the ruling of events—an egregious folly of which
history affords many an example—and it is probable
Shakespeare meant us to understand this, when, having
overcome the wise advice of Cassius to wait a day at least
before joining battle, Brutus backs up his mistaken view
by that well-known passage—

> There is a tide in the affairs of men
> Which taken at the flood leads on to fortune ;
> Omitted, all the voyage of their life
> Is bound in shallows and in miseries.
> Ou such a full sea are we now afloat,
> And.we must take the current when it serves,
> Or lose our ventures.

The statement is good philosophy; but Brutus misapplies
it to the affair in hand.   On the rock of its half truth
he wrecked his ship.   He mistook the tide.   Had he
waited, as Cassius advised, he might have caught the
flood.   As it was, he took the ebb and thought it was the
flood.   That is one development of the character—an increase, under the fierce pressure of circumstance, of the
original weakness of the thinker when pushed into practical affairs.   On the other hand, the gentle affectionate-
ness, especially in friendship, which underlies the stoicism
of Brutus, also increases and is developed into charm.
Portia's death smites his heart, but it softens its outgoings.
Defeat and the ruin of his cause are met with Stoic
courage, but it is a new thing to find that they strengthen
the deep loving-kindness of his nature.   Brutus gains a
double soul in Shakespeare's hands.   A similar development is wrought in Cassius.   He too in great trouble wins
back his soul.   Gentleness, lovingness in friendship, a
gracious humility, are born in him.   It is easy to illustrate
these changes.   The celebrated quarrel of Brutus and
Cassius is, as it were, a study of friendship; and Shakespeare almost suggests this when Lucilius tells Brutus

how Cassius received him—with courtesy, but not with
the old familiar freedom.   Brutus answers—

> Thou hast described
> A hot friend cooling ; ever note, Lucilius,
> When love begins to sicken and decay,
> It useth an enforced ceremony.   .
> There are no tricks in plain and simple faith :

This is close to the philosophic sententiousness of Brutus,
and the little dialogue, in Shakespeare's preparing way,
sounds beforehand one of the clear notes of that scene
between Brutus and Cassius, to which he means to give
his full strength.

I need not enter closely into it.   It is almost a household word; and it is most nobly conceived and expressed.   But I mark a few things—Cassius, pressed by
the times, has used tricks of policy, and supported
bribery.   This is quite in his character as Shakespeare
conceives it at the beginning of the play.   There he is
shown as believing in the corruptibility of all men.   He
is now himself corrupt.   It is a natural development.
He who believes in any evil being universal in men
ends by himself practising that evil.

Brutus meets this immoral expediency in his friend
with stern rebuke.   He is not modern but ancient Rome;
and Cassius feels that with so honest a leader their last
chance of success is lost.   But since all is lost, he cannot
bear that Brutus and he shall not be friends.   In the
ruin that at least shall be kept.   This tragic motive is
slightly but clearly wrought.

Then there is a fierceness in the words of Brutus which
is greater than the error of Cassius deserved.   Why is
the Stoic unjust?   We know why when we hear Brutus
say, 'Portia is dead.'   That which was behind the words—
the bitter grief within—made the words of Brutus fiercer
than justice demanded.

Again, we have seen Cassius, as yet, in an unamiable light. He has been the envy-ridden man, grim, harsh, and scornful. Now, that he is about to die, we are shown the depth of his heart. The reproaches of Brutus break through the ice of his angry experience. They might have made him furious; they make him as tender as Brutus. The divine genius of Shakespeare thus lifts him into our pity and affection. For the rest of the play he has left all his old nature behind him—that envious aigreur which had grown over him like a crust; and he becomes that which he probably was as a young man. This recurrence (when the end of life draws near) to that which a man was before he was spoiled awry by the world, is not unfrequent in experience, but few writers have used it as Shakespeare, who loved us, has used it in his plays. Cassius thinks of his birthday, reviews his life, and is content to die since he has failed. He was a sceptic; now he is partly superstitious :—

> You know that I held Epicurus strong,
> And his opinion ; now I change my mind.

He was old in heart; now he is fresh in spirit; and resolved, like a - young man, to meet all perils constantly. Nothing can be more tender, with more of the grace of a boy, than his farewell to Brutus—

> For ever and for ever farewell, Brutus !
> If we do meet again, we 'll smile indeed ;
> If not, 'tis true this parting was well made.

And then he dies, and Shakespeare, in his poetic fashion, makes Nature sympathise with his fall—

> O setting sun,
> As in thy red rays thou dost sink to-night,
> So in his red blood Cassius' day is set,
> The Sun of Rome is set !

And Brutus speaks his epitaph—

The last of all the Romans, fare thee well!
It is impossible that ever Rome
Should breed thy fellow. Friends, I owe more tears
To this dead man than you shall see me pay.
I shall find time, Cassius, I shall find time.

With that last line, beyond all praise in its thought-
embracing beauty of love, Brutus is left alone. He fights
to the end in a second battle. But the day goes against
him, and for the moment his stern self-restraint is broken
through. It was wonderful of Shakespeare to mark this
momentary rush of excited physical passion, conquering,
in the heat of battle, his stoicism. Cato runs into the
fight shouting like a madman—

I am the son of Marcus Cato, ho!
A foe to tyrants, and my country's friend;
I am the son of Marcus Cato, ho!

Brutus bursts forth, for the first and last time, into a
similar excitement—

And I am Brutus, Marcus Brutus, I;
Brutus, my country's friend; know me for Brutus.

And he rushes into the battle. That violation of his
character is a piece of pure truth.

And now the end is come. The great mistake, political
not moral, is closed in death. Cæsar has conquered.
'Cæsar, now be still,' Brutus cries as he runs upon
his sword. As he looks back, his tenderness and his
conviction of the rightness of his cause are both
undiminished.

Countrymen,
My heart doth joy that yet in all my life
I found no man but he was true to me.

No words are more loving, nor more nobly proud. The
rest is of his cause, and it is Shakespeare's comment on
his own conception of Brutus—

> I shall have glory by this losing day,
> More than Octavius and Mark Antony
> By this vile conquest shall attain unto.
> So, fare you well at once; for Brutus' tongue
> Hath almost ended his life's history :
> Night hangs upon mine eyes ; my bones would rest,
> That have but labour'd to attain this hour.

Even his enemies thought more highly of him than he thought of himself. They mark his isolation; his care only for the common good, not for himself; his tenderness, the many-sided fulness of the man.

> This was the noblest Roman of them all :
> All the conspirators, save only he,
> Did that they did in envy of great Cæsar ;
> He only, in a general honest thought
> And common good to all, made one of them.
> His life was gentle, and the elements
> So mix'd in him, that Nature might stand up
> And say to all the world, 'This was a man.'

It is Antony says that. It is Antony's plain condemnation.

IV

HAMLET

I DO not suppose that there is any product of modern genius that has been more written about, or created a greater curiosity than *Hamlet*. The *Divina Commedia* may perhaps, at those points, rank with it, but both derive the eager impulse they have given to curious search, and to the impulse to write about them, first from the extraordinary simplicity of the main lines of humanity in each character they delineate, and secondly from the equally extraordinary variety and subtlety with which, always within those simple lines, each separate character is imaged and wrought into a living soul.

The simple lines, for example, on which the characters of Hamlet, the King, Horatio, Ophelia, and the Queen are drawn, and on which the plot is made, are within the comprehension of the most uneducated intellect, and for this reason, as well as for the striking simplicity of the *mise en scène*, we find that *Hamlet* is as great a favourite with the gallery as with the stalls, with the village audience in a barn as with an audience of academies; when it is acted by a strolling company, or by the leading actors of England, Germany, or France. Every one understands the story, is interested in its action and characters, in the vivid and fatal movement of it. A child would comprehend the outline of Hamlet's story. An alert boy or girl, on seeing the play, would probably ask the same questions we ask. Did Hamlet believe the Ghost? Was he really in love with Ophelia? Why did he talk such nonsense and such sense together? If he thought the King had really murdered his father, why did he not kill the King at once? Was he mad or only pretending? These and many others are simple questions which naturally arise. And I am not sure whether the answers to them are not quite simple also. They would be so, if Shakespeare had not troubled our answers and confused our minds with his addition to the simple outlines of the most subtle and complex representation of the thoughts and feelings of the characters. The more we hear of their inner life, the less are we able to say clearly why they did this or that; the more subtle and the less simple seems the true answer to the questions.

Within the simple outlines is the filling up of the outlines—the delineation of the inner life of men and women —all that lies silent behind the action—and this is like an Oriental web for fineness, for involution of pattern, for delicacy of line, for subtlety of change and colour, for a bewildering crossing and intercrossing of thoughts, motives, passions, arguments, intuitions, imaginations, impulses, reasoned conclusions, unreasoned dreams and driftings, sane thoughts which adopt the expressions of insanity, insane wanderings like Ophelia's in the sub-conscious world, and the terrible mixture, as in the King, of the terrors of conscience and the consolations of self-deceit. These are but a few of the inmates of the inner world of the human soul which Shakespeare opens to us, and chiefly in the soul of Hamlet, who is the heightened concentration into one sensitive person of the main characteristics of thought and action in one of the great types into which humanity may be divided. An immeasurable variety then exists within the simplicities of this drama.

There is another thing to say in this connection. Hamlet is supposed to be entirely different, both in intellectual power and in strangeness of phantasy and feelings, from the common run of educated men—to be in a class apart. It is not really so, and one proof of that is that so many hundreds of thousands of men and women, when they listen to him, listen to their own souls. The thoughts he has they have had; the imaginative dreams and fancies he expresses have passed through their minds. The questions he puts to life, the questionings he has had about death, those he has about suicide when he is alone; the impatience he has with the troubles he is called upon to face, and the demands which they make upon him; the impulses he has to perform the demands and to battle with the troubles; the fading of those impulses as fresh thoughts occur to him and make him glad to forget them—are all common to millions of men and women who belong to the pensive, sensitive, imaginative, contemplative, idealising type of humanity, which thinks rather than acts, is quiet rather than stirring, dreaming rather than practical; to whom the soul is more than the body, the mystic more than the material life. Wherever persons of that type exist, in poverty or in riches, among peasants or princes, we find Hamlet, and they find themselves in Hamlet. And the wonder of the play consists not in the mental apartness of Hamlet from the rest of the world, but in the amazing power of the poet who made him, who embodied in him the representation of one million-peopled type of humanity; who made him so act, so speak, that he set before us not only the type, but almost all the variations within that type, almost all the main directions of their thoughts and feelings about the life of man. Shakespeare himself, not Hamlet, is the marvel. There are millions of Hamlets, but one Shakespeare. Moreover, the thoughts Hamlet expresses are not of exceptional range or excellence. They do not set him on a pinnacle above other men. They are, as thoughts alone, the ordinary thoughts of his type in a cultivated youth with a turn for philosophy. What does make his thoughts apparently greater and deeper than those of other young men of his temperament is the noble passion of their clothing, the splendour of words, like that of a starry heaven, by which they are made to seem uncommon. It is not a creature of deep philosophic thinking that we have in Hamlet; it is an undeveloped poet who adds to all he thinks and feels the spirit of a nimble and impassioned imagination which no one else in the play possesses, so that he shapes into splendid form thoughts, feelings, and problems common in the talk of educated young men, and makes them seem much greater than they really are.

There is the other type, containing also many diverse forms—the active, practical, quick-deciding, dry-thinking type, who use their intellect on the business of the world, on the investigation of natural or social phenomena; who put aside sentiment, who sometimes make love an episode; to whom this outward world is all; whom trouble does not much affect save to inspire them to get it out of the way; who recognise duty and do it often well, but who work it so as to increase their money or their reputation; to whom all dreaming is repulsive, all drifting a disgrace, all doubt a folly, all imagination and its works, not business, but entertainment for the moment; who rarely stay to question life, but do make it their own; who think of death as infinitely distant, till they grow old; who have no time to consider the world to come if it should occur to their mind; who think a man a fool who dreams of suicide; who sometimes recognise what is called the ideal, but are bored by it; who make intellect the judge of all questions; to whom the sensible is the real and the spiritual the unreal; and who, if they were put into their own soul, and forced to see it, would cry out with great naïvete, 'What is this place! where am I?'

This type (of a thousand more forms than I have indicated) is represented also by millions and millions of men and women in all the ranks of life, and not one of them can comprehend the Hamlet type. Claudius, till Hamlet made him afraid, the Queen, till Hamlet pierced her conscience, Polonius, Laertes, Ophelia till she became mad, belonged to this type; Hamlet and Horatio to the other.

Well, when a person of the one type meets a person of the other, and both are strong examples, each of his own type, neither of them can understand the other; and the easiest way to express their want of comprehension is to say: 'This person is mad, or half mad'—just what Polonius and the King and Queen and Ophelia, but not Horatio, said of Hamlet; just what a number of the critics of this play—more or less, in proportion as they belong to the type opposite to his—have said about him. They draw attention to many acts and words of Hamlet as tainted with madness; and the most eager to prove this point, and their own acumen, are the specialists in insanity who, believing themselves to be an unanswerable authority on what is madness and what is not, are the very blindest and most foolish of guides in this matter—men, some of whom at least, if they had their way, would end by shutting up in asylums all the poets, artists, and prophets, all the men and women who do not care for money, who are bored by science, and who think that the real fools are those who care for the things of this world.

These sapient folk are sure that Hamlet was mad, or all but mad; and do not ask themselves whether Shakespeare meant him to be mad, or why Horatio never thought him mad, or on the verge of madness; or whether a madman can be so sequent as he is in all that he says, or so continuously intelligent along with a weakened brain. At last, driven by a kind of demon, they end (like some of

the brain investigators of the present day) by saying
that any extraordinary imaginative power, which works
beyond the sphere of the analytic reason, is itself madness.
All men of genius are mad, genius itself is a kind of
madness.

Amazingly funny that is! And when we hear it, all that
is left for us to say is: 'That, in a world where the
humorist is at a discount, and where due reasons for
gaiety are only too few, it is very kind of Providence to
make men so amusing. If genius is a madness, Hamlet
was mad, but the maddest man that ever lived in
England was Shakespeare, who made Hamlet.'

The fact is that Shakespeare never intended to represent
Hamlet as mad or half mad or verging on madness. He
expressly made him a feigner 'of madness, and when he
wished to represent real madness and to contrast it with
feigned madness, he created the real madness of Ophelia,
and did it with wonderful truth and skill. There is not
a trace of madness in Hamlet. There is plenty of eccen-
tricity, plenty of fantastic thought and feeling, plenty of
wandering and roving imagination, plenty of wild and
even whirling phrases, and of those phrases which grow
out of a consciousness of a world beyond that of the
senses, into which consciousness penetrates unaware—
which, heard of by those who, like the specialists, are
looking out for madness, are quite sufficient to induce
them to suggest an asylum. Fancy a mad doctor asked
by Claudius or Polonius about Hamlet, hearing him
say à propos de rien, 'I could be bounded in a nutshell
and think myself king of infinite space, had I not bad
dreams.' What would he say, shaking his foolish head?
'Sire, with the deepest regret, I am of opinion that
Prince Hamlet is suffering from cerebral disease, likely,
at any moment, to become dangerous.' But if Horatio
were present, he would say: 'What an ass the man is!

What does he know? The Prince has thought this and talked of the idea in it a hundred times at Wittenberg.' And the same thing may be said of all the phrases which are used to prove the madness of Hamlet. These things, in a man to whom the soul is more than sense, who lives within rather than without, are not madness; otherwise almost half the world in which we live is mad. Moreover —when he lives in the outer world—Hamlet always knows what he is about; always sees his position clearly, always reasons, with following and linking intelligence, his point; always understands himself and his world, never gambols away from his thought on to another at the sound of a word as Ophelia does; and in all his soliloquies, however strange and apart from worldly life his thought, makes his meaning clear. After all, the main question with regard to this matter is—not whether Hamlet was mad or half mad, or not mad at all—but whether Shakespeare meant him to be mad—and to that there is but one answer possible. For my own part, those passages of thought which are used to prove that he was mad contain the wisest and deepest things he says; and those actions of his which are used to prove the same theory obey a higher law of reason than any mere logician has ever conceived.

How did Shakespeare imagine Hamlet? That is the real question. And, perhaps, the most interesting way of answering that question is not to isolate Hamlet's character for separate consideration, but to go through the play with him, taking up, along with him, the other characters, and the events which develop him and them. It is difficult to embody that in a single lecture, but it may be attempted.

The play opens about a month after the funeral of Hamlet's father, shortly after his mother had married King Claudius, his uncle, with 'most wicked speed.'

Hamlet had come over to Elsinore to his father's burial, and had with infinite disgust been present at his mother's marriage. He had been at Wittenberg, at the University, and had made a close student-friendship there with Horatio, whom he had left behind him, but who now, after a month's absence, has arrived at Elsinore. He had then been a student, with all the fresh ideals, and crude thoughts, and passionate hopes, and imaginative depressions, which belong to a young man of his type at the University. We see from his after-talk that his mind lived chiefly among those metaphysical questions which are so often the delight and eagerness of a young man. It is plain that he was an indweller of his own soul; that the outward world was visionary to him rather than real; that, thus dwelling chiefly in his soul, all the questions which belong to life and death, to the purposes of the one, and to what lay beyond the other; and all the depressions and excitements which cross and recross such an inner life—were his. This was his secret, sacred, hidden world. In this was his action, his thought, his passion.

There are in the Universities now—and elsewhere also —thousands of young men and women of a similar type, and living the same kind of honourable and secret life in the imaginative world of the spirit. And when, as in Shakespeare's time, a flood of new literature (filled and vibrating with new thought, and moved from without by the winds of a general national excitement) is let loose on the world, there are even a greater number of such young men, alive with the same spirit, swimming in such a flood, and blown on by such a genial wind. Shakespeare met them every day; he may—even now in his maturity—have become one of them and written this play out of that new experience.

In Hamlet at the beginning of this play, he realised himself and them. And now, he takes this silent, reserved, meditative, unworldly questioner of his own soul, of human life and of death, this inexperienced student, ignorant, except by hearsay, of crime and sin, unaccustomed to action, untrained in its struggles but accustomed to abstract thought, with only one friend to whom he speaks freely or at ease—and suddenly places him in the midst of terrible events, face to face with an awful revenge which duty seems to demand of him; with a father's murder, with a mother's incest blackening his life; with war threatening in the distance, with a wild and drunken court, such as seemed savagery to the quiet student.

His whole life was upturned; the very bottom of his soul was shocked and stained; out of his quiet he was flung into a filthy tempest! Every nerve must have been strained to the utmost, every fibre of his thought and feeling violated. Instead of metaphysical peace, unutterable disgust dwelt in his soul. That is what Shakespeare meant us to realise. His hatred and disgust of life begins before he knows that his father has been murdered. It is caused by the marriage of his mother to his satyr of an uncle within a month of his father's death. It is caused by the vile and wild disorder of the Court, by the revolt of his quiet soul against it, and by this drunken licence of mirth over his father's grave. The wrath and sorrow of this set him apart, and here his soul is opened, in this first soliloquy, in which his horror of the change from the meditative quiet of Wittenberg to the foul world of Elsinore is set before us. It is long, but it must be read. Remember, it is before he knows of his uncle's murder of his father—before the demand for vengeance is made upon him.

> O, that this too too solid flesh would melt,
> Thaw, and resolve itself into a dew !
> Or that the Everlasting had not fix'd
> His canon 'gainst self-slaughter ! O God ! God !

How weary, stale, flat, and unprofitable
Seem to me all the uses of this world !
Fye on 't ! ah fye ! 'tis an unweeded garden,
That grows to seed ; things rank and gross in nature
Possess it merely.   That it should come to this !
But two months dead ! nay, not so much, not two ;
So excellent a king ; that was, to this,
Hyperion to a satyr : so loving to my mother,
That he might not beteem the winds of heaven
Visit her face too roughly.   Heaven and earth !
Must I remember ?   Why, she would hang on him,
As if increase of appetite had grown
By what it fed on :   And yet, within a month—
Let me not think on 't—Frailty, thy name is woman !—
A little month, or ere those shoes were old
With which she follow'd my poor father's body,
Like Niobe, all tears :—why she, even she,—
O God ! a beast, that wants discourse of reason
Would have mourn'd longer,—married with my uncle,
My father's brother, but no more like my father
Than I to Hercules : within a month ;
Ere yet the salt of most unrighteous tears
Had left the flushing in her galled eyes,
She married.   O, most wicked speed, to post
With such dexterity to incestuous sheets !
It is not, nor it cannot come to good ;
But break, my heart, for I must hold my tongue !

For a whole month this has been simmering in his heart and brain.   Only two things have relieved the oppression of the accursed situation in which he was placed.   First, his love for the innocent grace of Ophelia, and, secondly, his habit, nursed by his quiet life in the past, of sliding away from any outward event or condition of things on to some river of meditative or abstract thought in which the actual present is forgotten, even does not exist for him.   This is constant throughout the play.   As constant is the way in which, suddenly recalled to the present, he bounds as it were out of his reverie into surprised contact with the actual world.

This is how Shakespeare first represents him.   The quiet student plunged into hateful noises, the young, even the

innocent thinker and idealist plunged into events, the
loathing and horror of which never leave him till he dies.
On the top of this—to double the trouble of his heart, to
add the supernatural to the natural horror, to bring his
young soul into murder and lust among those nearest to
him—his father's ghost appears to him at dead midnight.
The play opens with that vision, seen by others, in scenery
as fitting as it is effective.   The guard is being relieved on
the platform above the sea.   The night is cold; the stars
are bright

> When yond same star that's westward from the pole
> Had made his course to illume that part of heaven
> Where now it burns—

Horatio, Bernardo and Marcellus see the stately shade of
buried Denmark stalk by their watch.   They speak to it;
its appearance makes Horatio, the scholar, recall the portents which foretold great Julius's fall, and the classic touch
sketches the type of the man.   It crosses their watch again.
Horatio appeals to it with passion.   The cock crows, and
it vanishes away.   The scenery of the night is imaged to
our eyes in lovely poetry, and all the imaginative sugges-
tions that the coming morning brings, and the voice of the
bird of dawning.   No more delightful words were ever
written to suggest the growing light, the dewy freshness
of the dawn, than these two lines which add to the
beetling cliff, the platform and the sea, the vision of the
eastern hills now tinged with the colour of the northern
skies—russet, not golden.

> But look, the morn, in russet mantle clad,
> Walks o'er the dew of yon high eastward hill.

They tell the tale to Hamlet.   The condition of mind I
have sketched appears in his welcome of Horatio, his
memory of Wittenberg, his bitter references to his mother's
wedding, his scoff at the drunkenness of the court, and his
misery at this, and at his father's loss—

> Would I had met my dearest foe in heaven
> Or ever I had seen that day, Horatio !
> My father !—methinks I see my father.

And the word introduces in the easiest way the story of the
Ghost. 'O where, my Lord?' cries Horatio, full of what he
had seen. 'In my mind's eye, Horatio,' answers Hamlet;
and the unconscious phrase adds to the breathless expectation of the audience. I know nothing better in drama
than the conversation which follows. Its ease is as great
as its passion; its vividness as its clearness. Hamlet's
self-control, his trouble, his doubt, his intense, even his
contemplative questioning on every point of the appearance, as if it sometimes seemed to him only a story with
which he had a vague connection, and to which he was
listening; his resolution at the close—

> If it assume my noble father's person,
> I'll speak to it, though hell itself should gape
> And bid me hold my peace ;

his demand for silence—all his long disturbance within
and his hatred of what he has seen creating in him the
sense of some hidden evil—

> My father's spirit in arms ! all is not well :
> I doubt some foul play.

All, all is as admirable in conception as it is in execution;
most certain, in its dramatic appeal and passion, to awake
excitement and expectation in the veriest rustic in the
dullest village in England.

I pass over the third Scene for the moment. The
fourth is at midnight again on the platform; the moon is
in the sky, and the air bites shrewdly; it is very cold.
Hamlet is come to meet his father's spirit. As he waits,
he hears the sound of the revel in the castle where the
King drinks deep. 'Is it a custom?' asks Horatio—and
Hamlet (apparently forgetting that which he has come to
see), slides off from his blame of these drinking habits into

a meditative disquisition on the way in which one particular fault in men (not necessarily of their own, rather
of nature's making) spoils their whole lives, takes the pith
and marrow out of them. No actor should leave out this
passage, nor forget to represent Hamlet as gliding away
from the present into a reasoning in his soul on a question
which suddenly presents itself to him. It is one of the
key-notes of his character. This is the first example of
that habit on which I have already dwelt. In the very
centre of vital events, of times of crisis, he slips into such
questioning thought as filled his student days. He forgets
all about the Ghost in an academic question. He ought
to be thrilling with expectation. He has wandered away
into a vague disquisition on the force of habit. To
omit this passage in acting the play is to lose the intensity
of Hamlet's surprise at the apparition, the reason of his
overwhelming terror, and the uncontrolled passion of his
speech. He has been in the contemplative life of Wittenberg. He is plunged into the hell of Elsinore, from
abstract dreaming to dreadful reality in a moment.

The same sliding away into argumentative thought—
the same sudden shock out of it into the actual world,
occur again and again throughout the play. Even here,
after the first surprise, after the trembling passion, his
unconquerable questioning, his doubts of the reality of
things seen and heard, his forgetfulness, in side issues of
thought, of what has been and is, seize upon him, and he
wavers to and fro like a tree in the wind. He is shaken
by the sight 'with thoughts beyond the reaches of
his soul.'

> Say, why is this? wherefore? what should we do?

The Ghost beckons him away. Horatio urges him not to
follow. What does Hamlet care? Nothing the ghost can
do can be worse than his life, which, now transferred from

peace and meditation into the vile turmoil of a hateful world, is worthless to him.

> I do not set my life at a pin's fee.

And his soul, Hamlet's only reality, being immortal as any ghost, cannot be injured.

Again, it is characteristic of these dreaming, self-centred children of pure thought, that, when action is suddenly demanded of them, when they find themselves swept into the whirl of it, they rush into it with a far greater intensity than the man who has been accustomed to the movement of the world, who, trained to action, knows how to act. Such a man is quiet, collects himself, waits to understand before he acts; and the violent words and actions of Hamlet when he throws off his detaining friends would not have been used by him. His action would have been steady and continuous. Hamlet's excitement towards action is intense and whirling; but again it dies down as quickly as it rose. Thought, questioning, doubt, reasoning resume their sway. The native hue

> Of resolution is sicklied o'er
> With the pale cast of thought.

He cannot make up his mind as to whether the Ghost was really his father's, was a truth-teller, was not a devil. And he hovers to and fro, miserable in his confusion, hating and scorning life because it is not at peace—till he gets things clear at last after the play in which he proves the guilt of the King. Meanwhile, here, with the Ghost, he is on the very peak of excitement, every nerve strained to intensity by the terrible story, by the demand on him for revenge, and by the contact with the supernatural. The story gives consistency to the vague sense of trouble so long lodged in his thought.

> O my prophetic soul!
> My uncle !

It makes the whole world even fouler than he thought;
it stains his mother black, so that a son can cry—

> O most pernicious woman!

Yet it is curious and characteristic of the student that
what he thinks of most is not immediate action, but the
dismissal for ever of all the results of his contemplative
life as a student, the bidding good-bye to contemplation—

> Remember thee!
> Ay, thou poor ghost, while memory holds a seat
> In this distracted globe. Remember thee!
> Yea, from the table of my memory
> I'll wipe away all trivial fond records,
> All saws of books, all forms, all pressures past,
> That youth and observation copied there;
> And thy commandment all alone shall live
> Within the book and volume of my brain,
> Unmix'd with baser matter: yes, by heaven!

He takes out his tablets to write his observation down.
It seems an absurd action—but in reality it is a sub-
conscious recurrence to a habit of his student life. At
least, so I explain it.

The others now rush in, filled with fear and curiosity.
He receives them strangely, with wildered words of fantastic merriment. He seems to joke with them. When
he hears the Ghost crying 'Swear' underground, his wild
mirth welcomes the dreadful voice—

> Ah, ha, boy! say'st thou so? art thou there, true-penny?
> Come on: you hear this fellow in the cellarage:
> .   .   .   .
> Well said, old mole! canst work i' the earth so fast?
> A worthy pioneer!

It was audacious of Shakespeare to represent this, but it is
quite true to nature. When the strings of excitement are
on the point of breaking, it is a relief to play madly with
the cause of the excitement; and the more appalling the
cause, the greater is the relief playing with it affords.
And that relief is still greater in a character like Hamlet's,

to whose grave thoughtfulness of the inner life excitement was, till now, almost unknown. Even now the
excitement is beginning to lessen. He is returning to
his natural type. The rest of the scene is grave and
quiet. He even muses for a moment on the strange
event, turns it over, as if it were apart from himself, in
thought.

> There are more things in heaven and earth, Horatio,
> Than are dreamt of in your philosophy.

It might have been said over the fire at Wittenberg, if he
had only read of such a story. Then he explains how he
will act. He may bear himself ' strange and odd, and put
an antic disposition on.' He is going to pretend madness.
But only fools like Polonius, Rosencrantz and Guildenstern,
and foolish girls like Ophelia, think him mad. Claudius,
when he hears him talking wildly with Ophelia, understands that ' what he spake, though it lacked form a little,
was not like madness.' Even Polonius, though he was
convinced Hamlet was mad from love, says, ' though this
be madness, yet there is method in 't,'—method, the one
thing madness never has! No; what mad talk Hamlet
has hereafter is his own clever imitation of it. Yet, it is
a bad imitation. No sane man can imitate madness well.
His sanity forces him to link thought to thought; Hamlet
always does that. No madman ever does—in the sphere
of his madness. What he resolves on here, is resolved on
partly to give him time, partly because he shrinks from
violent action, partly because his doubts begin to beset
him, and partly because his nature and his past life have
caused him absolutely to abhor the position in which he
is placed, and unfitted him to meet it. Revenge is
demanded from one who has only discussed revenge.
The most resolute action is demanded from one who has
always been up to this moment a doubter, a questioner,
a natural sceptic.

The time is out of joint : O cursed spite,
That ever I was born to set it right !

When next we hear of him, he has been with Ophelia, and she describes his apparent madness to her father. Ophelia is the sensitive, impressionable, innocent, graceful, commonplace young girl, whom Hamlet, before he has seen the Ghost, has wooed and perhaps loved, finding, as I have said, a great pleasure, in the midst of the horrible life he now shares, in her innocent beauty and youth. She is never interesting, has little character, till love and sorrow make her mad. Her brother lectures her, her father lectures her. She replies with some sharpness to her brother, she obeys her father without a word. Her brother, Laertes, is the young man, just setting out into the world, whom Shakespeare has so often drawn, full of youth's sap, and eager for life; fond of his sister, and jealous of her honour and his own; obedient to his father, but scarcely listening to his advice— and with a certain worldly wisdom and insight into affairs of state, which lift him above the ordinary, and prepare us for the swift action he takes when the sister he loves is drowned of her pain, and the father he honours is slain by Hamlet. As to Polonius—he has, as he shows in his advice to his son, a wisdom gained from a long experience of life, or borrowed from the experience of others, cut and dried, bottled up for occasions, having no real ground in thought—the wisdom of the senile and cunning politician. In all else, he is a fool, and vain of the folly he believes to be wisdom. What thought he has, he cannot hold fast to; it slips from his brain. He believes he is always right now, because he has been right when he was young. He leaps to conclusions, and the conclusions are to him unshakeable. He thinks he is fooling Hamlet, and does not even imagine he is being fooled. He pushes himself in everywhere, and settles all questions. His policy is to lurk behind curtains and overhear what is said, to send his man to Paris to spy out his son. The only time he shows real good sense is in his talk to Ophelia about Hamlet's wooing, and then he is too harsh to his daughter, too thoughtless of her feeling, too regardful of himself. Now, when he hears of Hamlet's antics by which Ophelia has been frightened, he explains, to his satisfaction, all the humours which the court has observed in Hamlet by saying that love in its ecstasy has made him mad—the very conclusion Hamlet intended him to make in order to conceal his dangerous effort to discover the truth about his father's murder. With many wanderings of aged vanity Polonius prevails on the King, whose conscience has made him fearful of Hamlet, to test this matter, to hide and listen while Hamlet and Ophelia talk together.

Hamlet, who especially before Polonius plays the fool— folly lures the actor in him to caricature Polonius— sports with this tedious ass under the guise of madness.

> POL. Do you know me, my lord ?
> HAM. Excellent well ; you are a fishmonger.

'Have you a daughter ?' asks Hamlet, eager to encourage Polonius's view that he is mad from love ! Yet, he cannot help making his seeming madness talk good sense: 'Will you walk out of the air, my lord ?' 'Into my grave ?' asks Hamlet. And Polonius, suddenly puzzled by the sanity he feels in the phrase, answers—

> Indeed, that's out of the air. (*Aside.*) How pregnant sometimes his replies are ! a happiness that often madness hits on, which reason and sanity could not so prosperously be delivered of.

O fool, fool—no madman could have said it !

Finally Hamlet wearies of him, and of his own mad play with him—and all his sorrow rushes on him.

'I take my leave of you,' says Polonius—

> HAM. You cannot, sir, take from me anything that I will more willingly part withal : except my life, except my life, except my life. . . .

We hear in the words the terrible strain of his nerves—heightened by his being baited by a fool who wants he knows to find him out.

There is no relief for him, however. Rosencrantz and Guildenstern are now set on him. He is on his guard all through this scene, tensely on guard. Yet they have been youthful friends of his—and he cannot quite believe that they are spies. Even when he drags out of them the fact that the King has sent for them to interview him, he seems to forget that treachery from time to time, and speaks to them as if they were really friends, especially when the entrance of the players relieves the strain. At the beginning of this interview Hamlet is all alert with suspicion, quite close to the present events and to his purpose of revenge. He mocks the two men. But as it goes on he slips away, again and again, into the contemplative region of his soul. The present glides away from his grasp, and he forgets it or only sees it as in a mist—

> There is nothing either good or bad, but thinking makes it so.

This is another instance of that slipping away to his natural self. A still stronger one is this, where he slips out of the conversation into mystic thinking—

> O God! I could be bounded in a nutshell, and count myself king of infinite space, were it not that I have bad dreams.

They meet this—incapable of understanding it—with conventional talk about ambition; for the King, whose messengers they are, suspects Hamlet of wishing for the crown. Hamlet sees this trick, and meets them with a direct question—

> Were you not sent for?

It is a sort of appeal to their friendship. Will you be true to me? it seems to say.

> Come, deal justly with me: come, come; nay, speak.

They hesitate—he gives them up. And then he plays the half madman to them, confessing that he is changed within—

I have of late—but wherefore I know not—lost all my mirth, forgone all my custom of exercises : and indeed it goes so heavily with my disposition that this goodly frame, the earth, seems to me a sterile promontory ; this most excellent canopy, the air, look you, this brave o'erhanging firmament, this majestical roof fretted with golden fire, why, it appears no other thing to me than a foul and pestilent congregation of vapours.

It is quite true what he says; it exactly expresses his situation; but it is couched in so wild a poetry that the two men who are listening—and any mad-doctor who listened, wholly incapable of comprehending the imagination in the phrases—would believe him to be mad, as Hamlet wished them (with infinite contempt of them) to believe. So far he is close to the point, and the present situation. But now, excited by his own words, thrilled within by his own imagination, he slips away again out of the outward world into the inward world of contemplation. The present vanishes away in abstract consideration of humanity—

What a piece of work is a man ! How noble in reason ! how infinite in faculty ! in form and moving how express and admirable ! in action how like an angel ! in apprehension how like a god ! the beauty of the world ! the paragon of animals !

He might have said it — I repeat — at Wittenberg. Suddenly he is recalled to the present (perhaps by the amazement of these Philistines), and he comes home to what lies before him—

And yet, to me, what is this quintessence of dust ? man delights not me ; no, nor woman neither, though by your smiling you seem to say so.

The news of the coming of the Players relieves the tension of the scene, and Hamlet again, in his vital interest in play-acting, forgets the woeful situation in which he is— happy to forget it. At any moment he glides away from his tragedy into the intellectual or metaphysical world. Everything he says about acting is of a high intelligence, of the sanest reasoning; and he feels how too clear he has been, and cannot help saying to Guildenstern,

I am but mad north-north-west: when the wind is southerly I know a hawk from a handsaw.

Polonius comes in and irritates the sane man with his folly, so that, in Hamlet's wild humour—wild because, through the whole of this scene, underneath his passing forgetfulnesses, the terrible story of the Ghost is gnawing at his heart—he plays the madman with eagerness, with a kind of pleasure, before Polonius. Suddenly the Players enter; and as suddenly Hamlet forgets in this new interest all his trouble, enters fully into their business and into his own views of acting and of the drama, just as if he had never left Wittenberg. When they are dismissed, he gives them in charge to Polonius—'Use them well.'

POL. My lord, I will use them according to their desert.
HAM. God's bodikins, man, much better: use every man after his desert, and who shall 'scape whipping? Use them after your own honour and dignity: the less they deserve, the more merit is in your bounty.

Perfect sanity is in every word. How Polonius could listen to it, and not know that Hamlet was as sane as Plato (whom, indeed, he would have thought quite mad), only shows what a veritable fool he was—one of the half idiots the world thinks wise men.

When the Players are gone, Hamlet's thought recurs quickly to his father's murder, and he plots with the first Player to represent before the King the story the Ghost has told him. If the King blench at that, the story is true; the doubts he has had are nought. Then he is left alone, and all the horror—partly dimmed by social converse —surges up again in his heart. We must understand that throughout the scenes he has lately passed through he

has been kept at full tension; rigid to conceal what lies
in his heart, forced to play a part of madness, worried by a
fool, betrayed by his old friends, distressed by having let
himself go and perhaps betrayed that he was acting, holding all his little world at bay, angry with himself for delay,
smitten to the heart by the passion of the actor for the
woes of Hecuba, while he is moved to no effective passion.
Conceive the fierce and silent strain of all this, and you
will not wonder that when it is released, and the repressed
passion let loose like a torrent, it takes the form of that
wild, tumultuous soliloquy—close, close to his real self;
unlike that other academic thing—' To be or not to be.'

> O, what a rogue and peasant slave am I !

Doubt and questioning pervade it.   Underneath it lies
the deep debate in Hamlet's mind—partly caused, we must
remember, by his passionate hatred of the situation and of
the action it demands—as to whether the story he has
heard was true.   Was the King really guilty of this crime?
He tries to convince himself of that by furious abuse,
by words which, assuming his uncle's guilt, will work him
out of his doubt of it, and sting him into revenge—

> bloody, bawdy villain !
> Remorseless, treacherous, lecherous, kindless villain l
> O, vengeance !

Then he despises himself for his big words—words, only
words, when action seems demanded; seems, for he is not
sure—

> Why, what an ass am I !   This is most brave,
> That I, the son of a dear father murder'd,
> Prompted to my revenge by heaven and hell,
> Must, like a whore, unpack my heart with words,
> And fall a-cursing, like a very drab,
> A scullion !
> Fie upon 't !

Yet his very self-contempt conducts him not into action,
but into self-analysis—always gliding away from the hate-

fulness of the outward into his inward life—and then, in that inward life, finding only doubt, hesitation, wavering distress. Again he asks—Is the Ghost true? Is his vengeance justly asked for? If I kill the King, will it be murder done on the guiltless, or justice done on the guilty? I must prove the truth. The Players shall play that which will settle all my doubts. They shall represent before the King, as the Ghost told it him, his father's murder. Horatio, he says,

> Observe my uncle : if his occulted guilt
> Do not itself unkennel in one speech,
> It is a damned ghost that we have seen,
> And my imaginations are as foul
> As Vulcan's stithy.

By this time the King is anxious. He does not believe in Hamlet's madness. His conscience sees discovery in conduct so strange and unaccountable as Hamlet's. Wherefore he falls in with Polonius's proposal to bring Hamlet and Ophelia together. Then, hiding behind the arras, he will know whether love for Ophelia or something more dangerous is at the bottom of this strangeness. Hamlet comes in and thinks himself alone; and talks to himself in that famous soliloquy—

> To be, or not to be : that is the question.

To listen to it is not to listen to a madman—and the King knows this, and is not deceived when Hamlet, detecting that he is spied on, changes his whole manner to Ophelia, and does play the madman—

> Love ! his affections do not that way tend ;
> Nor what he spake, though it lack'd form a little,
> Was not like madness. There 's something in his soul
> O'er which his melancholy sits on brood,
> And I do doubt, the hatch and the disclose
> Will be some danger.

The King, led by his fear, sees justly. That soliloquy —known over all the world—does not arise straight

out of the situation. It arises from a side issue of the
situation, from Hamlet's loathing of life on account of the
hateful and cursed events which darken his life. Is it
right, is it advisable, is it foolish to put an end to life
in sore trouble, or to fight out, and beat down, the
trouble? He argues it almost as if it were an abstract
proposition, as he might have argued it with Horatio
in his student days. He has slipped away again in
thought from the present, save in so far that it is the
present trouble that has raised the question. But once
in the question, his meditative intellect and imagination
move over it with an interest so keen that he forgets
everything else. Point after point regarding life and
death suggests itself, point after point is followed—he is
far, far away in thought from Elsinore. Suddenly he sees
Ophelia; softened by his dreaming, he is gentle with her.
She speaks with tender grace, and returns his gifts. Sorrow has lifted her soul into a higher womanhood, love has
deepened in her since we saw her last. At that moment
he catches sight of Claudius and Polonius behind the
arras; and, furious with their spying, and disgusted with
Ophelia who, he thinks, is their partner in deceit, he acts
the rude, almost the savage madman—and, as he acts it,
seems to take an artist's interest in the way he plays it,
is kindled into fleeting passion by the sound of his own
words—and doubles and trebles, as he goes on, his violence
and rudeness. Even in this he runs away from reality.

Of course, we may make another conjecture to account
for his almost savage rudeness to the girl. He may really
have been in love with Ophelia before the revelation of
his father's murder and his mother's guilt had driven all
thoughts of love away. If so, mingled up with his rage
at the spying of the King and Polonius, would be the
agony of love betrayed. Ophelia, he would think, had
never loved him else had she never joined his enemies.

Her seeming love was not true. When a man is convinced of that, the ordinary courtesy and chivalry of a
man to a woman is dissolved. He and she meet outside
convention in the realm of truth alone, and passion
speaks to passion face to face on equal terms. And the
man will fling courtesies to the winds, and scorn and
cursing and violence will shape the agony he suffers.
So Othello speaks to Desdemona. So here Hamlet speaks
to Ophelia.

He leaves Ophelia in this storm, and poor Ophelia
thinks his mind quite lost. Her pathetic cry over him,
over herself, full of love, pity, and regret, prepare us for
the madness which follows when the man she loves slays
the father whom she respects. With what sadness, when
she comes in playing with her flowers, we recall her pity
now for Hamlet:

> Now see that noble and most sovereign reason,
> Like sweet bells jangled, out of tune and harsh ;
> That unmatch'd form and feature of blown youth
> Blasted with ecstasy : O, woe is me,
> To have seen what I have seen, see what I see !

Then, in the midst of all these wildered scenes of tumbled
thought and stormy feeling, of intellectual fantasy and
doubt and fear, Shakespeare, who loves to fill his play
with contrasts and variety, introduces in the scene with
the Players, the commonsense, the clear criticism, the
steady reasoning of Hamlet on the art of Acting.[1]

When the Players leave, Horatio comes in to Hamlet,
and in the quiet sanity of their conversation we see how
close their friendship is, how full of calm good sense.
This talk is another proof that there was no real madness
in Hamlet. Had he played his madman part alone, had

[1] When we read Hamlet's advice to the Players, we wish that all the
critics of the Drama, and all the acting-managers, were (if he was mad,
or half-mad) quite as mad as he. When also we read it, we understand
what Shakespeare was as an acting-manager, we hear his personal experience.

he been without a confidant in his plot to catch the King
—that would have been like a madman. But we now hear
that he has told all the Ghost's story and his own to
his one friend, consulted him throughout, made him a
sharer of all his thoughts and plans ; and has done this
on the sufficient ground of his long experience of Horatio's
steadfast, unflattering character, and of his tried judgment.
This is not madness, but wisdom—and it is plain that
Horatio never thinks for a moment that Hamlet is not in
his right mind.

The play comes on. The King and Queen see their past
on the stage. The Queen knows nothing of the murder.
The King alone beholds his secret unveiled. It is exciting to follow. To see it on the stage thrills the recesses
of the imagination. Hamlet's fierce excitement pervades
the scene with its fury. It deepens as the play goes on,
and as the King is more and more disturbed. His fierce
interjected phrases grow in wild savagery. At last he
interrupts the play, and himself tells the tale to the King
—tumbling out his words, trembling with excitement—

He poisons him i' the garden for his estate. His name 's Gonzago ;
the story is extant, and written in very choice Italian : you shall see
anon how the murderer gets the love of Gonzago's wife.

OPH. The King rises.
HAM. What ! frighted with false fire !
QUEEN. How fares my lord ?
POL. Give o'er the play.
KING. Give me some light. Away !
POL. Lights, lights, lights !

And Hamlet is left alone with Horatio—wild with excitement, wild with the discovery of the truth—seeking (as
it was after his scene with the Ghost) to drown the strain
of his passion in wild merriment. He bursts into singing;
he falls exhausted into Horatio's arms ; he calls for music.
He goes over the proof with Horatio—he cannot contain
himself—and no wonder. It would have moved to excite-

ment a mountain of granite. This is the centre of the drama.

Hamlet, after the King's discomfiture by the play, is borne beyond himself for the moment by his discovery that the Ghost's story was true.

O good Horatio, I'll take the ghost's word for a thousand pounds. Didst perceive?

His excitement continues when Rosencrantz and Guildenstern come in to summon him to the Queen. He knows he must conceal his secret from them, and he beats down his excitement. This inward struggle to appear calm when his soul and body are thrilling, is the cause of his broken phrases, of his mock courtesy, of his bitter but repressed scorn and hatred of the King, of that bitter but close-curbed wrath with the Queen, which are manifest in his talk with these spies of the King. He cannot help his scorn, but he can constrain his fury. It is a wonderful dialogue, and must be supremely difficult to act. At one point, however, he can let himself loose without endangering his secret. He can let those fellows know he looks on them as spies, and loathes them for that treachery. He offers one of them a pipe and bids him play upon it. 'I cannot,' he answers, 'I have not the skill.' And Hamlet answers half in contempt and half in rage.

It is characteristic of him now that when he is excited by the closeness of events, his excitement is always on the edge of doubling and redoubling itself. The smouldering ash takes fire, and blazes to the skies. He does not betray the secret passions within, or their cause; but he relieves their pressure by the furious words which he uses on matters other than his secret. And the words grow hotter and wilder as he speaks—as they do here.

Why, look you now, how unworthy a thing you make of me ! You would play upon me ; you would seem to know my stops ; you would pluck out the heart of my mystery ; you would sound me from my lowest note to the top of my compass : and there is much music, excellent voice, in this little organ ; yet cannot you make it speak.   'Sblood, do you think I am easier to be played on than a pipe ?   Call me what instrument you will, though you can fret me, yet you cannot play upon me.

But . he can play on others.   Polonius comes in, and he mocks him with feigned folly; his wild excitement runs into a bitter merriment—he makes himself foolish to a fool.

HAM.   Do you see yonder cloud that 's almost in shape of a camel ?
POL.   By the mass, and 'tis like a camel, indeed.
HAM.   Methinks it is like a weasel.
POL.   It is backed like a weasel.
HAM.   Or like a whale ?
POL.   Very like a whale.
HAM.   Then I will come to my mother by and_by.   (*Aside.*)   They fool me to the top of my bent.

And now he is left alone again, and night has fallen.   All his repressed fury breaks out of him.   His words are the words of a swashbuckler—

> Now could I drink hot blood,
> And do such bitter business as the day
> Would quake to look on.

He is thinking of the King; but his whole nature hates the bloody work he is called to do.   To every fibre of the being of this imaginative student it is repugnant.   It is the lashing of his nature up to do what he hates which is the reason and the excuse for his turgid phrases.   The next moment he thinks of his mother, and his violent speech becomes pitiful with his thought.   'O heart!' he cries, 'lose not thy nature.'   'I will speak daggers to her, but use none.'   The storm within is beginning to lose its fury.   It has been almost spent in that volcanic outburst.   His passion lowers its crest, and his habit of thinking over the problem of the situation instead of meeting it by , action, has now begun to resume its normal sway. But then, as he goes to the Queen, he sees the King alone, and praying. The full opportunity has come, but he is no longer in the full exaltation which would lead him to make use of it.

> Now might I do it pat, now he is praying;

But he does not do it. On the contrary, his exaltation is so lessened that now he argues the matter. If I kill him now, he goes to heaven. Is that revenge? I'll wait till I can catch him in mortal sin, and so send him to damnation.

It is plain the fury has died down, else he would not discuss the killing. It is plain that behind the ruthless argument there is the dislike to kill, now that his blood is colder. Hamlet, unless driven by a passionate impulse, will not act; but when he is quick with momentary passion, he acts instantly, as when he sacrifices Guildenstern and Rosencrantz, when he leaps into Ophelia's grave, when he kills the King, even when he kills Polonius. In a moment he springs into destroying act; in the next moment he falls back into his customary meditation—now a very quiet, now a most dangerous man.

He has now come to see his mother. His mood is grave, not furious; he does not suspect her of any knowledge of his father's murder. He is only indignant with her marriage with the murderer. And he is softened by the natural piety of a son. Yet below there is in his soul the ground swell of the dark situation into which he has been thrust against his will. In this atmosphere of many thoughts compact, he is liable to change, at any moment, from one mood into another, from one man into another, as he does in this interview. Moreover, he is also liable, at a touch, to wander away from the actual present into the imaginative world of thought in which he naturally lives. In such a medley in his soul he is outside of this world and its seeming realities. Life and death, love and sorrow, even his own pain are as dreams, are nothing. Hence Polonius's death is no more than an incident, his slaughter of him no matter. At first he is rough and rude with the Queen. He pushes her down into her chair. The Queen thinks she is dealing with a madman and cries for help. Polonius cries behind the arras. Hamlet whips out his sword. All in a moment action seizes on him—he leaps out of one world into another. It is his way. He lunges through the curtain. 'O me, what hast thou done?' cries the Queen. 'Nay,' answers Hamlet, 'I know not: *is it the King?*' I am told that when Edmund Kean said that awful word, the whole theatre rose in wild appreciation. I would I had been there. But Hamlet has no care for what he has done. He leaves the body, and turns, forgetting it, to his mother. Nothing can show more clearly than this the carelessness, the overmastering tyranny of thought, the grip upon him of the mystery of evil in which he is entangled. He flings one word of pity to the old man, and ends with a sarcasm—

> Thou wretched, rash, intruding fool, farewell !
> I took thee for thy better : take thy fortune ;
> Thou find'st to be too busy is some danger.

'Tis a light epitaph for a murdered man! Once the thing is done, Hamlet thinks no more of it. No remedy for it, it is ended—a mere incident in comparison with the overwhelming horror in which he is involved. And he turns, as if he had done nothing, to his mother, to tent her to the quick.

It is a strange scene. There is a certain staginess in the business of the two portraits which is like what a young man, who does not know the world, might fall into.

I do not think it effective, even as art, on the stage. It enables Hamlet, however, to dramatise the occasion, and this dramatisation already shows that he has begun to slip away a little from the stern reality into an imaginative picture of it. And as his imagination takes fire, his moral indignation takes fire also, and he glides on—so curiously—away from the pressing present into a half-philosophic contrast between the lust of youth and of a matron, and then into a blaze of raging words (to relieve his soul) against the King, such words as he has used before without shaping them into deeds—lapsing out of resolution into soliloquy—into an intellectual passion which, content with itself, does not drive the will to act. His father's spirit knows his temper, and enters suddenly. Terror comes with the ghostly presence, terror that merges into love,

> Save me, and hover o'er me with your wings,
> You heavenly guards ! What would your gracious figure ?

And in the vision Hamlet knows and describes himself:

> HAM. Do you not come your tardy son to chide,
> That, lapsed in time and passion, lets go by
> The important acting of your dread command ?
> O, say !
> GHOST. Do not forget : this visitation
> Is but to whet thy almost blunted purpose.

That is Shakespeare's own description of Hamlet's state of mind. Every explanation of Hamlet's nature must take it as a test. And Shakespeare takes care to clear Hamlet of madness—indeed, of any wild ecstasy that might, for the moment, run into madness.

> My pulse, as yours, doth temperately keep time,
> And makes as healthful music : it is not madness
> That I have utter'd : bring me to the test,
> And I the matter will re-word, which madness
> Would gambol from.

And his speech now is quiet and to the point. But again, it slips away into disquisition. That ineradicable habit of his—to moralise, to philosophise, as if he were in his rooms at Wittenberg—again seizes him. Again, he forgets, momentarily, the matter in hand, and preaches about habit, and the breaking of habits; again, he repeats his bitter cry against his mother living with the King; then runs into a scorn of a woman's loose tongue—with a menace in it—and ends with a fierce threat of what he will do with those treacherous schoolfellows whose craft he will outcraft; and with a bitter mock which is half of sorrow for Polonius.

A multitude of motives! His soul is a tossing sea and every wave a thought. One thought undulates after another—thoughts of philosophy drawn from his student life, of misery at its breaking up, of horror and hatred of his mother's incest, his father's murder, of the breaking of his love, of the feigning of madness, of the King's self-betrayal, of his father's supernatural appearance, of his own delay in revenging him. They come and go; he slips from one to another. He cannot hold any one of them enough to shape it into present act.

Is this the man who could fulfil a revenge? But, all the same, having once dipped his hand in blood, having passed the Rubicon which he thought never to have passed, a new and unknown element is added to his life; he no longer shrinks from giving death to his foes. A new element, brought by some chance into life—who that has ever known what that experience is, can tell what changes it will work within; what it will force us to do in the world without? With this within him, Hamlet is now a danger to his foes. In slaying Polonius, he has at last overstepped the bounds which held him back from blood. He will not be squeamish again, and he proves that soon by handing over Rosencrantz and Guildenstern to death.

I cannot quite get over that affair. I believe there are critics who, desirous, in contradiction to Shakespeare, to prove that Hamlet was prompt and resolute in action, folk who seem to imagine that Hamlet was a real character, and not made by Shakespeare, aver that when he rewrote the letter, and sent Rosencrantz and Guildenstern to death, and himself escaped on board the pirate, he showed quick resolve passing into immediate action. But he had meant all along to hoist these engineers with their own petard, if he proved them traitors.

It is also said he proved by this his intellectual sharpness, his clear brain; proved that he was a man not of impulsive but of calculating action. I only see in it the cunning almost of a madman. That action of his—an action of treachery and of mean treachery—is so apart from the rest of his magnanimous character, that, if ever Hamlet passed the limit between feigned and real madness, he seems to me to have passed it then. The punishment he inflicted on Rosencrantz and Guildenstern was far too heavy for their guilt—the sort of punishment which just reasoning would not have imposed. The event does not prove Hamlet's clearness of intellect, but on the contrary. At no other point of the play does he act in this unintelligent, unmoral way. It is said in excuse of Hamlet's conduct here, that the age in which he lived was savage, and human life of no importance. That is true; but Hamlet, as Shakespeare made him, was not of that age. He is not naturally fond of blood or war, of drink or feasting, of such treachery, for ambition's sake, as the King's. He does not belong to this crew; nay, it was part of Shakespeare's idea to place in the closest contact with them this young man who differed at every point from them, to whom they were naturally repugnant, and to work out his drama within that outline. This action of Hamlet's with Rosencrantz and Guilden-

stern is not in harmony with Shakespeare's conception,
nor with the rest of his drawing of Hamlet.[1]   I am told
that there are those who call it heroic, in a vain endeavour
to make a hero out of Hamlet.   I hope a hero is built
on other lines.   It is still more absurd, as I believe some
American has done, to make him heroic because he
leaps into Ophelia's grave in rivalry of Laertes' sorrow,
or because he kills the King, when not to kill him were
ridiculous.   I do not care where Shakespeare got this
episode; it is a blot on the play.

In the King, on the contrary, we have drawn one to
whom for the sake of lust and ambition treachery was
native.   He does not act by open murder, but by furtive
stealth; bloody, but not bold or resolute.   He hangs
behind curtains to spy out those he fears.   As his fears
increase, his treachery deepens.   He makes Hamlet bear
letters to England which carry Hamlet's death-warrant.
He makes a vile plot to do away with Hamlet by Laertes.
He draws that young fellow into dishonour, guarding
himself from blame or danger.   He approves Laertes'
suggestion of oiling the rapier's point with poison.   He
plans, to make all sure, a poisoned cup for Hamlet, should
Laertes fail—a secret, traitorous villain.   All his talk is
of a bluffing honesty.   He is a half-Iago; he plays the
part of a bold, open-hearted King.   It is the scented
grease of the traitor which smoothes his words.   With
his treachery is mingled, in equal parts, sensuality.   He
drinks deep, and feasts high.   He has seduced the Queen
while her husband is alive.   He marries her within a
month.   It is to his credit that he loves her, and not
only her body—

---

[1] Moreover, it is a mistake in art to link Hamlet up with the King in
a treacherous and murderous action.   He is for the moment hand in
hand with the King; and Shakespeare should not have done this.
Moreover the act is not in Hamlet's character.

She 's so conjunctive to my life and soul,
That, as the star moves not but in his sphere,
I could not but by her.

Let that be recorded on his side of the account. Shakespeare did not mean to make him altogether bad. His
first speech is statesmanlike; the foreign affairs of Denmark
are safe in his hands. This also is to his credit. But his
claim to be thought a father to Hamlet, his long preach-
ment to Hamlet against overweening grief, delivered on
a high moral, even a religious note is—since he has
murdered the father of the man whose grief he blames—
a piece of detestable and unforgivable hypocrisy.

In such a treacherous soul Fear is a common in-
habitant; and fear, as it grows, doubles the action of
treachery. Nothing is too bad to do in order to keep
past guilt still concealed; and whatever is done at the
bidding of this fear, is done with exhaustive treachery,
as, for example, the doubling of the poison to slay Hamlet
by the hand of Laertes—Laertes whom the King would
also have slain the next day, for the traitor never spares
the accomplice in his treachery. Again, fear is clear-
sighted. The King, and only the King, suspects Hamlet's
transformation as having danger to him behind it. All
the rest are deceived by Hamlet; the King is not. He
sets Rosencrantz and Guildenstern on Hamlet to find out
' whether aught unknown to us afflicts him thus.' When
Hamlet plays the madman with Ophelia, the King suspects more deeply. When the *Mouse-trap* is played
before him, he knows. Fear then drinks up his heart;
and fear awakens his drugged conscience into idiotic
speech. The King's conscience, for Shakespeare does
not leave him without a semblance of it, totters about,
uttering confused contradictions, and falls back again
into its drugged slumber. It seems to have been already
touched by Polonius's phrase—

POL.   That with devotion's visage
      And pious action we do sugar o'er
      The Devil himself.
KING.   O, 'tis too true !
      How smart a lash that speech doth give my conscience !

What sort of a conscience it was we hear in his soliloquy
when (after the terror of his discovery) he tries to pray.
Shakespeare opens the secret chamber of his soul. He
confesses himself to himself, his murder, his inability to
pray. But there is forgiveness in heaven, he says, else
what were the use of the existence of mercy; and to pray
is to be pardoned. So will my fault be gone. But then,
I keep all the pleasant results of my crime, and I doubt
that one can be pardoned and retain the offence. That is
often the way with earthly law, but not with heavenly—

> *There* is no shuffling, there the action lies
> In his true nature, and we ourselves compell'd
> Even to the teeth and forehead of our faults
> To give in evidence.

What then; I'll try repentance, but I cannot. 'O wretched
state! Help! angels! make assay!' change me, force me
to be good. 'All may be well.' He prays, but his heart
and its fear keep his thoughts to earth. He cannot get
away from his dread of discovery.

> My words fly up, my thoughts remain below :
> Words without thoughts never to heaven go.

All the same, it has been a great relief to him to have had
it out with his conscience, to have listened to its wail and
bid it go to sleep; to have confessed in speech his crime;
to have bluffed heaven with a desire for repentance.
When we have not a priest to open our sins to, and get
rid of them by speech of them, we make ourselves priest
as well as penitent, and gain a great relief, even a renewed
power of sinning again. Or, perhaps, it is that the self-
deceit we then practise is so vile that it makes the whole
character much viler; and then, in the added vileness,

worse sins than we did before are easier henceforth, and are done with even a certain gusto. The King is certainly, in his murderous treachery to Hamlet and Laertes, twice as bad as he was before his prayers. He has earned a greater damnation.

The fourth Act is very long-winded—so many threads have to be gathered up and woven together, in order to get home to the conclusion. It might have been made shorter and more effective had Shakespeare managed it better. It contains the episode of sending Hamlet to England, of the treachery of Hamlet to Rosencrantz and Guildenstern, of the awkward pirate story, which has made the play linger and crawl, and forced on the writer a number of needless explanations in needless scenes. Hamlet could have been got rid of for a time in some other fashion which would not have exacted so much delay. It is true, the play was never intended to move swiftly, like *Macbeth,* or to be knit closely together in almost a unity of place and time, like *Othello.* Shakespeare, who loved variety, meant it to linger, and the nature and character of Hamlet, as he conceived them, could only be developed slowly. Hamlet himself is a lingerer. His presence alone detains events. His incessant thinking forces the other characters to move slowly. Yet, the delay is too great. The Queen, the King, even Laertes, seem in their conversation to be infected with Hamlet's over-thinking and under-action in this fourth Act. I can fancy even an Elizabethan audience crying to the dramatist—'Get on, get on!'

The introduction in this Act of the army of Fortinbras meeting Hamlet on his way to the sea, if it be necessary to account for his appearance at the close of the play, need not take up so much time. It certainly motives another soliloquy of Hamlet's by which we understand that he is as far away as ever from taking any action for his revenge. So far as the Drama is concerned, this new soliloquy only repeats, in the main, the two former ones. It is a wail over his delay. This army, led by an eager prince, runs quick to his ambitious goal, and the thought of it 'spurs his dull revenge'—and then he glides away to ask, What is a man if he only lives to sleep and eat?

> Sure, he that made us with such large discourse,
> Looking before and after, gave us not
> That capability and godlike reason
> To fust in us unused.

And he applies this to his delay. 'Oblivion'—a curious reason, but a true one—or 'A craven scruple'—also true —or 'Thinking too precisely on the event'—the truest reason—have held back his hand. But while he is thus on the point, seeing himself clearly—he slips away, as before, on thoughts about greatness and fame suggested by his own words, and then comes back again to his own problem—but only to thinking of it—waves of thought running after one another without clear direction—

> O, from this time forth,
> My thoughts be bloody, or be nothing worth!

Dramatically, all this is quite unnecessary. But, as fine thinking on Shakespeare's part, and as fine poetry, it is excellent. I cannot help thinking that this episode and soliloquy were never intended to be acted, but were inserted by Shakespeare, in his revision of the play, in order to add some further metaphysical thoughts to his delineation of Hamlet. And I believe that this is also true of other places in the play.

Whatever we may say about the rest of the Act, it is made beautiful by the pity of Ophelia's fate. Never did madness take a more delicate, a more gracious shape. Pretty Ophelia, cries the King. Thought and affliction, says her brother, passion, hell itself,

> She turns to favour and to prettiness.

Her littleness, her commonplace is gone. She is in the invisible, the supersensible world, among the spirits beyond the earth; a child now of the gods; no fear in her heart, only a vague sorrow; of an infinite kindness to the world; in love with the beauty of flowers, closer to them in thought than to anything else; a child within a maiden; touching with frankness that which a sane maiden might think or dream, but would conceal; singing through life, for she loves sweet sound; gay with a pitiful gaiety; slipping without any link of thought from one fancy to another;—all the deep fineness of her loving nature, now unladen of convention, visible on the surface of her girlhood. Were it not so beautiful, it were too piercing in its pathos. Were it not so pitiful, it were not so beautiful.

Hamlet, speaking to the Queen, describes what madness is, and admirably; a thing a madman could not do. Ophelia is mad; and whence Shakespeare drew the power to represent it in its gentlest form, yet in its completeness, and so as to wake pity, not repulsion, the philosophers may try to discover; I will not. But he does not only represent it in her; he states by the mouth of the *Gentleman* of what sort it is.

> She speaks much of her father, says she hears
> There's tricks i' the world ; and hems and beats her heart ;
> Spurns enviously at straws ; speaks things in doubt,
> That carry but half sense : her speech is nothing,
> Yet the unshaped use of it doth move
> The hearers to collection ; they aim at it,
> And botch the words up fit to their own thoughts ;
> Which, as her winks and nods and gestures yield them,
> Indeed would make one think there might be thought,
> Though nothing sure, yet much unhappily.

That is an admirable sketch, and especially the picture of those people who, listening to insane wanderings, try to fit them into sanity, or to find out the origin of the broken images the madman uses. They fail, for what we hear

said is generally only half a thought—the first half of it,
or the latter half of it—and this because any thought,
when it is not seized and retained by the will, is succeeded
by another with extraordinary rapidity. Each matter
then runs into the brain and runs instantly out of it, and
another takes its place before it is finished. Ophelia's
speech bears the same relation to sane speech that the
pieces of a broken jar bear to the unbroken jar. One
thing is, however, dominant—her father's death; and it is
dominant because it was that which broke up order in her
brain; done as it was by her lover. Of her lover she says
nothing, but that he also underlies her pain is marked by
her songs about St. Valentine, and the strange slips, so
common in delirium, into a certain grossness, which is
primeval nature speaking, when the restraint of convention is removed. It is so plainly innocent that it does
not injure the beauty of her delicate sorrow, her piteous
gaiety. Oh, how mingled of many drifts of pain and
pleasure, of memories remembered to be forgotten, of
forgetfulness intruded on by memory—and all broken, all
astray—is her speech! Here is one instance—

I hope all will be well. We must be patient: but I cannot choose
but weep, to think they should lay him i' the cold ground. My brother
shall know of it: and so I thank you for your good counsel. Come, my
coach! Good night, ladies; good night, sweet ladies; good night, good
night.

And her gracious, graceful play with the flowers—was anything more beautiful ever written? She dies with flowers,
in a stream banked in with flowers, and singing snatches
of sweet song. In loveliness she died; and the world went
on, the better for her madness, since it was beautiful. She
came, in her innocent grace, in her feeble maidenhood, into
the path of great events, when they were clashing in
storm, and she perished in the wind of them. Hamlet
says of the death of Rosencrantz and Guildenstern—

'Tis dangerous when the baser nature comes
Between the pass and fell incensed points
Of mighty opposites.

It is as dangerous for an ignorant sweet maid to be innocently involved in the beating together of such opponents as the King and Hamlet. She, like the others, like Polonius, Laertes, Guildenstern, Rosencrantz, the Queen, meets the fate of the crystals between the pestle and the mortar. The innocent perish like the guilty; 'tis a strange world. Yet Ophelia lives on—it is her reward— in the high region where the generations of men find that happiness in contemplation of beauty which after no repenting draws. The others we do not care to think of; they are not our inspiration. But Ophelia remains, with Hamlet, in the hearts of men. There are none who have not heard her say to us, in secret hours—

There's rosemary, that's for remembrance ; pray you, love, remember : and there is pansies, that's for thoughts.

It is characteristic of Shakespeare to knit up the humour of his play with her death in order to preserve the continuance of thought and the unity of action. The fifth Act begins with the humorous talk of the two grave-diggers who are delving Ophelia's grave, and who discuss whether she ought, or ought not, to have Christian burial. What to them is all this misery ? what matter Kings and Queens, murders and adulteries to them ? Shakespeare has made their apartness from the terror and pity of the circumstance around them almost shocking ; yet this apartness of theirs seems to enhance the tragic elements.

Then, too, the gulf between the upper and under classes —that gulf which makes the tragedy of states—was never made more clear than he has done in this scene. The death which the rich see with terror, which the King fears so much that he will do murder to rid him of its fear, is nothing to these men but a matter of rough humour. They

joke and sing as they dig graves. They have a pride in
their business; the houses they make last till doomsday.
Has this fellow, says Hamlet, with the sensitive feeling of
his class, no feeling of his business that he sings at grave-
making?   And again (still feeling what his class feels),
he answers Horatio, who has said that custom has made it
easy for the clown to sing amid graves—

'Tis e'en so : the hand of little employment hath the daintier sense,

—the idle man of our class has time for fine feeling.   It is
now, in this half-philosophic mood, that we meet Hamlet
again by the grave of Ophelia.   He does not know of her
death.   He is quite grave and interested in the churchyard and the thoughts it engenders.   Shakespeare has felt
that if the joking of the grave-diggers went on much
longer, without the introduction of a serious element, the
tragic atmosphere would be injured.   Therefore the conversation of Hamlet and Horatio turns to the seriousness
which befits gentlehood when it finds itself among the
dead.   The light song of the sexton accompanies the grave
reflections of the thinker, and sets them into clear relief.

Nothing in the play is stranger than Hamlet's apartness
through this scene from the trouble in which he is
involved.   Even when his father and himself are spoken
of by the grave-digger, this does not seem to awaken him
out of philosophising into the reality of things.   His
voyage seems to have wiped away his agony.   Here, with
his friend, he meditates aloud on what he sees, just as he
might have done when he was a student.   His revenge
is replaced by contemplative thought.   Who were these
dead, and what are they now? a politician, a courtier, a
lawyer? and now their skulls are jowled on the ground,
knocked about the mazzard with a sexton's spade—

Here's fine revolution, an' we had the trick to see 't.

It is curiously tragic to hear him wander away into an

imagination of the eager life of the men whose skulls lie at his feet, and to know, as one listens, that round the corner waits his father's demand for vengeance. It is still more curious to be sure from his meditative talk that for the moment he has forgotten all about it. One little remark, following on the cool indifference to him of the grave-digger, shows how, in continuous thought, he has followed in the past what we call 'the tendencies of the age.'

How absolute the knave is l we must speak by the card, or equivocation will undo us. By the Lord, Horatio, this three years I have taken note of it ; the age is grown so picked that the toe of the peasant comes so near the heel of the courtier, he galls his kibe.

But the main thought of his meditative hour is persistent, and the famous address to Yorick's skull best enshrines his customary musing on life and death—their contrast and their interchange—which his late experience has intensified.

Alas, poor Yorick ! I knew him, Horatio : a fellow of infinite jest, of most excellent fancy : he hath borne me on his back a thousand times ; and now, how abhorred in my imagination it is ; my gorge rises at it. Here hung those lips that I have kissed I know not how oft. Where be your gibes now, your gambols, your songs, your flashes of merriment, that were wont to set the table on a roar ? Not one now, to mock your own grinning ; quite chop-fallen ?

Shakespeare's heart must have been bitter with pain to have written that, and bitterer still when, wrenched with curious cynicism mixed with indignation, he finished it with a savage touch—

Now get you to my lady's chamber, and tell her, let her paint an inch thick, to this favour she must come ; make her laugh at that.

Hamlet wanders on, multiplying thoughts, in his fashion, round his main thought, varying it, illustrating it, absorbed in meditation—when suddenly—all the actual world rushes on him with King, Queen, the procession following the corpse of Ophelia, and Laertes wild with sorrow.

What will Hamlet do now ? He will do what he has done before, when the agony of the present is suddenly rushed upon him. Quiet for a little, there will follow an out-burst of unbridled passion, expressing itself in wild and wilder words. This is what takes place when Hamlet hears the furious sorrow of Laertes, as he leaps into Ophelia's grave. He says so himself. 'For sure, the bravery of his grief did put me into a towering passion —I am very sorry that I forgot myself.' It was not the bravery of Laertes' grief which made the storm. It was that he had forgotten, and suddenly remembered all.

Laertes has also been excited by events. He has headed a revolution. He has been lured into a plot to slay Hamlet. His father's death, his sister's death, he attributes to Hamlet. A tempest roars within him : and in those days, when men were not reserved, they drove the inward tempest into high-swelling words and acts. Both, as here given, seem unnatural to us. Laertes is painfully rhetorical. He leaps into the grave [1]—

> Now pile your dust upon the quick and dead,
> Till of this flat a mountain you have made
> To o'ertop old Pelion, or the skyish head
> Of blue Olympus.

Hamlet hears, and his ancient love simmering in his heart, rushes into a like excitement, and leaps also into the grave :

> HAM.   What is he whose grief
> Bears such an emphasis ? whose phrase of sorrow
> Conjures the wandering stars and makes them stand
> Like wonder-wounded hearers ? This is I,
> Hamlet the Dane.
> LAER.   The devil take thy soul !

They struggle, and the physical rage of the struggle doubles Hamlet's mental excitement, which, as it doubles,

---

[1] Quite a little disquisition might be written about the conduct of Laertes, and why Shakespeare is so very rhetorical in *Hamlet*. But it is scarcely worth while.

annihilates by its supremacy the lesser passion of Laertes, the lesser man.

> I loved Ophelia : forty thousand brothers
> Could not, with all their quantity of love,
> Make up the sum.

Once started, his passion mounts and mounts, climbing the sky, till, having reached a wildness of imagination, in which he outsoars Laertes' image,

> And, if thou prate of mountains, let them throw
> Millions of acres on us, till our ground,
> Singeing his pate against the burning zone,
> Make Ossa like a wart !

it falls as suddenly. He realises his loss of himself—

> Nay, an thou 'lt mouth,
> I 'll rant as well as thou.

It is very characteristic. If outbreaks of this kind, or liability to them constitute madness, Hamlet was mad at these times. If such outbreaks do become continuous and frequent, sanity is in danger. But hosts of men and women are subject to them, and recover from them, as Hamlet did, with a certain shame. ' I have lost myself,' they say. We cannot call them insane; they still retain the grip over their will; they recover themselves; they are under no illusion. The transient fury is conquered, and, for the most part of life, they are, like Hamlet, quiet enough. But if, like Hamlet, who was naturally a still and pensive person, they are subjected, as he was, to the continual surging within of a secret tempest of battling thought round a repugnant and hateful subject, then any exciting cause, coming from without, flings them into gusts of passion, makes them forget themselves; and this is even a relief to them. It enables them (in a sphere of thought not connected with their secret trouble) to relieve its pressure, to blow off its steam; and, in doing so, they avoid the betrayal of their secret.

It was so here with Hamlet at Ophelia's grave. When

we find him again, he confesses that he lost his head. He
talks quietly with Horatio, telling him how he dispersed
Rosencrantz and Guildenstern—and full of wise remarks—

> Our indiscretion sometimes serves us well
> When our deep plots do pall ; and that should learn us
> There's a divinity that shapes our ends,
> Rough-hew them how we will.

Finally, as he tells of the treachery of the King, his long-
protracted revenge, of which we have lost sight of late,
recurs again—but still with a questioning of conscience
in it, or with an allusion to a previous questioning of
conscience,

> Is't not perfect conscience,
> To quit him with this arm ? and is't not to be damn'd,
> To let this canker of our nature come
> In further evil ?

So Shakespeare, recovering the main motive of the play,
prepares us for the last scene. But Hamlet, before half
an hour has passed by, Hamlet, the creature of moods,
the victim of the moment, seems again to forget all about
his slaying of the King, in appraising, playing with, and
mocking Osric, who brings him Laertes' challenge to a
bout with the foils.

Osric is the dandy, the decadent euphuist, the rich
hanger-on of the court, the water-fly. Hamlet sketches
him, almost as a socialist would do—

> He hath much land, and fertile ; let a beast be lord of beasts, and his
> crib shall stand at the king's mess : 'tis a chough, but, as I say, spacious
> in the possession of dirt.

He mocks his subservience as he mocked Polonius; he
imitates, with confounding cleverness, Osric's plumed
speech, his dainty phrases ; and he finishes by a meditation on the whole of Osric's tribe, who represent one
tendency of the time. He is again miles away from his
revenge. It comes in the end, all of a sudden, as it were
by chance; quite unpremeditated at the moment, as if

the gods, and not he, had slain the King. In a rush of dying fury, he does that slaughter of the King over which he has thought and questioned and doubted for so long a time, which he has forgotten and remembered so often, from which he has receded so far, and to which he has approached so nearly; does it almost without knowing what he does, with no satisfaction in his revenge. And he drags down with himself, and with the King, owing to his delays, the Queen, Polonius, Ophelia, and Laertes.

There were from the beginning only two things to do— and to do at once—either to obey the Ghost, and kill the King quickly, and take the consequence—or else to say the Ghost was wrong in urging vengeance ; and to disobey him, leaving to the justice of God the punishment of the King. Hamlet did neither. And it is plain, as Shakespeare conceived him, that he could do neither the one nor the other. He acted, or did not act, within his character—acted, or did not act, inevitably.

Dying, he felt this ; and felt he might be mistaken by the world. I have been fantastic, he thought, and the world does not understand the fantastic in one born to great position. I have been drawn from a quiet life into a tangled web of stormy events and hateful crimes, and the world does not understand the story, and how a Prince of my character was not made to ride the storm or to endure the horror of the crimes. Therefore live, Horatio, to tell the truth and explain me to the people.

> O good Horatio, what a wounded name,
> Things standing thus unknown, shall live behind me !
> If thou didst ever hold me in thy heart,
> Absent thee from felicity a while,
> And in this harsh world draw thy breath in pain,
> To tell my story.

> Fortinbras : he has my dying voice ;
> So tell him, with the occurrents, more and less,
> Which have solicited. The rest is silence.

So cracked a noble heart, thinking with his last breath of the peace of his country, himself at last at peace.

He has drifted through the play till the hour when the infinite happiness of death removed him from himself, and from a world where he had done all that his nature could have done.

V

MEASURE FOR MEASURE

THE date at which *Measure for Measure* was written is uncertain. But there are some passages in the play which are supposed, on very little evidence, to refer to the conduct of James I. and to his character, at the time of and after his entry into London. The Duke is at certain places credited with a likeness to James (Act I. sc. 2, 68). Also, the fantastical spying of the Duke resembles the spy-fever in which James found a chuckling pleasure, and which Walter Scott tells of in the *Fortunes of Nigel*. These allusions are part of an argument which places the date of this play in the years 1603-4. A better evidence for this late date lies in the style and metre of the drama, but this evidence might just as well date it earlier, or even later, in, let me say, 1606, after *King Lear*; and some reasons might be suggested for such a conjecture.

There are also many resemblances in the thoughts on death, and on grave problems of life, and even in words and phrases, between this play and *Hamlet, Macbeth*, and *King Lear*, which suggest that *Measure for Measure* belongs to the years between 1601 and 1606, the period of the great tragedies. It is commonly put between *Othello* and *Macbeth*. I might put it alongside of either *Troilus and Cressida* or *Timon of Athens*—after the first, before the latter. This, however, is conjecture, and the conjecture is only based on a feeling, which may be called literary, that the style, the metrical movement, the not

139

infrequent abruptness and comparative obscurity of the verse, and, above all, the temper of the play, are not as much in harmony with *Othello* and *Macbeth* as they are with *Troilus* or *Timon*. Moreover, *Othello* and *Macbeth* are written with Shakespeare's highest power, and in every part of them the power is equal to that which he desired to represent. In *Measure for Measure* the power is not the same as it is in *Othello* or *Macbeth*. It wavers: great in one page, it is at a much lower level in the next. Nor do the characters always explain themselves. In *Othello* and *Macbeth* they do. Again, the poetry, its imaginative reach, its grip on the heart of the thing or thought in hand, are, beyond expression, penetrating, equal, and splendid in *Othello* and *Macbeth*. In *Measure for Measure* these qualities are sometimes as great as they are in *Othello* and *Macbeth*, but they are so in patches. There are passages where this high poetry lags behind, where clearness and splendour seem not to have deserted the house of Shakespeare's imagination, but to be less at home in it. This is strange, I repeat, if this play was written between *Othello* and *Macbeth*. However, the critics may be right. Shakespeare, like Homer, sometimes sleeps.

Perhaps the subject influenced Shakespeare wrongly. An artist sometimes seizes a subject which he thinks will suit his mood, or which suddenly attracts him, and it comes to pass, when he has been at work on it for some time, that he finds it is not in sympathy with his genius, or that it does not turn out, and come home to him, as well as he expected. He would like to throw it aside, but either it seems to him that he ought to finish it, that it is due to his genius to master it; or the work may exercise a kind of tyranny over him. In any of these cases, he is sure not to do as good work as he would do did he love his subject, or did his subject at the time altogether suit him. And this **may** be true of Shakespeare and *Measure* *for Measure.* If it were, I do not wonder, for the subject was eminently disagreeable.[1] A society eaten to its core by mere fornication, which is the social basis of the play, is not a delightful milieu for a great artist to choose his subject from; nor, in itself, does the subject contain or produce any of the deep-striking passions whose presentation arrests the souls of men. No great, noble, or terrible tragedy such as we find in *Macbeth, Othello,* or *Lear,* could come out of it. In order to get into the subject an arresting representation of the passions, he is driven to create extremes of human nature—Isabella, of enskied but exaggerated chastity; Angelo, of revolting, though sudden sensualism; Claudio, shamefully dishonoured by the fear of death. The subject carries with it, and perforce, elements of sensationalism. It was also predoomed, though naturally tragic, to be turned into a Comedy, and *Measure for Measure* wears with extraordinary awkwardness the garments of Comedy. Shakespeare did his best with it. He so arranged events as to make this ugly story into a representation in the characters of high-souled chastity; of the break-up of mere outward virtue into sensualism; of the fear of death; and, as a side issue, of the danger and limits of authority,—and these are subjects which underlie the Drama. But they have, in an extreme representation of them, been foisted into the story. They do not grow naturally out of it. Isabella's chastity is mingled with an ascetic severity. Angelo's hypocrisy is almost out of nature. Claudio's fear of death borders on meanness; is not in character with his training, his rank, and his honour as a gentleman. Shakespeare, in this play (even in the minor characters), is, not unfrequently, a little outside nature. He owed that, I think,

---

[1] An old play, *Promos and Cassandra,* is said to be Shakespeare's original. If so, he has transformed it. Also, the romantic image of Mariana in the moated grange is his own invention.

to the choice he made of a subject. It was a sword which
did not quite fit his hand. Whenever he struck with it
his blow went somewhat awry.

I believe, as I have said elsewhere, that there was a
twist in Shakespeare's life at this time, of which we know
nothing, and which turned into gloom and sometimes
into a transient cynicism the charming nature of the
man. There is no reason, some may say, to make this
conjecture; it is sufficient to say that, having reached
middle age, his thought turned to the stern aspect of the
world, and resolved to write about the greater passions
which afflict men, and the deeper sins which tempt them.
It may be so, but this does not explain the immense change,
within a year or two, from the spirit of *Twelfth Night* to
that of *Macbeth* or *Othello* so well as the first conjecture,
and it conceives Shakespeare more as a contemplative
moral philosopher than as an artist. I do not believe
that he deliberately set himself, while he was the same
man within who wrote the *Twelfth Night* or *Julius Cæsar*,
to describe with an extraordinary and heightened passion
the agonies of Lear and Othello, the crime and terror of
Macbeth. No artist, working out of his own soul, would
do that; or if he did, he would not do it well. No;
Shakespeare chose his subjects in accordance with the
passionate emotions and drift of his own soul; and the
tragic of these plays, and the cynicism of *Troilus* and
Timon, were the expression (I do not say of his own
personal circumstances or feelings—it was plainly his
habit to conceal these) but of the general temper of his
soul, changed, by events of which we know nothing, from
a cheerful to a grim outlook on the world. The atmosphere of his life was charged with rain and storm, with
lightning and thunder; and out of it came *Othello*,
Macbeth, Lear; and out of them came intervals of cynicism.

It is characteristic of such a temper of mind to pass at

times into self-contempt, and to transfer that contempt to the world. A man then becomes ~~hard, sarcastic,~~ cynical or savage. And then he writes, while the bitterness lasts, in the mood which rules *Troilus and Cressida* or *Timon of Athens*; and the result is that he gets rid, by such expression, of the cynicism which, if he has a beautiful soul such as Shakespeare had, he hates with all his heart.

Further still, there may be a period of transition between the noble sympathy with the sorrows of the world's sin and error which appears in the great tragedies and the full cynicism of Timon or Troilus; and then the dramatist is likely to write a play like *Measure for Measure*, which is half cynical, which has the tail of a comedy and the body of a tragedy, neither quite one nor quite the other.

Whatever it was that troubled Shakespeare, it did not trouble his intellect or his imagination. It seems, on the contrary, to have stimulated and expanded them. *Macbeth, Othello, Lear* reach a level no man in England ever reached. But in *Timon of Athens, Troilus*, and in *Measure for Measure* neither his intellect nor his imagination seems to work with a similar power. I should like to repeat more fully what I have already said. These plays are unequal, and their elements are not as harmoniously mixed together as they are in *Macbeth, Othello*, or *Lear*. Nor is there the same certainty of touch or the same inventive variety. Their language also is frequently more obscure than it should be, and their metre is sometimes broken and unmusical. It seems as if Shakespeare did not care to take them up afterwards, and to correct and polish them. The style, when it is concerned with great matters, is as good as it is in *Macbeth* or *Othello*, but it is not so steadfast throughout, nor so consistently excellent. On graver subject-matters (as, for example, the Fear of Death in *Measure for*

Measure), his thought is as deep and far-reaching as in the large tragedies; and the subtle play of his intellect (as in the scenes between Isabella and Angelo) is equally great; but this intellectual power does not grip the situation so closely in other parts of the play. There are times, that is, when the sails of his intellect are not as full of wind, do not draw so well as usual. The power wavers—now steady, now unsteady.

I cannot put this down altogether to Shakespeare's wrong choice of a subject. It is, I suggest, due to the wave of cynicism which now and then at this time passed over him, and which, after this play, and when he had written *Troilus* and his part of *Timon of Athens*, ebbed away from him for ever. There is not a trace of it in *Antony and Cleopatra and Coriolanus*, which (according to the investigators) followed on *Timon*, and preceded the three last dramas.

Cynicism, even of this transient kind which I impute to Shakespeare, lowers all the powers of genius. It has its own powers, powers of the pit, but they are jealous and envious of the heavenly powers in genius; and they taint and depress them. They did so now to Shakespeare. *Othello*, *Macbeth*, *Lear*, *Hamlet* are not cynical. Pity overrides their darkness, and we feel that human justice is done, even if the gods, as in *Lear*, seem unjust. In *Measure for Measure*—intercalated among the great tragedies—we are in contact with this transient cynicism, and we are not touched with pity for the sorrowful or the guilty. We can feel little compassion for Mariana's pain; and her conduct at the end of the play, though natural enough, is wanting in womanly dignity and honour. Her excited desire to have Angelo for life as her husband (knowing, as she does, his baseness in and out) could only exist in a society which had lost good taste, honourable feeling, and the common sense of

life. I have no pity for Claudio. He dishonours himself.
Angelo is too vile for pity, and Isabella too austere. Moreover, justice is not done in the play, and too light a treatment of natural justice, as if it did not matter, is a main
characteristic of cynicism. Angelo, whose criminality is
almost overdone, who violates his solemn oath to Isabella,
who promises at the price of her dishonour to save her
brother's life, and who takes that life within a few hours
of his ravishment of the sister—lest Claudio should hereafter reveal his iniquity—this Angelo is saved, married,
and lives at ease in Vienna. It is the end that cynicism
would make. We are defrauded of justice; and we feel
with indignation that we are defrauded. And then
every one who stands by at the end when this failure of
justice takes place, even Isabella, is lowered in our eyes.
The whole society where such a pardon was accepted is
in a degraded state, and we are asked to accept it as all
right. Indeed, this degeneration of society is plain in the
play. From the Duke down to Barnardine (with the sole
exception of Isabella), none of the characters belong to a
noble society. They are all weak or wicked. The Duke
has not enough intellect to rule rightly, though he knows
what is right. Conscious of his want of force as a governor, he becomes a student, and then when things become
too bad to be endured, the only way he can think of
to discover or mend them is to become a spy, sniff about
in the prisons, and try to detect Angelo, whose goodness
he suspects, in sin. We must remember, during the
whole conduct of the play, that the Duke knows, even
when he hands the government over to Angelo, the
dishonourable way in which Angelo had some years
before acted towards Mariana. He has been affianced
to her; she is greatly in love with him. Her brother
was drowned, and with him Mariana's dowry. Angelo,
when her money was lost, threw her away, and to

excuse this, spread evil reports about her reputation. This villainy in the past is in the Duke's knowledge; and it is plain that one of the reasons he disguises himself is to find out whether Angelo is all he seems to be. 'Lord Angelo,' he says, 'is precise':

> Stands at a guard with envy ; scarce confesses
> That his blood flows, or that his appetite
> Is more to bread than stone ; hence shall we see,
> If power change purpose, what our seemers be.

Very good business for a friar—but surely quite unworthy of a great ruler; and so thinks Friar Thomas to whom the Duke reveals his trickeries. The Duke succeeds in his aims, but we do not like his way; and his scenic business, with its low cleverness, at the end of the play is equally unworthy of a high-minded ruler. Then, Escalus is a good-natured piece of commonplace. Angelo, a hypocrite in grain, slips into an odious villain, without a trace of the gentleman, till he is condemned to death. Claudio is a weak-minded gentleman, who has lost the fibrous stuff of a man in a dissipated life. Lucio and his friends call themselves gentlemen, but their conversation is as abominable as it is feebly cynical. Nor has it the saving grace of humour. When we read what these etiolated gentlemen say, how deeply do we regret Sir Toby Belch! Lucio, who shows some sparks of gentlehood at the beginning of the play, falls towards the end into gross blackguardism of mind. What he is *then* does not fit in with himself as we first see him. This is an instance of the wavering hand of Shakespeare of which I have spoken. Then Abhorson is as his name, and Barnardine is a picture of the brute in man, in whom the brutal elements, accompanied by even the lowest ray of intelligence, are far worse than in any animal. As to Mariana, she is a nonentity. Isabella alone shines clear and pure.

an unapproached star; but when Shakespeare marries her to the Duke, his irony is almost too deep.

What possessed Shakespeare, if not a passing wave of cynicism, to descend to this base and ugly realism, unrelieved, as he would have made it at another time, by humour? Humour lifts the base; where laughter is, wickedness is redeemable. But the sole worthy effort of humour in this play is in the sketch of Elbow the Constable; and it is below the ordinary level of Shakespeare's humour. Where is, we ask as we read, the hand and the mind which created Dogberry and Verges?

There are, it is true, some snatches of natural humour in the lower characters. Pompey, Froth, as well as Elbow, make us smile at human nature. Abhorson is not without his fantasy. He objects to a bawd like Pompey being associated with him as the executioner. 'A bawd, sir? Fie upon him, he will discredit our mystery.' Even Barnardine has a touch of humour. He refuses to be executed because he has been drunk all night. He refuses to die except at his own consent.

> BARNAR. I swear I will not die to-day for any man's persuasion.
> DUKE. But hear you,—
> BARNAR. Not a word: if you have anything to say to me, come to my ward; for thence will not I to-day.

And they are true to their nature. In the state of society Shakespeare is painting, the lower ranges of the people who are consciously vicious are really much better folk than the upper classes who are vicious and conceal it. The frankness with which they maintain that their vice is natural, and that they mean to continue it, has much more chance of change into a higher life than the hypocrisy of Angelo, or the calculated looseness of the rest of the gentlemen of the play.

These were the elements and characters Shakespeare chose to combine in this play; and as none of them, save

Isabella, were noble enough, or strong enough in passion or in intellect, in what they did or in what they suffered, to be woven into the loom of Tragedy, Shakespeare was forced to make his work into a Comedy; Angelo and Claudio are saved from death, Isabella is married to the Duke. To do that, Shakespeare, with great cleverness (too great, I think, for noble art), invented the story of Mariana, which saves Isabella's chastity, and by a side issue Claudio's life, and in the end Angelo's.

The play makes a poor comedy—one of the amorphous things they call a tragi-comedy. It ought to have been a tragedy. But in order to be that, Shakespeare would have had to have conceived all the characters on nobler lines, even Isabella's. Angelo would then have accomplished Isabella's ruin; Claudio would have been really sacrificed to Angelo's fear; Isabella would have slain herself like Lucretia; the Duke would have had to be lifted out of a spy into a steadfast justicer—and Angelo, despairing and accursed, been carried away, like Iago, to meet his death. Every one, on the contrary (after all the odious business), departs home in peace, to go on, no doubt, in the same fashion as before; the Duke and Claudio just as weak, Isabella even more austere, Lucio and his friends just as dissipated and degraded, Mariana as foolish, and Angelo frightened into a deeper hypocrisy. The happy ending is really a more wretched ending than that of *King Lear*. After the tragic horror, the social convulsion of that play, the society in which these dreadful things were wrought will improve. After the close of *Measure for Measure*, the social state will worsen. Its guilt will be more concealed, but it will not be less, but more.

Again, with regard to this play, I have sometimes wondered if Shakespeare, for once in his life, wrote with a moral aim—to paint the baseness of a society in which fornication flourished, and ate away the power, greatness and magnanimity of a State. If so, this aim being mixed up with an artistic one, would partly account for the broken, unequal work, for the want of grip on the main issues. If a man's aim be single, his whole work is full of light; if it be double, his work is in twilight, and confused in it.

And cynicism is often very fond of being moral. It never lays before us the unreached perfection, but it does enlarge (like the writer of Ecclesiastes) on morality, on the impropriety and unprofitableness of vice, on the peace that comes from obedience to law, from harmonising oneself with the ordinary course of things, however wretched an affair the cynic may think it to be. And then, if this cynic, in this mood, be a writer of plays, he would write, if he could, just such a play as *Measure for Measure*, with a good worldly ending, to warn men against the foolish vices which make society less comfortable, more disagreeable, more difficult for clever men to manage. Perhaps Shakespeare, for a brief period, fell into this error. If so, let us be for ever grateful that he never did it again. He has certainly failed to make outward morality interesting or attractive. Angelo's morality breaks to pieces before a sudden temptation, and is replaced by hypocrisy. Isabella's morality never succeeds in making us love her. The Duke's morality, which is that of a philosopher ignorant of human nature or its passions, awakens repugnance in every one on whom it is imposed. His discourse to Claudio concerning the indifference with which the wise man should look on life, is very well put as ignorant philosophy, but is ludicrous to a young man in whose veins life was running fast and dearly. Claudio endures it (being from one whom he thinks a priest), but it has no influence on him. Mariana's morality is on her lips, not in her desire. On the whole, though there are excellent things said about morality in the play, though the thoughts expressed in it on moral questions are profound and ennobled by genius, morality itself is, in this play, left without attractiveness; and as if to emphasise this, its highest form in Isabella is made by Shakespeare to be the cause of Angelo's worst immorality. It is because she is so good that his cold nature is, at last, kindled into evil desire. This is a dramatic turn which is, I think, not far removed from cynicism. Shakespeare himself must have smiled a little bitterly when he made Angelo, on Isabella's leaving him, discuss himself, with great surprise, in this fashion—

> What's this, what's this? Is this her fault or mine?
> The tempter or the tempted, who sins most?
> Ha!
> Not she; nor doth she tempt: but it is I
> That, lying by the violet in the sun,
> Do as the carrion does, not as the flower,
> Corrupt with virtuous season. Can it be
> That modesty may more betray our sense
> Than woman's lightness? Having waste ground enough,
> Shall we desire to raze the sanctuary,
> And pitch our evils there? O, fie, fie, fie!
> What dost thou, or what art thou, Angelo?
> Dost thou desire her foully for those things
> That make her good?
>
> .   .   .   .   .   .
>   Most dangerous
> Is that temptation that doth goad us on
> To sin in loving virtue.

Finally, before I come directly to the play, the fifth Act, in which all the tangle is undone, is, in its universal forgiveness of the odious wickedness we have gone through—as if justice were of no matter in comparison with ease and peace—the most cynical part of the play. It is really, in the matter of Angelo, more like a light scoff at justice than a display of mercy. The Duke retires with Isabella as his wife. It seems a most unfitting marriage. We may hope she gave him some strength of character, and stopped his spying expeditions. The marriage of Angelo and Mariana would have been quite right had Angelo's life been immediately put an end to. As it is, it is most unfitting; and Isabella had better have been silent than speak for it. Then, the whole conduct of the Act by the Duke is to the last degree fantastical; a piece of unworthy trickery. All the same, it would be effective on the stage; full of action, surprises, unexpected situations, ceaseless movement; and Angelo's terror, during the slow revealing of his sin, would supply a good actor with plenty of business. Shakespeare has in it sacrificed high dramatic simplicity and dignity to stage cleverness and sensational efficiency.

The play opens with the Duke handing over his powers to Angelo and Escalus; but chiefly to Angelo whose austere and honourable worth is known to all Vienna. The Duke does this in one of those philosophic and moral speeches which are characteristic of this play; which occur in it like golden patches on a somewhat dirty gown; and which do not always fit happily into the circumstances. These half-orations are full of Shakespeare's wise and serious thought on life and death, and many of their profound phrases have become texts for the household uses of mankind. The Duke is one of their chief speakers. But the more he speaks in this fashion, the less do we think him fit to be a ruler of men. He is a thinker, not a man of action; a dilettante philosopher in a wrong place. He makes an excellent Friar, and it would have been well for Vienna had he continued a Friar—to console the dying, to help poor maidens out of trouble, and to preach to naughty people. But to manage a State, to set its evils right—one has only to think that he let Angelo off the judgment to see that he is not fit to be a Duke.

Here is his first little piece of philosophic morality; and an excellent thing it is. He is urging Angelo to make full use of his virtues in affairs—

> Heaven doth with us as we with torches do,
> Not light them for themselves ; for if our virtues
> Did not go forth of us, 'twere all alike
> As if we had them not. Spirits are not finely touch d
> But to fine issues ; nor Nature never lends
> The smallest scruple of her excellence,
> But, like a thrifty goddess, she determines
> Herself the glory of a creditor,
> Both thanks and use.

With that, the Duke departs, not on a journey, but to take up his office as an ecclesiastical spy on his Dukedom. And Angelo, as we hear from the next scene, has put into practice an old law against fornication which had fallen out of use, and under which he condemns Claudio to death, though Claudio's offence against it had been committed in the past when the law was not enforced. But Shakespeare makes it plain that natural justice would consider the penalty of death too severe for this sin ; that its infliction would bring justice into disrepute; and that it was still more unjust to make the penalty retrospective; and finally, in the mouth of Pompey—Act II. Sc. 2—that such a law was absurd. Vienna would be depopulated. Sexual appetite is stronger than the fear of death.

Then, another view of the matter is presented. Claudio, who is condemned by this unjust law, repents his deed, though he had made the woman his wife in all but ' outward order '; and, being an honest gentleman, tries to persuade himself that the law is just. Yet Shakespeare, by his mouth, shows how an unjust law lowers the high prestige of the lawgivers, and with that, the honour of justice. Claudio thinks that Angelo, who, by the way, has sinned twice as deeply as Claudio, is seeking for mere popularity by this severe morality. Like a new broom, he does too much; or he wants to sting the 'body public' into the belief that at last they have got a governor. Therefore he puts into force a law which has hung unused on the wall for nineteen years.   There's yet a chance however of my life, he tells Lucio; go and beg my sister, who is to enter the cloister to-day, to persuade Angelo to be less strict.   Her youth has a 'prone and speechless dialect' which moves men, and her discourse is persuasive. Thus Angelo and Isabella are brought into touch with one another.

Both Angelo and Isabella, who meet like black and white, are sketched, in Shakespeare's preparing fashion, before they come together.   They are both severely chaste, but chastity in Isabella is part of a noble and good nature quite capable of passion; in Angelo part of a mean and bad one.   Angelo's blood is said to be very snow-broth.   He does not feel the stings and motions of appetite; chaste because he is cold, not because he is in love with virtue. Therefore, when temptation does come, he has no guard. Once his blood is heated, the very novelty of it is greatly attractive; he yields at once to the sensual impulse, and with so great an intensity that all his seeming virtues topple into odious vices.   Great is the fall of this house built upon the sand.

As to Isabella, we meet her first at the convent.   Her severity at once appears in her conversation with Sister Francisca.

ISAB.   And have you nuns no farther privileges?
FRAN.   Are not these large enough?
ISAB.   Yes, truly: I speak not as desiring more;
         But rather wishing a more strict restraint
         Upon the sisterhood, the votarists of Saint Clare.

The impression she makes on Lucio, that wild gentleman, accords with this.   He does not dare to play with her cold serenity.

I hold you as a thing ensky'd and sainted.

And when he tells her Claudio's story, and begs her to
soften Angelo's harshness, she shrinks at first from interfer-
ing.   The sin is so hateful to her she can scarcely bear to
plead for pity.   But at last she yields.   Then they meet—
Angelo and Isabella—he resolved to maintain his authority
by holding fast to the sentence he has pronounced on
Claudio, she to induce him, for the sake of mercy, to reverse
that sentence.   It was a situation that Shakespeare would
love to tackle; and indeed it has brought out all his
powers.   There is not a subtler piece of work in all the
plays.   We must remember that Isabella was a young
girl, forced to speak of a subject she blushed to think of
before a grown, grave man; and moreover feeling, in her
young and ignorant austerity, that the law is just which
condemns her brother.   This accounts for her seeming
coldness at the beginning of her pleading, and for the
shyness as well as the conviction with which she suddenly
gives up her effort, when Angelo declares the law—

> O just but severe law !
> I had a brother, then.

And she turns to go.   You are too cold, says Lucio.
And Isabella, while confessing that the law is just, now
pleads that it should be tempered with mercy, and that
mercy ought to be an attribute of authority.   Angelo has
the right, she thinks, by law to modify the law.   And
henceforth her appeal is directed to him as a ruler.   Like
Shylock (not for revenge, but to support his austere
reputation), Angelo stands for law.   Like Portia, Isabella
maintains the sanctity of law; but claims that mercy is
a part of eternal justice, and may very well be a part of
earthly justice.

  Indeed, it is worth remarking that through the whole
of this play the question of Authority and its limits, of the
temptations it brings to those who possess it, and of the
sins it may fall into, is debated and illustrated by Shake-

speare. It is one of three great subjects which engaged his thought, as he, musing on the world of men, wrote this play. The second is the Fear of Death, and the third is the terrible rapidity with which sin, and especially sensual sin because of its public shame, generates sin; with which seven devils are born of one, and fifty of seven.

The Duke, as we have seen, in handing over all authority to Angelo, has spoken of its duties. Claudio, on his way to prison, says that this demigod Authority claims to slay or save as it will, like a deity—and he meant that this claim is more than ought to be made by any man. It is only divine authority which may say, 'What I will, I will.' Then, he touches the temptations to abuse of authority. He feels that Angelo's death-sentence on him is to prove to the people how active he is as a ruler, how severely just; that is, Angelo is unjustly using his authority to exalt himself. Then Escalus, pleading for Claudio, bids Angelo consider whether he has thought enough of what he himself might do, had he been similarly tempted. Let the source of authority think, when it censures sin, whether its own life is clear. It is one thing to be tempted, answers Angelo, another thing to fall. When I, that censure Claudio, fall, let me die his death. Thus, in an awful ignorance, he pronounces his own condemnation.

Then, again, the Duke has his say on the matter. Great authority is the target of the world it rules. All arrows, barbed with pain, are shot into it.

> O place and greatness ! millions of false eyes
> Are stuck upon thee ! volumes of report
> Run with these false and most contrarious quests
> Upon thy doings ! thousand escapes of wit
> Make thee the father of their idle dreams,
> And rack thee in their fancies !

This is the Duke's philosophic turn, and it has little force in real life. But now, the whole question is presented to us in a vivid, passionate, human situation, with life and death dependent on its solution. Isabella stands, pleading for her brother's life before severe authority; and she confronts authority with the equal duty of mercy, and joins with this the personal appeal and demand which Escalus has already made—that the executor of the law should consider whether he also might have sinned in the same way as the man he condemns. If he consider the weakness of his human nature, he will be led towards mercy. Mercy! why, it belongs to great place. Nothing becomes authority like mercy. Let Authority on earth think what the highest Authority has done.

> Why, all the souls that were were forfeit once ;
> And He that might the vantage best have took
> Found out the remedy. How would you be,
> If He, which is the top of judgment, should
> But judge you as you are ? O ! think ou.that :
> And mercy then will breathe within your lips,
> Like man new made.

The law, the law, cries Angelo, quite untouched. Then Isabella, whose passion has been deepening minute by minute, who has now lost all her coldness, whose own eloquence and voice have wrought her into the natural intensity of her character, turns to a scornful wrath. She feels that this severity is not justice but its counterfeit, and she holds up the authority which says ' What I will, I will,' to blame and ridicule. I wonder how James the First liked that ? Let authority beware lest it become tyranny—

> So you must be the first that gives this sentence,
> And he, that suffers. O, it is excellent
> To have a giant's strength ; but it is tyrannous
> To use it like a giant.

LUCIO.   That's well said.

ISAB. (*in scorn*). Could great men thunder,
> As Jove himself does, Jove would ne'er be quiet,
> For every pelting, petty officer
> Would use his heaven for thunder.
> Nothing but thunder ! Merciful Heaven,
> Thou rather with thy sharp and sulphurous bolt

> Split'st the unwedgeable and gnarled oak
> Than the soft myrtle : but man, proud man,
> Drest in a little brief authority,
> Most ignorant of what he 's most assured,
> His glassy essence, like an angry ape,
> Plays such fantastic tricks before high heaven
> As make the angels weep ; who, with our spleens,
> Would all themselves laugh mortal.

Intellect and imagination are married in the words. Into a full power of both her passion has kindled her. And Angelo seems touched. But it is the woman not the matter of her speech which touches him. Sin is already crouching now, like a wild beast, at the door of his heart. One more touch, and the brute will be within! And this touch is given by Isabella's bold attack on his authority, and on him. She suddenly changes from imaginative soaring to sharp sententiousness; and this with a keenness and swiftness enough to trouble any man. And still her subject-matter is Authority. Great authority thinks it has licence to do what in lesser men is wrong, and to call it a slight error. Great men—so runs her sarcasm—may jest with saints, and think it wit; in lesser men 'tis foul profanation.

> That in the captain's but a choleric word,
> Which in the soldier is flat blasphemy.

And she looks straight at Angelo, whom she, like Claudio, now suspects of making advantage to himself out of his severity, of using his power to increase his repute,—and her keen eyes and words probe him to the soul.

> Ang. Why do you put these sayings upon me ?
> Isab. Because authority, though it err like others,
> Hath yet a kind of medicine in itself,
> That skins the vice o' the top. Go to your bosom ;
> Knock there, and ask your heart what it doth know
> That 's like my brother's fault : if it confess
> A natural guiltiness such as is his,
> Let it not sound a thought upon your tongue
> Against my brother's life.
> Ang.   She speaks, and 'tis
> Such sense, that my sense breeds with it.

Angelo is not thinking now of law or justice, but of the woman. She has youth and beauty, but so had many in Vienna. But now he has seen her youth and beauty glorified by passion, imagination, and intellect. Also, her soul has made her supremely beautiful as she pleaded ; and her fire and scorn and wrath have added to her loveliness. All that is noble and good in her has so enhanced her personal charm, that it stirs, in this base nature, not reverence and noble love, but sensual desire ; and when she ends by saying that her prayers for him will enter Heaven, he is thinking of leading her down into Hell.

Then comes Shakespeare's presentation of the tremendous rapidity with which sin, and sensual sin especially when it is accompanied by personal dishonour, doubles and redoubles its progeny. It is not in youth, but in middle age, that the fiercest temptations come, that the worst overthrows are wrought. And the temptation arrives with appalling suddenness, like the typhoon out of a clear sky. All is commonplace life and peace at noon. Before the afternoon has come, the certainties of life have suffered earthquake, the soul is devastated. It was so with Angelo. I have quoted his soliloquy when Isabella leaves him ; here is his soliloquy when he waits her next morning. He is no hypocrite to himself. He knows and reveals how irresistibly his evil passion has gripped his will.

> When I would pray and think, I think and pray
> To several subjects. Heaven hath my empty words ;
> Whilst my invention, hearing not my tongue,
> Anchors on Isabel : Heaven in my mouth,
> As if I did but only chew his name ;
> And in my heart the strong and swelling evil
> Of my conception.

Weary of State affairs, he would give all his gravity of which he is proud, to be as light as an idle feather. Place and form, once everything to him, only wrench awe from fools, and tie the wise to hypocrisy. The surging blood of sense commands him altogether, and disenables all the powers within him of their fitness to resist or command his appetite. In that temper he meets Isabella the second time. The dialogue is even more subtle than the last, but finally Angelo is stung by his furious senses out of all delicate approaches, and is grossly clear. His first guilt begets brutality — and his brutality begets cruelty. 'I have begun,' he cries,

> And now I give my sensual race the rein.

'And if thou dost not yield, Claudio shall not only die, he shall die in torment!' So quick, so desperately quick, does baseness follow on baseness. He can scarcely be worse, we think, but he becomes viler still. When he has fulfilled, as he supposes, his sensual desire; then, when one would have imagined that dishonour could go no further, the multiplication of guilt increases. He gives swift order for Claudio's hurried death—Claudio whom, at the price of his sister's honour, he has sworn to save. And the reason for this damnable villainy makes it still more damnable. It is lest Claudio hereafter might tell the story and injure his repute. Isabella, he thinks, will, for her own sake, not dare to betray him. With this almost inconceivable rapidity, to this multitudinous hurry of guilt on guilt, one temptation, yielded to, may bring a cold, precise, and steady man in twenty-four hours. It is a terrible study, but it is true. Morality is not always virtue.

The third matter Shakespeare dwells on is Death, and the fear of it. He does not debate it; he presents various aspects of it in his characters.

It first appears in Isabella's talk with Angelo. Death is nothing, no, nor tormented death, in comparison with honour—

> were I under the terms of death,
> The impression of keen whips I'ld wear as rubies,
> And strip myself to death, as to a bed
> That longing have been sick for, ere I'ld yield
> My body up to shame.

Then the Duke, as philosopher and priest, urges Claudio to be content with death. After all, what is life but a long death? and life is something that only fools would keep. Our life is servile to the elements that hourly afflict it. We labour to shun death, yet run to it all the while. Death is no more than sleep. And life is not really happy, nor certain, nor rich, nor kindly. Disease makes our organs of life desire death.

> Thou hast nor youth nor age,
> But, as it were, an after-dinner's sleep,
> Dreaming on both ; for all thy blessed youth
> Becomes as aged, and doth beg the alms
> Of palsied eld ; and when thou art old and rich,
> Thou hast neither heat, affection, limb, nor beauty,
> To make thy riches pleasant. What's yet in this,
> That bears the name of life ? Yet in this life
> Lie hid moe thousand deaths : yet death we fear,
> That makes these odds all even.

This is cheap philosophy on the Duke's lips; he is in no danger of death. And a thousand philosophers, comfortable in their studies, have cheaply said the same things, and never influenced the world of men. Those are not the considerations which make men despise death. Not one of them drove the Japanese up the forts at Port Arthur.

Claudio, in courtesy to the priest, and having no hope, accepts them with a certain irony :

> To sue to live, I find I seek to die ;
> And seeking death, find life : let it come on.

But we know how little impression they have made when he sees a chance of life—how even dishonour seems better than death to his youthful blood. For now Isabella comes in to tell her story, and her view of death being an unconsidered trifle when dishonour is in the other scale, conflicts with his. In this vivid conversation, where two souls meet in a dreadful reality, the love of life, the fear of death are tossed as subjects to and fro.

'Is there no remedy?' asks Claudio.   'None,' answers Isabella, 'but such as will strip you of honour.'   'Let me know the point,' Claudio replies.

> ISAB.   O, I do fear thee, Claudio ; and I quake,
> Lest thou a feverous life shouldst entertain,
> And six or seven winters more respect
> Than a perpetual honour.   Darest thou die ?
> The sense of death is most in apprehension ;

Oh, answers Claudio, with a young noble's habitual courage,

> If I must die
> I will encounter darkness as a bride
> And hug it in my arms.

Then she tells him how Angelo has encountered her, and how

> If I would yield him my virginity
> Thou mightst be freed.

Thou shalt not do it, cries Claudio.   If it were my life, she answers, I would throw it down for your deliverance as frankly as a pin.   But now the fresh youth in Claudio calls on him to live.   It is not the fear of death, but the force of life in him which makes him say—'Sure, it is no sin, O Isabel.'   One sees her face, as she looks into his eyes, change every moment.   It is a terrible face and hour.

> ISAB.   What says my brother ?
> CLAUD.   Death is a fearful thing.
> ISAB.   And shamed life a hateful.
> CLAUD.   Ay, but to die, and go we know not where ;
> To lie in cold obstruction and to rot ;
> This sensible warm motion to become
> A kneaded clod ; and the delighted spirit
> To bathe in fiery floods, or to reside
> In thrilling region of thick-ribbed ice ;
> To be imprison'd in the viewless winds,
> And blown with restless violence round about
> The pendent world ; or to be worse than worst
> Of those that lawless and uncertain thought
> Imagine howling :—'tis too horrible !
> The weariest and most loathed worldly life
> That age, ache, penury and imprisonment
> Can lay on nature is a paradise
> T₀ what we fear of death.

ISAB. Alas, alas!

CLAUD.   Sweet sister, let me live :
  What sin you do to save a brother's life,
  Nature dispenses with the deed so far
  That it becomes a virtue.

ISAB.   O you beast!
  O faithless coward! O dishonest wretch!
  Wilt thou be made a man out of my vice?
  Is 't not a kind of incest, to take life
  From thine own sister's shame? What should I think?
  Heaven shield my mother play'd my father fair!
  For such a warped slip of wilderness
  Ne'er issued from his blood—Take my defiance!
  Die, perish! Might but my bending down
  Reprieve thee from thy fate, it should proceed ;
  I 'll pray a thousand prayers for thy death,
  No word to save thee.

CLAUD. Nay, hear me, Isabel.

ISAB.   O, fie, fie, fie!
  Thy sin's not accidental, but a trade.
  Mercy to thee would prove itself a bawd :
  'Tis best that thou diest quickly.

That sounds almost too harsh on a sister's lips to a brother who is to die to-morrow! And many have blamed Isabella for unwomanliness. But chastity such as hers, which repudiated all union with a man, even in marriage, as impure, was directly against nature, and has always induced into its advocates and practisers an unnaturalness in their actions and judgments. Moreover, she was young, and the young have not known yet the weakness of human nature, and therefore do not excuse it. And she was innocent, and her innocence had been so insulted that she was on the top of rage and misery. And innocence is not merciful to sin or to dishonour. It is the experience of one's own guilt that awakens in us mercy and tenderness. And she was bitterly disappointed in her brother who should have thought her honour dearer than his life. And such strength as she possessed is severe on weakness, because it does not comprehend it. And she was austere by nature. Her defiance of Claudio, her wrath, are in right harmony with her previous character; and finally, her native austerity on this special matter of chastity had been deepened by convent religion. I do not think that these considerations wholly excuse her fierce outburst, her flashing refusal to speak to Claudio any more. After all, he is her brother, and she seems to violate natural piety; but they *do* lessen the offence of her words. She has been wrought to the very ultimate thrill of nervous strain by a desperate situation, containing the blackest insult to her womanhood. She who could then be careful of her words, who would not be lifted into a region where all human relationships, brothers, husbands, fathers, were nothing in the balance, would not be true woman at all. Isabella is none the less noble for her outbreak. Its motives are sufficient, given the nature born with her, but her nature was a little unnatural. And Cordelia, Desdemona, Imogen would not have put her reproach into these violent words. They would, however, have felt the greater part of it.

The Duke, Isabella, Claudio have thus, driven by events, imaged before us their thoughts on Death and the fear of it.

There is yet another presentation of the matter. Claudio's bottom thoughts (when the chance of escape is offered to him) are those which in a soft luxurious age, when sensual immorality has corrupted every rank in society, cultivated men think with regard to death. Shakespeare now contrasts this type with its extreme opposite. He paints, still haunting this question of death, the brutal man, hopelessly material, in Barnardine. Death to him is nothing at all. He thinks less of the deprivation of life than he thinks of the deprivation of drink. He has no care for the past, the present, or the future. He makes his roaring joke in the presence of instant death. The sketch is rapid and vivid. No one can mistake Shakespeare's intention to contrast him with Claudio. Yet both, in different circumstances and rank, are the direct products of the kind of society Shakespeare has painted in this play.

Lastly, we are allowed to see how a man feels with regard to death, when, having been on the summit of repute, he is cast hopelessly down into an abyss of shame. Then Angelo cries out—

> good prince,
> No longer session hold upon my shame,
> But let my trial be mine own confession :
> Immediate sentence then, and sequent death,
> Is all the grace I beg.
>
> I crave death more willingly than mercy ;
> 'Tis my deserving, and I do entreat it.

In the last depth of shame, as well as in the last height of ideal joy, death is welcome.

These are grave subjects, and though they awaken our thought, they do not stir us to delight. Nor does the picture of a base society give us pleasure. Both have no charm ; nor have either the stern loveliness they might have had if the play had been a tragedy. There is but one thing in the whole play which has romantic beauty. It is the image of the moated Grange where Mariana mourns, and the song which her attendant sings. Its music shall close this essay, that, after much distress, the reader may have some pleasure—

> Take, O, take those lips away,
>   That so sweetly were forsworn ;
> And those eyes, the break of day,
>   Lights that do mislead the morn :
> But my kisses bring again,
>   bring again ;
> Seals of love, but seal'd in vain,
>   seal'd in vain.

VI

OTHELLO

WHATEVER we may say about Shakespeare's apartness from his own personality in his art or as an artist, the man who wrote the four great tragedies, of which *Othello* is one, has but a very little resemblance with the man who wrote *Romeo and Juliet*, or *As You Like It*. Eight years, twelve years, have done their work upon his soul. What their result was no one can fully explain.

These years had also brought their experience into his art. During their passage he was incessant in practice and production, and as an artist had reached all he could of excellence in versification, in construction, in presentment, and in characterisation. The change in art power between *Romeo and Juliet*, 1592, and the four tragedies, especially *Othello*, 1604, is immense. All that his early work promised has been more than fulfilled. He stands now on the summit of the Genius of England.

There was an equal change in his soul. There are artists who through practice of their art develop steadily in power of execution, but whose imagination is moved chiefly by their intellect; whose thinking does not develop an emotion of an equal power to their thought; whose emotion, when it rises, does not enter vitally into the human life which surrounds them; who practise their art for the sake of their art alone. In these men the level of the soul does not change. They have no fresh personality to put into their work; their personality has become mannered into sameness, incapable of change. Exquisite,

perhaps perfect, in technique, their art is rarely simple ;
it is sensuous by rule; it cannot be impassioned.

There seem to be some folk who think that Shakespeare
was such a man. They say, or appear to say, that the
change from plays like *Twelfth Night* to *Hamlet, Othello,
Macbeth* and *King Lear* was owing only to an artistic
desire in Shakespeare to make use, for art's sake, of his
knowledge of the darker side of human life; that when he
wrote these tragedies he was much the same man within
as when he wrote *As You Like It*; that he had only taken
up these tragic subjects in order to try his artist hand
upon them. He beheld these fates of men, and recorded
them, with the artist's externality.

I look on that statement as almost incredible. The
terrible passion, searching, unsatisfied emotion, which
informs and burns in these four tragedies, which is
clothed in words which seem hot from the furnace, now
of one passion, now of another, did not, I believe, arise
out of a soul at case. It, with all its questing thought,
arose out of a soul in trouble, it may be, tormented; out
of darkened thought, bitter questioning, intense and
sympathetic feeling with the suffering and mysteries of
humanity.

I do not say that in these tragedies Shakespeare represented any personal experiences of his own, or that we can
trace in any historical circumstances the causes of his
tragic representation of life. It would be nonsense to say
that. But I do say that when he wrote these terrible
dramas, the foundation of his soul was entirely different
from what it was when he wrote the *Merchant of Venice*,
or *Twelfth Night*, or even *Julius Cæsar*. There had been
that in his inward being which made his view of human
life and of its fates dark instead of bright. The subjects
he took were dreadful with guilt and pain; his treatment
of them was unrelenting. His joyousness, his play with

life, had vanished as if it had never been. His belief in
a divine Justice is shaken in *Hamlet*, is almost mocked at
in *Measure for Measure*, is really absent in *Macbeth*, is
replaced by a belief in Chance as at the root of the
universe in *Othello*, and in *Lear* it is altogether gone.
He does not quite say that in the play, but it is like a
creeping mist in it. All the more, because of this, he is
in a great grief for mankind. He has a deep and personal
sympathy with the sorrows he records, and this is unmis-
takable—a hundred passages are steeped in it—but it is
a sympathy which sees but little light beyond; and which,
at least in *Othello* and *Lear*, walks in darkness and weeps
as it walks.

In the midst of his change, this profound sympathy
with humanity was unchanged. It had been sympathy with joy, with love and lovingness, and the sorrow
of love; with his country's history and fairyland, with
the movement and clash of outward life in war, in courts,·
in the streets of the city. It was now as close, as vital
a sympathy with the crimes, the temptations, the in-
effable sorrows, the deeper passions in the souls of men
and women. That sympathy was perennial; in these four
tragedies it is intense; its head of waters was always full.
Like Charity it never fails in them.

Another thing which lasted from the past was the
executive power of the artist. We might, perhaps, think
that a troubled soul would lose the artistic powers—
conception, construction, representation, imaginative
creation, execution—that these would at least be confused or weakened. But that is not the case with an
imperial genius. Nay, the inward pain of such a man
stimulates, agonises his powers, drives them to the
summit of their energy, as Shakespeare was driven
in these plays. As to the executive power—when a
great artist has been working for many years, and is

in constant practice, and has improved in capacity every
month, his executive power works almost of its own
accord; it would work in hell; and the pangs of hell
would only make its doing more magnificent. It would
build without an effort the frenzy of Lear, the agony of
Othello.

This being said, I repeat that Shakespeare was not, in
these tragedies, the impersonal artist. He chose these
grim, awful, piteous, and fierce subjects because his
mood towards humanity was grim with pain; because
the questioning of mortal doubt and trouble which he
did represent in *Hamlet*, had left him without an answer
to give to the problems of misery and evil. His early
sense that

> There's a Divinity which shapes our ends,
> Rough-hew them how we will,

which lingered still on the lips of Hamlet in *Hamlet*,
has vanished away in *Lear* and in *Othello*. The noble,
the good, and the beautiful are there sacrificed without
any good arising from their sacrifice. Lear makes a vain
old man's mistake and pays for it by torture and madness. Cordelia perishes by a villain's love of cruelty;
Desdemona dies of her frank innocence; Othello of his
love and of his foolishness, the blind victim of a
miscreant. And there is no explanation, no reason why
such things happen in the world; nor is there any use,
any far-off interest in these tears. That, I believe, was
now the temper of Shakespeare.

Is that a full account of his temper at this strange
time? No; it omits *Measure for Measure, Troilus and
Cressida*, and *Timon of Athens*. Where and how shall
we class these plays? Well, when a man, like Shakespeare in these four tragedies, is in the temper I have
spoken of—the temper of 'black choler'—there will come
intervals when the state of things will seem more than he

can hear, when either sorrow for humanity will pass into rage with the gods who are indifferent to the pains of men, or when his own sympathy with men is changed into anger with their villainy, or scorn of their weakness, or hatred of their falseness—into contempt of humanity at large. This is natural enough and not uncommon. And it makes the cynic. It is some such state of the soul which underlies *Measure for Measure*, which deepens into scathing scorn in *Troilus* of human nature, and which is black with wrath against all the world in *Timon of Athens*. In these plays Shakespeare's sympathy with humanity scarcely exists, and, owing to its loss, his executive power as an artist is weaker than it is in the four tragedies. It works unevenly, uncertainly. His hand wavers. His view of the situations is not inevitably right.

In natures not nobly built, who have not a solid foundation of healthy humanity, to whom cheerfulness and joy and love of human nature are not native, such cynicism when it comes is cherished, grows, and finally masters them. Their genius, if they have had any, is ravelled away, and finally dispersed. But in natures that are of an opposite character—noble, healthy, joyous, loving—such cynicism is transient. It is like a close and gloomy cloud-veil which, after violent storm, makes grey the landscape, and is silent from the exhaustion of the forces which preceded it. It broods, like a curse, over the land, and takes all colour out of everything. Then a clear wind arises from the west; the black vapour thins, breaks upwards into soft cloud-flakes, sun-smitten into tender beauty; and in the quiet sky the evening sun is shining with a lovely and delicate light, more lovely and delicate than was its radiance in the morning.

That was the course of the soul of Shakespeare after the tempest out of which the tragedies arose. The intervals also of cynicism which brought forth *Troilus*

and Cressida—that strange, mocking, fierce play, with
so grim and weighty a thoughtfulness, so sardonic an
exposure of the baseness of the world's heroes, and so
savage a contempt of human nature—had passed away.
So also the terrible denunciations of mankind and the
gods, which make the Shakespearian work in *Timon* the
ideal of searching hatred and scorn of humanity, cease
their raging.

With these the cynicism of Shakespeare exhausted
itself; devoured its own brood. In *Coriolanus*, in *Antony
and Cleopatra*, the wind of a new temper in his soul began
to blow. Love of human nature, tolerance for its follies,
even for its guilt, pity for its sorrows, a deep sense of its
natural nobility, even joy in its beauty, revived; with an
added dignity, a wiser experience, a solemn sense of the
permanence of goodness, a balanced temperance in the
judgment of men, an exquisite mercy—elements which
had settled themselves now into his soul through his
conquest of the tempest and the cloud. And then came
the soft, sweet gentleness, the peaceful happiness, the
immeasurable kindness of the evening light in his soul
—the tender twilight of *Winter's Tale*, of *Cymbeline*,
and of *The Tempest*.

But we are far from that delightful time when we are
engaged with *Othello*. There is, it is true, nothing in it
of the dark grin which peers out from the corners of
Troilus and Cressida, nothing of the *sæva indignatio*
which in *Timon* rains black damnation on all mankind;
but everywhere in it we seem to feel in the writer's soul
his dark consciousness of the inexplicable aspect of the
world, of the answerless problem of evil and sorrow; of
his doubt, with the dismay that companied it, whether
there was any intelligent Good-will behind the life of
man, or whether all that happened was by soulless
Chance, or by ruthless Fate. Fate dominates *Macbeth*,

but here in *Othello* Chance or Unreason, blind and deaf, is at the centre of human life.

That the history of mankind or our personal life should be subject to mere Chance, without reason, law, or direction, is infinitely less tolerable, and more irritating, than that it should be subjected to Fate, whose decrees and movements are unalterable, and which, being unalterable, imply reason at their back. We may, in the end, bend before Fate, because it moves by Law; but nothing will ever induce us to be otherwise than in angry rebellion against unreasoning Chance. We abhor a universe which is without any law at all; and if, for a moment or a year, we think we are in such a universe, we despise ourselves and our race. That way lies, if it continue, black cynicism or insanity.

Something of such questioning and the temper which arises from it seems to have been in Shakespeare's mind when he wrote *Othello*. The conception of the play, the movement of it, the events in it, the bringing about of the catastrophe, are all apparently in the realm of Chance. There is a shocking unreasonableness about them, which is all the more curious when we consider that the construction of the play, the linking and the sequence of its scenes, is so eminently clear, so closely ordered by the imaginative reason and the logic of passion. This is a wonderful combination.

But I dwell at present on the unreasonableness, the chance-strangeness of what occurs. There is a *prima facie* improbability in Desdemona's love for Othello, even if he were only a brown Moor, much more if he were intended by Shakespeare to be a thick-lipped Negro, as he is called in the play by those who hate him. But even as a Moor, the strangeness, the unreasonableness of her love is great. It is as if Chance were at the back of it. The natural, indeed the rational feeling of the world is against such an

affection. And Shakespeare makes every one in the play,
except Desdemona, feel how odd it is, how out of the
natural way of things. No amount of greatness of mind,
of nobility of character, in Othello can entirely—as some
think it can—do away with the natural improbability, the
physical and racial queerness of her love for the Moor.
And I venture to say that this is the first feeling of those
who read the play, however they may, in their admiration
of Othello's noble nature, persuade themselves afterwards
to the contrary.

Then there is Iago. It is odd that a young man of
twenty-eight years should be capable of such cool hypocrisy, unreasonable hatred, such luxuriousness of cruelty;
should have such advanced experience of evil, such lip-
smacking pleasure in plotting it and fulfilling it; should
so soon have arrived at the pitilessness of grey-haired
inhumanity. It is possible, of course, but it is very improbable; as if a monstrous mind had arrived by chance
in the body of a non-commissioned officer. It is all the
more improbable that the reasons of his wickedness cannot
clearly be discovered by us, nor indeed by himself. End-
less discussion has gathered round the question—'Why
did Iago torture Othello?' Even when he is proved in
the play to have done so, no one can quite understand
why. His wife is lost in surprise. Othello cries—

> demand that demi-devil
> Why he hath thus ensnar'd my soul and body.

Iago himself cannot tell. Hate is his native air; the
desire to torture stings him within. He seeks to explain
it; he searches for his motives; 'motive-hunting,' Coleridge
calls it. He finds this and that motive, but not one of
them explains what is in his heart, not one of them is an
adequate reason for the devilish pleasure he has in putting
Othello on the rack, in egging him on to kill Desdemona.
His suspicion that the Moor was intimate with his wife is

an invented suspicion. To give it some colour he accuses Cassio of the same sin. His action is outside of probable humanity, even of wicked humanity. It is like that of a soulless devil in a man, that is, of the last improbability. Envy is the most real of his motives, but is in him excited to a height almost incredibly beyond its ordinary nature. Cassius was envious, so was Casca, but they only desired to slay Cæsar, not to torture him. All this is the more improbable when we find that every one believes Iago is especially frank, honest, and open; that every one, and especially his chief victim, trusts him to the bone.

I intercalate Emilia as another of the improbabilities. It is surely passing strange that she should have lived with Iago for some years, and never thought any ill of him, or imagined him capable of deceit. She thinks him 'wayward.' Wayward! His wickedness bursts on her like a thunderbolt. Till Othello mentions the handkerchief, she has not the slightest suspicion of the unhonesty or cruelty of the man she has lived with as a wife. Of course, he would have deceived the very elect. Still it is vastly improbable that she should have thought him only wayward, and at times impatient.

The writer who devised all this was in doubt while he wrote that any rational Will, or Justice, or even a fixed Destiny, was at the helm of the Universe; but a general Unreason which one might call Chance, and which made a more muddle of the course of humanity and of our personal lives.

Then take Othello. When we live with him through the first two Acts, we live with the great and experienced soldier, with a grave and noble character. He has arrived at full middle age, and has won the trust and respect of the most jealous and difficult of governments. All men honour his integrity, his skill in war, his ability in governing men, his self-governance, his temperate nature, a ruler of men

who rules himself.   He has also seen the world and mixed
with many men and events in an adventurous youth, as
he relates to Desdemona and to the Signiory of Venice—
a man then not liable to give his trust rashly, to act on
mere suspicion, without inquiry, to be ignorant of the evil
which is in men.   Yet this is the vast improbability which
Shakespeare creates for him—this is the blind, deaf,
unreasonable chance which happens to him.   He places
his unquestioning trust, to the ignoring of every one else,
in a young man of twenty-eight, whom, in spite of interest
made for him, he has put in a lower position than his
lieutenant, Cassio.   It never occurs to him that he may
have angered Iago.   He entrusts his wife to Iago's charge,
he keeps him always by his side, he consults him in the
circumstance of the riot; he cashiers Cassio, who has
fought with him as a faithful comrade, on the report of
Iago; he listens to his first innuendoes against his wife
without one symptom of distrust in the man who makes
them; he believes even in that foul dream which Iago
invents.   He attributes to her, on the mere hearsay
evidence of Iago, coarse and common lustfulness, revolting appetite.   He turns his young wife, in his
thoughts, into a common harlot; and his belief in Iago
is so unshaken that he slays Desdemona.   Nothing,
given Othello's character in the first two Acts, can be
more improbable.

Then it is amazingly improbable that a grave, experienced, world-worn man like Othello, of so magnanimous a nobility of thought and character, should not
have felt the innocence of Desdemona, should have been
immediately disturbed into suspicion by Iago's phrase
' I do not like that'—by his 'Indeed'—should, in an
hour, at the hints of a raw young man, be tortured into
distrust of the woman who had given up all for him,
broken with her father, violated the customs of her

society, and followed him to the war. It is equally improbable that he should have made no inquiry concerning the handkerchief from Emilia, but believed that Cassio, having received it from Desdemona, gave it carelessly away to his mistress Bianca. The matter of the handkerchief bristles with improbabilities, and Othello— this temperate, grave man—never looks into it, drives his wife by his violence about it into a lie, and takes his only refuge in his hopeless trust in Iago.

The improbability of the whole affair is shocking. It is one more of the mass of improbabilities Shakespeare has chosen to rest his play upon. Yet, I repeat, while he yielded to a mood which thought men were involved in a world of chance, he never ceased to be the artist. There was no chance in his work. What he constructed, he constructed with the finest imaginative logic. Not a trace of want of reason is in the building or conduct of the play. The art-powers in him wrought with complete independence of the mood of his soul ; as if they were led by a separate being in him. He combined all these improbabilities with so creative and formative an imagination that the whole play seems eminently probable. We are hurried on so fast from the first suspicion of Othello to his death that we have no time to ask questions, to doubt or debate anything. Our interest is so caught by the artist that we resent even a moment's delay. Still, Shakespeare made the improbabilities, and they are so great that it seems as if at the bottom of his mind he believed that a reasonless Chance prevailed in this world.

I turn now to the conduct of the drama.

It begins with a rush into the main subject. Shakespeare mostly starts on his way with a scene or two of quiet preparation, but here, as if his dreadful conception of the wild passions which were to rage in his drama had cast their atmosphere back to the beginning of its action, his opening scene is full of noise and shouting. The silence of the night around Brabantio's house is broken into a tempest of anger by the fierce summons of Roderigo and Iago to tell him that his daughter is gone, and with the Moor. Iago is in full blast, brutally gross, shouting the scandal at full voice, pitiless of the father, rejoicing in the scandal which will hurt Othello. This is the tumultuous opening of the tragedy, and it suggests, mixed up as it is with the ill-fated marriage, the storm-swept atmosphere of human passion in which we are to live from the second Act until the end.

The streets of Venice now affront the quiet night with noise. Brabantio and his clan are out seeking Desdemona. In another street Othello with attendants and torches goes to meet Brabantio and out-tongue his complaint. Cassio with a troop meets Othello to summon him to the Senate. On them comes, full of fury, Brabantio and his men with swords drawn, to accuse Othello of practising on Desdemona with drugs. It is a mêlée of passion and noise, and is again an outward prologue to the inward and dreadful turmoil in the soul of Othello and the spirit of Desdemona. In the whole scene Othello, as if in contrast, is calm and dignified, the master of the disturbance, and it is piteous to think of him, as he is a few days later, racked and torn with misery, all his quiet lost, all his dignity departed.

In the next scene, in the council chamber, when Brabantio accuses Othello, and the Senate send him to Cyprus, he still preserves his noble quietude, his soldier bearing, the frankness of his nature. His defence is full of self-confidence, and yet there is in it a curious simplicity as if a child in a man was speaking; as if, loving Desdemona so well, something of Desdemona's spirit had lodged itself in him. Again, we think of what this stately, quiet man will soon become, and the contrast shakes our soul.

And here for the first time we meet Desdemona, and she is a surprise. We expect to find her, like her father's description of her,

> A maiden never bold ;
> Of spirit so still and quiet that her motion
> Blushed at herself ;

and we find no such person.[1] No one is more surprised than Brabantio by her dignity, her firm grasp of the situation, her unshrinking attitude before the Senate ; not one at all of spirit so still and quiet that her motion blushed at herself. All these years he has never known her, no more than Lear has known his daughters. Love has not transformed her, but brought to the surface the deep powers of her nature—strength of loving, strength of will, firmness in act, clear vision of what to do in difficulty as when she settles the question before the whole Senate of what she is to do when Othello leaves for Cyprus. She is frank and bold and firm; not a girl, but a steadfast, clear-eyed woman. But in her boldness there is no immodesty. It is the boldness of deep love. It is the boldness of innocence. It is the boldness of one who is ignorant of the wrong and wickedness of the world, and this innocent boldness in her character accounts for the pleasant frankness of her conversation with Iago in the next Act, and for her natural relations with Cassio, and alas, for the ease with which she slips into the net of Iago. With what pity then we read, with what foreboding, Othello's trustful words—

> My life upon her faith ! Honest Iago,
> My Desdemona must I leave to thee.

---

[1] This description has been foolishly taken by many great actresses as the basis of their presentment of Desdemona. It is Brabantio's idea of her, not Shakespeare's.

We are now left with Iago and his gull Roderigo,
who is in love with Desdemona. We have seen Iago
shouting coarse insult in the streets of Venice to bring
injury on Othello. At the bottom of him is a natural
brutality, a pleasure in gross lust and soulless cruelty.
His talk smells of the barrack and the brothel. He
maddens Othello with the grossest pictures of his wife
and Cassio. He has not one shred of belief in faithfulness, chastity, or purity. There is no goodness—is
the only truth of which he is certain.

Roderigo, seeing Othello and Desdemona, thinks his
love hopeless, and will drown himself. Iago laughs him
to scorn. Desdemona will soon tire of the Moor, and
seek for other flesh; Othello will also change, and then
you shall be happy. Lust is master. 'Think first of
yourself, and then of love. I'll drive Othello and
Desdemona apart; I'll help you; I hate Othello. Put
money in your purse. Virtue? Virtue is the getting of
one's own way.'

There we are alone with Iago. Shakespeare is fond of
soliloquies, and this self-communing, in which Iago bares
his soul, is a habit with him. He plays before others
so hypocritical a part, with such intense a falseness, that
it is a great relief to be true in solitary speech, and to
chuckle over his own cleverness in lying. And here he
smiles as he engenders his plot to make the Moor jealous
of Cassio and Desdemona, to get Cassio's place, and to feed
fat his envious hatred of Othello. Thus ends the first
Act, and the foundation of the whole tragedy is closely
knit together in it. It could not be better conducted, nor
with a firmer and a more experienced hand. All the
characters are drawn not only in the clearest outline, but
the outline is filled up with a multitude of subtle touches
like those of a great painter; nor can the politic and
human character of a great council, such as the Senate of

Venice, be better indicated than Shakespeare has done it here.

The second Act, in which Iago arranges and outspreads the events which will enable him to make safe and probable his attack on Othello, is full of business, hustle and noise, and in a general turmoil all the personages are brought on the stage. The only steady thing is Iago's supremacy as maker of the riot. Othello, however, when he comes on the stage, is still pre-eminent, quiet, self-contained, and determined. It is the last time we see him as the master of men. In a short day, his peace has gone for ever; he can no longer rule men, he has lost all power to rule himself. He has been like an impregnable tower, four-square against all the winds; he is henceforth like the same tower breached, ruined, and all the stately rooms within destroyed.

The storm-atmosphere of the first Act is thus carried by the riot into the second Act. The impression of a great tragedy to come falls like a shadow on the soul, and when we listen to Iago at the end of the Act—alone and darkly talking to himself—we know what dreadful sorrow is in the wind, and what infernal will will make and direct the storm. To harmonise with this human tumult, Shakespeare begins this Act with a great storm at sea. All the way from Venice, down the chafing Adriatic, Othello's fleet has been molested by the gale, and the Turkish fleet destroyed. He and Desdemona land on the island of their misfortune in a tempest when—

> The wind-shaked surge, with high and monstrous mane,
> Seems to cast water on the burning Bear,
> And quench the guards of the ever-fixed Pole.

Nor is the end of the Act left without words which seem to insist from without on this sense of wild disturbance

in the atmosphere of the play. When Othello comes in
to subdue the quarrel, the great bell of the town has
begun to ring.

> Who's that that rings the bell?
> The town will rise.
>
> . . . . .
>
> Silence that dreadful bell : it frights the isle
> From her propriety.

I cannot tell why these words have always seemed, to my
ear, to be charged with a picture of a town waking to
wild riot, and to a tempest in the sky bearing fire from
street to street. It thickens the tempestuous atmosphere
I speak of. It recalls Iago's pleasure when he bids
Roderigo shout his dishonour to Brabantio. 'Cry,' he
says,

> 'Cry, with like timorous accent and dire yell
> As when, by night and negligence, the fire
> Is spied in populous cities.'

And now the third Act opens, and all this outward
storm in nature, and in the riot and quarrels of men,
becomes inward in the soul of Othello. There, in his
tortured spirit, the tempest rises, grows and deepens,
rages fiercer and more fierce, agony on agony, till it breaks
into murder and dies of its misery. And the spiritual
tempest is more terrible than the natural, as that in the
spirit of Lear is greater than the hurricane.

I say no more on the conduct of the play.[1] I turn to
the main characters as I think they were conceived by
Shakespeare.

---

[1] I should like to draw attention to the *mise en scène* at the beginning
of the second Act. Shakespeare's stage was naked of scenery. But the
dialogue makes the scene spectacular. We see the town in the background, and the cliffs outside lined with the people looking for the ships.
Below is the tempestuous sea, and the great waves roaring. A group of
gentlemen talk in the foreground, and in their talk we see Cassio's ship
arrive, then Iago's, then Othello's. Cries of 'A sail! a sail!' guns going
off, a trumpet sounding, announce these arrivals. Nothing is seen, but
the dialogue paints all, as in a cinematograph.

With the exception of Hamlet, no characters in Shakespeare's plays have been subjected to so much analysis, discussion, and theories as Othello, Iago, and Desdemona. In no play are there two such leading and tremendous parts, each challenging the actor's utmost study, as those of Othello and Iago. The most famous actors have chosen to act both parts, as if they were equally worthy of the best efforts of their genius. What each of these characters say from point to point, the meaning of each phrase, how it came to be said, how it is to be acted, with what intention, with what gestures, have been studied, varied, criticised, opposed and defended for nearly three hundred years.

That means that the characters are not only exceedingly complex underneath their boldly drawn outline, but also that Shakespeare's multitudinous thoughts about them, as he wrote and attempted to express each of those thoughts, even if it were only in an interjected phrase, have made them even more complex to us than he originally intended them to be. At this time of his life, when he was burdened with incommunicable, unresolvable thinking concerning God and man, his writing was so charged with passion, meditation, and the matter of humanity, that it often became obscure, not so much in its expression, as in its intention and its goal. Men have never yet satisfied themselves with regard to what he meant Othello, Iago, and Desdemona to be.

There are those who say that one cannot understand Desdemona or Othello till Iago is understood; that Iago's native wickedness lies at the root of the play. It is a probable supposition and arguable. But I think, with natural diffidence, that Shakespeare's idea was not that. The deepest source of all the woes and guilt of the play lay in Desdemona's extraordinary innocence of the world, and the sin of the world. It is on seeing that innocence,

and by play upon it, that Iago conceives and carries out
his plot. It is plain, in spite of his blasting hints of
Desdemona's unchaste nature to Roderigo, to Cassio and
Othello, that he knows she is innocent. Yet what would
Venetian society have said had it heard her say to Cassio—

> If I do vow a friendship, I'll perform it
> To the last article : my lord shall never rest ;
> I'll watch him tame and talk him out of patience ;
> His bed shall seem a school, his board a shrift ;
> I'll intermingle everything he does
> With Cassio's suit : therefore, be merry, Cassio ;
> For thy solicitor shall rather die
> Than give thy cause away.

We feel her innocence in every word, but Othello, with
Iago beside him, would not feel it; and her persistence in
her friendship kills her. She takes Cassio's defence so
eagerly that she maddens her husband ; and does this
twice at the most unlucky times, even at the hour of her
death. It is owing to her innocence that Iago makes her
his easy tool. It is owing to it she thinks of every explanation of Othello's fury except the right one ; that she is
quite ignorant of jealousy, and cannot, when it is suggested,
conceive it in Othello. It is owing to this that she
has that frank, unquestioning trust in Iago, in Cassio, in
Emilia, in Othello, which leads her straight to death. Her
innocence is her bane. It is owing to it that Othello—who
does not understand innocence and has evidently never
met it—suspects her so easily. It is owing to that ignorance of the world which goes with innocence that she half-
woos Othello, and bids him speak to her, which afterwards
comes up against her. It is owing to this that she abandons her home when she loves, forgets her father's love, and
marries a Moor against all the traditions of her society—
every one of which actions are used by that villain to
defame her in the eyes of Othello. Is such innocence
believable ?—that is Iago's argument to Roderigo, to

Othello. The dames of Venice are not like that. 'In Venice,' says Iago, 'they do let heaven see the pranks,'

> They dare not show their husbands ; their best conscience
> Is not to leave 't undone, but keep 't unknown.

Desdemona is not like these Venetians, and it is her destruction. The only man in the whole play who sees her as she truly is is Cassio; and he is the man with whom she is supposed to be false to Othello.

O, what was Shakespeare thinking of the world when he invented this, and laid it all upon one innocent head? Is this the result and the fate of innocence? Alas! too great innocence in a woman is a most dangerous factor in a society which is not innocent, or, not being guilty, is well acquainted with guilt. Desdemona's innocence, quite unconsciously, ruined the lives of men. Her path was strewn with the dead. A little knowledge on her part of the world; a little knowledge of the passions of men, of the impurity of men and women, of hatred and jealousy, a little common sense such as comes of handling daily life in the world, would have dissolved Iago's villainy, saved her own life and saved Othello. O, I say again, what was Shakespeare thinking of the course of things when he made this representation? With what an infinite piteousness he has clothed it; and yet how deeply, combined with the stupidity of Othello, it irritates the reader, how deeply the injustice of the situation irritated Shakespeare —for part of the irritation we feel is the irritation in his soul with a world of mere chance transferred to us. Yet who has not felt the loveliness of Desdemona's unconscious innocence? In scene after scene, with Cassio, Iago, Othello, Emilia, in a great variety of circumstance, it is bright and clear as sunshine. It goes easily with the frank boldness on which I have dwelt. I sometimes think that her pleading for Cassio is overdone, that we might have less of it, but nevertheless the presentation of Desdemona as she passes through the unveiling to her of wickedness and sorrow and passion to her death, is of an unearthly beauty. To the end she is whiter than the driven snow. The last scene with Emilia is pathetic beyond words. Innocent she loved and lived, and innocent she died. In a world of Chance she died.

To turn from her to Iago is to turn from light to darkness. Shakespeare has given to his character infinite care, minute artistry. Its variety, within its low range, is almost incalculable. Every sentence adds a new touch, a new complexity, a new thought to it. Yet, it seems simple enough as we read the play, so great is the art which represents it.

Iago is raised by some writers into the representation of almost absolute evil: a Satan incarnate, with a majesty of evil surrounding him, of which I think Shakespeare had no notion at all. He is again represented as a great artist of evil, who is enthralled with the pleasure of his own artistry in wickedness. He is also called a silent poet, who works out the dreadful tragedy of which he is the cause with all the joy of a great dramatist.

I think these views are strangely exaggerated, and that Shakespeare would not accept them. There is no majesty in Iago. He is a low and cunning beast. Nor is his intellect of a high character; it is keen and subtle, partly of the fox, partly of the snake, but there is nothing great about it. It enables him to disguise his real nature, to wear the mask of the honest man, of the bluff, open-speaking soldier; but that kind of cleverness is not uncommon, and needs no special intelligence.

Views of him, such as I have mentioned, arise partly from seeing Iago against the background of the white innocence of Desdemona, and the noble simplicity of Othello. When Iago is near Desdemona he looks blacker than hell. If Othello had not been so simple, so stupid, so devoid of any intuitive sense that he trusts Iago and distrusts his wife, Iago would not have seemed so intelligent. But he is always in contrast with good people, or with fools like Roderigo.

He does not deceive Roderigo. He is his own gross wicked self with him; but then he holds Roderigo in the hollow of his hand, because of his dishonest love of Desdemona. He stimulates that love, and the more he stimulates it the more does Roderigo become his gull, his slave; and the more frankly does Iago revel in his natural wickedness, and boast of it with pleasure. It is quite an agreeable exercise to speak of himself as he is, without his mask, to a comrade, and at the same time to rob and make a tool of this comrade. This additional betrayal is nuts to Iago. There is no special cleverness in his treatment of Roderigo. A fox can easily outwit a rabbit. Had Iago met ordinarily intelligent folk, he would have been found out in a day; and once or twice Shakespeare suggests that view of him. His plot against Othello and Desdemona is founded on their noble nature, and is skilfully worked out, but it is a plot of low cunning, not of fine intelligence. Othello had no defence against it, because he was entirely incapable of conceiving or understanding anything so ignoble. Fortune supplied Iago with trustful folk to work on—on Desdemona, ignorant of evil, and Othello, dull of intelligence while noble of character.

Again, Iago's plot was not so intelligently constructed but that the slightest chance would have undone the whole tangle of it, and it is undone at the end by his not having been sufficiently clever to guard against Emilia's knowledge of his possession of the handkerchief. He ought to have stolen it unknown to her. On the whole, the notion that Shakespeare meant Iago to be an imperial force of evil, a monarch of the pit, an embodiment of masterly intelligence subtle and powerful to destroy, or an artist in evil, is not in the play. Not intellectual power then, but the power of base cunning in a greedy nature, was of the essence of the man.

But the very centre of Iago is that self-love which is the excluder of all other love, and therefore absolute evil. Himself alone is Iago's universe. 'I never found man' (till he found himself) 'that knew how to love himself.'

Of course, then, since the absence of love is the absence of all goodness, everything he does and thinks is evil; and when he sees innocence or goodness, he hates them, blackens them, and desires to injure them. 'Virtue! a fig!' he cries. 'Love is merely a lust of the blood and a permission of the will.' To him self-sacrifice is sin, all true love and goodness unbelievable. He is sure that Cassio is false to Othello, and that Desdemona and Othello will soon seek for fresh blood when they are satiated with one another. The only other character in Shakespeare who cannot love, but is for himself alone, is Richard III., and he is less evil than Iago, for his conscience awakens when he is asleep. No touch of conscience ever disturbs Iago. Where there is no love there is no conscience.

Combined with this is sensuality; not sensuality united to love, or somewhat spiritualised by imagination, but the common appetite of the brute intensified by the memory, the intelligence, and the experience of the man. Only one thing in Iago is stronger than sensuality. It is his will to live for his own success, for his greed, for the satisfaction of his envy and his hate. For the sake of quenching these thirsts, sensual appetite is mastered; and he enlarges on this to Roderigo. But it is vital in Iago, as vital as men say it is in the goat and the monkey, as this vile brute tells Othello it is in Desdemona. To her, to Cassio, to Othello, to his wife, to all the dames of Venice, he imputes this appetite as their conqueror. What they call love is bodily lust, and that only. He has used women, but never loved them. His conversation, his soliloquies, are full of hateful phrases, images, innuendoes, gross and abominable. He is a dirty dog, and his vile ability leaves him still indescribably vulgar. How two noble creatures like Othello and Desdemona did not feel a natural repulsion from him I cannot understand. But there is no trace of even an unconscious antagonism to him. Their high and noble soul cannot imagine Iago. They hold him to be 'honest Iago' till the very end. This is another, however, of the strange improbabilities of the play.

Again, the sister of sensuality is cruelty. The lust of the one induces the lust of the other. The exercise of cruelty produces the same thrill of the nerves and senses as the exercise of the other. Iago may not have been cruel in the past, but when he begins to carry out his plot and feels that he has his victims helpless in his hands, cruelty born of his sensual nature awakes in him, and when he has once begun to be cruel, he has an increasing pleasure in it. He loves it for its own sake. He is not satisfied with making Othello jealous; he turns his weapon in every wound he makes, he puts irritant poison on the blade. His words are chosen to torture, and to vary the torture. His appetite for cruelty grows by what it feeds on. I do not think when he began to make Othello jealous that he desired to bring him to the murder of Desdemona, but his cruelty, becoming more luscious by habit, grows into that, and he urges his victim into that ultimate misery. Once he has tasted blood, he thirsts for more and more of it insatiably. He is always the brute, at the root of him: the hyena, with the brains of a loveless man.

This is Iago in himself. Outwardly, he is incarnate envy. Such a nature when thrown into the movement of men is certain to be envious of all who are more fortunate or better than himself. Envy is raised to its highest power in Iago. In other men it is modified by some forms of love, but Iago is incapable of loving, and because of that his envy has no check, no bounds. It makes him feel himself the enemy of all his world, and he knows the danger of this position. Therefore he puts on the mask of one who is the very opposite of that which he knows he is—the honest, bluff soldier who is the friend of all. His keen cunning enables him to succeed in this, and he plumes himself on his knavery and its inventiveness. He utterly despises all the crowd he has to do with, fools whom he can play with as he pleases—Othello, Cassio, Roderigo. 'Who are they,' he says, 'to stand in my way? I'll drag them down till my envy is satisfied. I can outplot them, I'll wring out of them all my greed desires.' His envy has been general, but when the play begins it has become particular. An incident has given it a particular direction, and awakes it into fury against a set of persons who have injured his self-love. Othello has passed him over in favour of Cassio, and instantly his natural envy leaps into tenfold energy. When an evil passion sees its prey, it concentrates itself into deadly action. 'I have 't,' cries Iago,

> It is engender'd. Hell and night
> Must bring this monstrous birth to the world's light.

Then, next in order, hatred is born of envy, and hatred calls to her side all the keen cunning of Iago's brain to weave pain and shame, torture and death for those he hates. Envy, greed, and hatred, lashed together like hounds, Iago lets loose upon Cassio and Othello, and on Desdemona.

This is born in his brain before the play opens. It

gives its fury to the shouts with which he betrays Othello to Brabantio. It fills all his reasoning with Roderigo. 'I *hate* the Moor,' he cries. It is developed into the full means of his treacherous plot in his soliloquy. And his hatred never relaxes till his end is reached. He reaches that end, but he overreaches himself. He holds all those he hates in supreme contempt. In that contempt he breaks down. There is no one whom he despises more than Emilia, and Emilia causes the discovery of his villainy. In his rage he slays her, and passes unrepentant to his death. There are plenty of Iagos in the world, but there are not many, fortunately, who combine with a foul and loveless nature a base but keen intellect. It is a deadly combination, and when it is driven by the love of power, by greed, by envy, and by hate, Iago is discovered.

Othello, when the play begins, is a great partisan, one of those leaders of soldiery whom cities like Venice or Florence employed in their service, faithful, even to death, to the state that employs him, and of so high and magnanimous a nature that Iago hates him as naturally as Cassio and Desdemona love him. There were noble Moors of this type, as the history of Spain proves—men of romantic honour and dignity. Calm in battle and riot, aware of his power-to master them, he is self-confident from long management of men and wars. At the same time he is curiously simple, even childlike, as his speech to the Senate displays him, when he opens his heart to the wondering senators. A stately, noble, self-contained, quiet figure! It is of the very essence of the tragedy that, when a few days have passed, this dignified image of the man is miserably reversed. Othello has lost all dignity, all quietude, all self-command, all power to see clearly, all simplicity; and the happy child in him is replaced by dark suspicion of his innocent wife passing swiftly into her brutal murder. The contrast is terrible and heartrending to the audience, who, listening, know the truth.

What has happened? On this grave, mature man, in full middle age, who has probably never known an innocent or well-bred woman in his incessant warring, falls the dreadful misfortune of a young girl's love, and of one who is of a different race and colour, so that her love seems to him from the beginning a little strange, as it does, he knows, to every one else. He has never quite understood why she loved him. He feels in contact with her his colour and his race, and his soul is forced to feel this by the accusation of Brabantio that he must have practised by drugs on Desdemona, otherwise she could not have loved him. Strange reasonings would beset him from time to time, and he is prepared to receive the insinuations of Iago. This explains and partly excuses the quickness with which he receives them. Moreover, he is all of a tremble, every string of his heart is over-tense with the advent of love. Love, when it comes, charged with all its witcheries, on a sensitive and imaginative man who has long past his youth, upturns the whole nature of such a man, throws every element in his character into new positions, new relations to life, is like a despotism in a soul which has been free. If his path of life be smooth, such a disturbance settles down into a peaceful rearrangement. But if any bitter circumstance then touch the agitated soul, if any doubt of the truth or love of the woman arise, if jealousy, above all, enter its house, the man will suffer torture; the waters of the great deep within will overflow, and every wave will be fire of sulphur; his intelligence will tremble on its throne; his moral nature will lose its power to command or act; his insight will be blinded; every suspicion will agonise him

into a passion for certainty; his sense of honour will
dissolve into baseness; his courtesy, all social conventions
of gentleness and good breeding, will be flung to the
winds; his love will not perish, but it will add so much
bitterness to his hatred that it will seem to be an incredible hatred; the whole world will be black as night, and
against that blackness he will see Cassio and Desdemona
in the red light of murder, while every nerve in his body
will tremble with a maddening intensity. He will fly into
furies of act and speech; strike Desdemona before the
nobles of Venice, call her devil, curse her.

> Damn her, lewd minx, O, damn her.

He will fall into trances of miserable thought; the ancient
brute in man will spring into life, and issue in foulness of
thought, hunger for revenge and murder. It is a hopeless
degradation. Jealousy is a hell, and its victims writhe
and curse in its waves of flame. This was Othello's fate,
as it has been the fate of a thousand thousand other
men and women. It is a piteous sight, and if we had not
followed Iago's infernal work on him, it would awaken some
contempt in the pity. For Othello has lost his intelligence. He is stupid with pain. The slightest inquiry,
the exercise of common judgment, the smallest thought,
would have, in a moment, undone Iago's net. We are so
angry with his stupidity, that when Emilia calls him at
the end—

> O gull, O dolt! As ignorant as dirt.   O thou dull Moor!

we are grateful for the truth in spite of all our pity.
There are those who suggest—to save the noble nature
of the man—that he was not the victim of what they
call vulgar jealousy. But he *was* in Shakespeare's mind,
and Iago's stories and hints would have made a saint who
believed them jealous. Othello is lashed into the extremity
of jealousy. For it is not only rage that Desdemona's

love and thought should be given to ·   ʰ·· fury
that her body should be his; and this stings and maddens
him more than the other. Again, again, again Shakespeare marks that into clearness, and Iago whips that
element in jealousy into fierceness. But both forms of
jealousy are in Othello, and when both mix together
jealousy reaches its extremity. The man is not mad, but
he is running at full speed, with disordered hair and torn
clothes and flaming eyes, on the waving line which divides
sanity from insanity. It is a border-land where every
breath is torment, and Othello was wild and whirling in it.

The root of jealousy is selfishness—self-love which
believes itself to be love; which claims all for itself alone.
'All that I love is mine and only mine. Her body and
soul are mine. Her kisses are mine, her thoughts are
mine. No one shall share the one or engage the other.
I claim all, and if she give her love away to another, I'll
defend my own tooth and nail and make her suffer the
pain I suffer. "I'll tear her all to pieces," cries Othello.
"I'll chop her into messes!" I'll strike her dead. Then
if we ask why, the jealous wretch answers: "Because I
love. It is love which drives me on."'

It is not love, but self-love. Nay, it is the reversal of
love. With that reversal of the essence of all goodness,
all other goodness is reversed, for the time, in Othello.
His faith changes into suspicion and distrust, his love into
hatred. His intelligence becomes stupidity, his stately
quiet the blind fury which strikes his wife; his free and
noble nature the slave of an ignoble passion, his gentle
courtesy savage cruelty, his dignity indecent coarseness,
his balanced judgment blind revenge. All is reversal.
What he was is lost, is no more. Iago knows it—[1]

---

[1] A few phrases, such as this, of imaginative quality, or of apparent
pity, are given to Iago by Shakespeare. They are out of Iago's character,
but they are eminently effective on the stage, and Shakespeare wanted
that.

> Not poppy, nor mandragora,
> Nor all the drowsy syrups of the world,
> Shall ever medicine thee to that sweet sleep
> Which thou owedst yesterday.

Othello feels he is no more Othello, and the vast misery of that breaks into that piteous farewell to all that he has been—I wish it were less rhetorical:

> O, now for ever
> Farewell the tranquil mind ! farewell content !
> Farewell the plumed troop and the big wars
> That make ambition virtue !   O, farewell.
> Farewell the neighing steed and the shrill trump,
> The spirit-stirring drum, the ear-piercing fife,
> The royal banner and all quality,
> Pride, pomp and circumstance of glorious war !
> Farewell !   Othello's occupation 's gone.

The great soldier is no more.

And now, yet more unhappy, the great lover is no more.   Othello bids farewell to love.   Welcome, in place of love, revenge and hate; and the dreadful passion in his unhappy soul lifts his words into verse which sounds like the rolling sea.   Iago thinks he may change his bloody purpose :

> Never, Iago.   Like to the Pontic sea,
> Whose icy current and compulsive course
> Ne'er feels retiring ebb, but keeps due on
> To the Propontic and the Hellespont ;
> Even so my bloody thoughts, with violent pace,
> Shall ne'er look back, ne'er ebb to humble love
> Till that a capable and wide revenge
> Swallow them up.

The happy lover is dead.

Yet, now and then, even in the furious fire, he remembers how he loved, and love rushes into him, and, with love, an infinite pity for himself.   This is a common characteristic of jealousy at its height, and Shakespeare does not forget it.   Othello recalls how he had lain beside her.

> I found not Cassio's kisses on her lips,

N

he cries in an utter misery of love. And then again, in
the very midst of his rage,

O, the world hath not a sweeter creature: she might lie by an
emperor's side and command him tasks.
Iago. Nay, that's not your way.
Oth. Hang her! I do but say what she is: so delicate with her
needle: an admirable musician: O, she will sing the savageness out
of a bear: of so high and plenteous wit and invention —
Iago. She's the worst for all this.
Oth. O, a thousand, thousand times: and then, of so gentle a
condition!
Iago. Ay, too gentle.
Oth. Nay, that's certain: but yet the pity of it, Iago! O
Iago, the pity of it, Iago!

It is pity for her; pity full of recollected love. But for
us who listen, it is pity for the situation, pity for both, but
our greater pity is for Othello. Then, finally, in that last
scene before he slays Desdemona, there is an unspeakable tenderness below every word of Othello's soliloquy.
He is no longer furious; he is deadly quiet; and he is
quiet because, after long tossing to and fro in doubt, he is
resolved to kill. In that fixed resolve jealousy is for the
moment half-asleep, and he lets his memory slip back
into praise of her perfection and into pity for her fate.
These two interchange their passions from verse to verse,
but in both his heart is overflowing with love.

It is in this strangely mingled temper that he attempts
to prove that his killing of her is a sacrifice, a judicial act,
the execution of a weak and wicked woman, who must die
lest she should betray more men; and there are critics
who take this view in order to save the noble nature of
the man, even when he blindly murders Desdemona in
order to prove that he was not the victim of what they
call vulgar jealousy. He had been noble, but for the last
two Acts he had been ignoble, with fleeting moments of
nobility. And here, in this majestical soliloquy, there are,
like bursts of sunshine in a black sky, passages of the

ancient nobleness in Othello. But it does not last. Underneath the real cause why he blots his wife out of the
world, his unintelligent, coarse, revengeful, cruel jealousy
lies like a tigress, and leaps at a touch into brutal fury.
The notion of a grave justice to be done on her is evapor-
ated in the heat of his personal rage. He has mentioned
Cassio in his accusation. Desdemona replies so that it
seems she is sorry for Cassio. This maddens the jealous
man.

OTH. Out, strumpet! weep'st thou for him to my face.
DES. O, banish me, my lord, but kill me not!
OTH. Down, strumpet!
DES. Kill me·to-morrow ; let me live to-night !
OTH. Nay, if you strive,—
DES. But half an hour !
OTH.   Being done, there is no pause.
DES. But while I say one prayer !
OTH.   It is too late. [*He stifles her.*

There's no sacrifice offered up to honour in that, no
judicial calm. It is jealousy that slays, jealousy which
has conquered the infinite sorrow, love, and pity which has
filled his soul before the deed, and made us half believe
that jealousy was dead. We know the rest, when, the madness over, he is himself again, again the noble creature he
was of old. He judges himself, and his sword dissolves
the inexplicable chance in which the blundering universe
has entangled him.

> I kiss'd thee ere I killed thee—no way but this ;
> Killing myself, to die upon a kiss.

Deep pity is left with us for the ill-fortuned whose
suffering was unreasonable, whose death was a mistake.
Our pity is so great, it rises into love. And the more we
pity and love, the more deeply do we realise how dark,
grim, and inexplicable seemed now to Shakespeare the
cruel irony of life. He does not complain of it himself,
but he writes down with unrelenting realism one example

of things as they are, if haply he may purge his spirit of the black choler which possesses it. It is no use to say that he writes only as an artist, with a cool temper. He writes in a passion of pity for men, in a passion of resentment for their pain. His soul was dark with tempest, and the tempest deepens in *King Lear*.

VII

KING LEAR

THERE is a faint, a pathetic touch of association between *Twelfth Night* and *King Lear*. The Fool, in the midst of the storm, sings a verse of the same song with which the Clown c'oses that comedy—and the verse fits the pitiless night, and the madness and sorrow of Lear.

> He that has, and a little tiny wit,—
>   With hey, ho, the wind and the rain,—
> Must make content with his fortunes fit ;
>   Though the rain it raineth every day.

I wonder if Shakespeare, when he wrote that into *King Lear*, thought of the last time he had used the song, and of the temper half-jovial, half-romantic, in the atmosphere of which he wrote *Twelfth Night*. We, when we read it, cannot help thinking of the contrast between the spirit of the two plays. Yet there are only about four years between them. *King Lear* was composed in 1605 or 1606, and is known to have been acted before King James at Whitehall on December 26, 1606. *Twelfth Night* was acted in 1601-2.

What Shakespeare passed through, within his soul, in those four or five years we cannot tell. It led him through *Hamlet, Troilus and Cressida, Othello, Measure for Measure* and *Macbeth*. It brought him now to *King Lear* and *Timon of Athens*. It was a terrible journey, and the goal at which he arrived was even more terrible than the journey. There is no drama in the whole range of modern literature, perhaps of ancient, which can equal

King Lear in the tragic imagination which has there clothed with chaotic darkness and godless sorrow not only Lear and all the characters that make his mighty pains, but also the whole of humanity, even the gods themselves. The eternal Justice which, we trust, lives beyond and above our sorrow and our crime; which the Greek Drama permits us to feel as holding in its hands a far-off hope—is not to be found in *King Lear.* Its outlook over the world that was, and is, and shall be, is of blackness and darkness for ever. The gods have not only forgotten man; the gods seem dead. The stars alone—the destroying planets who hate the human race—rule the world.— And the loveliness of Cordelia's love, and the loyal truth of Kent, and the tenderness of the Fool, and the pity of Lear's madness, while they redeem human nature from the horror of Regan and Edmund, Goneril and Cornwall, only deepen the dreadful aspect of the world, for they suffer for their goodness more than these vulture-men and women for their crimes. The world of *King Lear* is a world from which all the conceptions which create a just God are expunged. In it also Nature herself is as blind, as pain-stricken, as helpless, as left to herself as Lear; and if she is not blind, she is as wicked, as pitiless as Goneril and Regan.

What brought Shakespeare to this dread? How came it to pass that, like Dante, he went down into Hell, and with, it seems, even more personal suffering than Dante? I do not know that we have any right to inquire (though we cannot help it), and certainly it is quite fair that we should not know. It is enough for us to know that, like Dante, having seen Hell, and set Cordelia shining like a star above its brown and fiery airs, he climbed out of it, and saw the stars again in *Cymbeline,* and *Winter's Tale,* and in the *Tempest.*

Whatever it was, it took him down, in imagination, not

only into the infinite tenderness of Cordelia, but into the
primeval brutalities of uncivilised man, into the unre-
strained lust, cruelty, and greed of savage humanity; even
into their unnatural violation of natural piety. Moreover,
during these years he went down into the slums of human
nature. And there, in his realism, he found Thersites,
and Pandarus, and the vile things he made men in
Measure for Measure. And these, Thersites and the rest,
belonged to a decaying, but a civilised society. The vices
in *Troilus and Cressida*, in *Measure for Measure*, and in
Timon of Athens are the vices of a decadence.

In *King Lear* the social scenery is quite different.
The evils are those which characterise the beginnings of
a society when men are emerging from savagery and
retain much of its brutality. Gloucester's light talk
before his bastard son of his lust with his mother is a
slight instance of this. The tearing out of Gloucester's
eyes by Cornwall and Regan (the woman urging on the
hateful deed) is a piece of primeval cruelty. The hanging
of Cordelia belongs to a brutal society. So does the lust
for Edmund of both the sisters in its bold expression.
And the unnatural absence in Goneril and Regan of any
shred of filial piety towards their father, combined with
cruelty to him, and plotted against him by both from the
beginning, is such guilt as could not be openly practised
in a society which had been civilised. But here it is
open, boasted of, rejoiced in by its doers, claimed to be
statesmanlike. This is pure savagery developing itself
with frank selfishness in the atmosphere of irresponsible
power. We are at the beginning, not at the end of a
nation, midst of antique barbarities. Whether Shakespeare deliberately put in this local colour (knowing that
his story belonged to early Britain), we cannot tell, but
we are certainly placed in the midst of a primeval society,
where gigantic figures and gigantic pains pass across the

stage, and speak a gigantic language; where all that is said and done arises out of the first unmodified elements of human nature. And this last is as true—on the other side—of Cordelia's love and Kent's loyalty as it is of Regan's hardheartedness and Cornwall's treachery. The good in the play is also of early human nature.

The tragedies of Æschylus do not place us in quite so savage, so unmoral a world as we are in *King Lear*. Their world is more civilised. The murder of Agamemnon is accounted for. It is by no means unnatural, as the conduct of Goneril and Regan. A Greek audience would not have borne to look on this drama.

It may be said that the central horror which drives the Œdipus of Sophocles into a desolate world is as ghastly as the cruelty which drives Lear into a ruined world, but Œdipus takes with him his daughters' love; and in the end the just gods give him peace. There is no such close to Lear. We are left in darkness that may be felt. Cordelia suffers for her goodness as Goneril and Regan for their guilt.

There is reason for Orestes' slaying of his mother, and a rude Justice demanded her death, yet the sinner against natural piety is driven to madness by the Furies, till, after terrible days, he is solemnly judged and purified. But no Furies, not even the inward snake of Remorse, pursue the unnatural impiety of Goneril and Regan. They die of their own lust. And no God lives in *King Lear*; no divine Justice interposes to save Cordelia. There are many who think Shakespeare might have saved her. But he was not in the temper to do that justice. As the world is, the best for her, he thought, is that she should leave it.

Or if at times the gods are spoken of, they are gods who make their sport out of the tragedies of man. Not even the abstraction *Nature* avenges on Goneril and

Regan their violation of her earliest law. Lear appeals
to her in vain; and himself violates her call upon him.
In the unchecked ill-temper of absolute power, he is
unnatural to his well-loved daughter, and flings her in a
moment out of his heart. And when he finds himself
flung away in turn by the daughters to whom he has
given all—his language, in its intellectual splendour and
passion, is the language of one who has gone beyond
Nature in his anger. He is not mad when he pours his
curse of ardent sulphur on the head and womb of Goneril.
The soul of an audience shudders (almost as much as
when Goneril and Regan drive the King forth into the
storm) when Lear, in unforgettable grandeur of savage
imagination, calls on Nature herself to blast his daughter.

> Hear, nature, hear ! dear goddess, hear.

Furious passions, wild lands, untilled society, savage
beginnings of the world !

Edmund belongs to that world by the cool cruelty
with which he orders Cordelia to be hanged, but his vices
are rather the vices of a civilised society. Greedy of
power and wealth, no motion of conscience troubles him
till he has received his. death wound. Then his repentance is modern. His speeches then seem out of harmony
with the general note of the play. Even at the beginning,
he is not of the ancient world. His soliloquy about his
bastardy, and his claim to be the lusty child of Nature;
his scorn of custom, convention, and law, because he is
himself an illegality; his call on the gods to stand up for
bastards, are far removed from the earlier world. They
breathe of the reckless life of that Italy which Shakespeare knew from the stories of the novellisti. His
deliberate and soulless treachery is also apart from the
rough vices and antique honour of a half-savage society.
Treachery is a vice of civilisation; and the cunning and

conscienceless traitor who sacrifices father and brother for his lust of power, who carefully weighs whether Goneril's or Regan's love will be most to his advantage, without any love for either of them, is entirely in tune with the Italy of the Borgias. He is also intellectual enough; and sees his own blackness, and the self-cheating of the men of the world, with the clearness and coolness of Machiavel himself. That self-excusing hypocrisy of society which Lear in his madness sees, and slashes as with a sword, Edmund also sees and mocks at, not only in others, but in himself. But Lear hates hypocrisy and treachery; Edmund loves to wear them, and use them for his self-advancement.

To this antique world belongs also the rough-speaking loyalty and faithfulness of Kent. But his rugged manners are born of his love for Cordelia, and of the incredible folly of Lear not only in banishing her but in giving away his power—

> Be Kent unmannerly,
> When Lear is mad. What wouldst thou do, old man?
> Think'st thou that duty shall have dread to speak,
> When power to flattery bows? To plainness honour's bound,
> When majesty stoops to folly.

Kent is the plain, faithful man, who has never minced his words nor filed his mind; and it is characteristic of Shakespeare's insight that when Kent is in disguise he exaggerates his plainness of speech. His disguise sets him loose from the restraint his high position imposed on him, and he pleases himself by his freedoms of speech and act. His attack on Oswald, whom he abhors for his flattery and knavery, is ferocious, but it delights him to make it. No servant, such as he seems to be, would have dared it, but the Earldom of Kent is at the back of his boldness. With all this bluntness, he is as tender as he is faithful. He never leaves the King who has banished him; tends him like a nurse through storm and madness; and Cordelia is always in his heart. When Edgar meets him near the end of the play, his love of Lear and Gloucester, his surcharged pity, break down his sturdy strength. His grief grew puissant and the strings of life began to crack. At root, he is half Cordelia. He says but little as the Earl of Kent in the play, but all the political conduct of its affairs is in his hands—one of those steadfast men, with the gift of fidelity to persons and to long-established ideals, and with the gift of silent common sense, who, when affairs are stormy, holds the helm quietly, directs the ship, and brings it safely to land. Shakespeare was sure to make a little study of such a man. It is true that Kent is, when he is acting as a servant, opulent of abusive words, and talks like a torrent. But that is because he is in disguise.

When, for any reason, we get into such a disguise that no one knows us, or can compare us with the character we have built up before society—then our loosely-held thoughts, our individual imaginations, the convention-shocking things we have concealed, the queer tempers we have hushed to rest, tumble out in our words and ways, because we are no longer shy or afraid of society. We are delighted to have the chance of free expression, of being quite true to ourselves. This is true of Kent in the scene in the courtyard when he trounces Oswald.

It is still more true of Edgar when he disguises himself as a madman. Edgar is at first the pink of propriety— as admirable in morals as in manners. He would not be out of place in a London drawing-room. His existence, alongside with Goneril and Regan and Lear, is an ana-chronism. Yet, what lay in him unexpressed? All that we listen to from the lips of Poor Tom! In his disguise he lets loose the original thoughts, the unconventional things which his soul had mused on and concealed. We get the Edgar which lived underneath the Edgar of

society. He plays the madman so well that he seems
to like it; and probably he did. He was free. In the
midst of his mad inventions, sayings appear pregnant
with meaning, vivid with a naked liberty. His account
of himself as a worthless, dissipated fellow is at every
point different from what he was in life. He sketches,
that is, what one of the natures in him might have made
him. He sketches another Edgar who might have ended
in beggary and been haunted by the fiends. He hits too
much truth when he says—'The Prince of darkness is a
gentleman.' Lear, who himself is then half-way to madness—a situation in which a man is keenly intelligent—
feels that Edgar's talk has strange reason at its back.
He cries,

> Noble philosopher, your company.
>
> . . . . .
>
> I will keep still with my philosopher.

When Edgar puts off his madness, having gone through
misery, starvation, and cold, he is more just in feeling,
higher in intellectual insight, than he was in his luxurious days. He knows what man is worth, and what is
best. We hear to what conclusion he has come, when we
meet him on the wild heath in his rags, alone.

> Yet better thus, and known to be contemn'd,
> Than still contemn'd and flatter'd. To be worst,
> The lowest and most dejected thing of fortune,
> Stands still in esperance, lives not in fear :
> The lamentable change is from the best ;
> The worst returns to laughter. Welcome then,
> Thou unsubstantial air that I embrace !
> The wretch, that thou hast blown unto the worst
> Owes nothing to thy blasts. But who comes here ?
>
> *Enter* GLOUCESTER.
>
> My father, poorly led ? World, world, O world !
> But that thy strange mutations make us hate thee,
> Life would not yield to age.

And at the close, his conduct is worthy of a noble gentleman who, while defending truth and loyalty, is tolerant

to his false and treacherous brother when he is dying and a little repentant.

I scarcely need to speak of Albany: he is almost a cipher in the play, but he comes to the throne at last. Nor is he so weak as he appears to be when seen side by side with the fierce violence of Goneril. ₁She seems to blot him out. When he is freed from her he is quite strong enough for affairs. He does shrink from the scenes Goneril makes him, and no wonder; and he seems a feeble person; but when all the violent men and women are destroyed by their own violence, the quiet man comes out at the top. He has made no enemies, and he has staying power. Moreover, it is worth saying that his shrinking from violent action serves to produce the one speech which renders, for a moment, Goneril endurable.

I pass on to Lear, and before the terror and sorrow of his tragedy one feels incompetent to speak. The genius who created it soars beyond our ken. When we meet him first, he is that wretched thing—an old man who, because he has, without one check, ruled for many years his kingdom and his household, thinks that his will is absolute wisdom. The serene vanity of this is only equalled by the folly into which his vanity leads him. He is blind to his own folly; blind to the fact that his two daughters hate him; blind when, with the embroidered eloquence of hatred, they tell him that they love him; blind to the character of Cordelia, though she has truly loved him; blind to the worth of Kent; blind to the political results which (even if his daughters loved him) would inevitably follow on the partition of the kingdom; and equally blind to the personal results which were sure to follow on an irresponsible person like himself, with a train of a hundred knights and with a violent temper, wandering about from one petty court to another.

Inevitable then would be the irritation, the quarrels, and finally the fury of the situation.   There are critics of the medical profession who say that Lear was already mad when he did this; and base their explanation of his character on this supposed fact.   But Lear was no more mad now than thousands of persons, perfectly sane in society, are, when, by long dwelling on themselves, they have become compact of vanity.

Lear is a sane and healthy giant of a man when first we meet him.   It is only after fearful and redoubled shocks which subvert everything he has believed, and after a protracted struggle against their maddening assault, that he finally loses his will-power over his brain.   And, even then, it is complete madness only for a time.   He slips in and out of madness.   Edgar, listening to his wild talk near Dover, cries

> O, matter and impertinency mix'd !
> Reason in madness !

Then he recovers sanity with Cordelia, but is shocked back again into merciful insanity by Cordelia's death. Violent temper, sure to be nursed into greater violence by unchecked power, may be called madness, and lead to madness, but it is not madness.   It does lead Lear to madness when it is lashed to overstrain by his effort to restrain it.   Its long indulgence in the past is shown by the ease with which he slips into immediate furies of wrath.[1]   He curses Goneril without a pause, without a question.   Even before these outbursts, we remember the petulant impetuosity with which in a moment he flings Cordelia out of his heart.

---

[1] Compare what the tribunes say of Coriolanus :

> Put him to choler, straight.   He hath been us'd
> Ever to conquer, and to have his worth
> Of contradiction : being once chaf'd, he cannot
> Be rein'd again to temperance : then he speaks
> What's in his heart ; and that is there which looks
> With us to break his neck.

Nevertheless, even in this first scene, we forgive him much because at the root of his follies he desires so strongly to be loved. For that, and moved by pity for the weakness of his violence, we do forgive him, but feel that indeed he needs forgiveness. Our forgiveness is in our pity, and our pity is touched with a just contempt. Afterwards we pity him altogether, because his trust in love is betrayed where he most believed, and his desire for love is crucified by those from whom he desired it. There is no pity in Goneril and Regan. Their short sharp consultation at the end of the first scene tells us that their cruelty has been long determined on. Their observation of their father's character has 'not been little'; and now they have got power, they will make him understand how 'slenderly he has known himself.' 'We must do something,' says Goneril, 'and i' the heat.'

Men put down the shameful conduct of Goneril and Regan to natural, inherent malignity. They are bad in grain, as Cordelia is good in grain; but their steadfast hatred of their father is not without some cause; and Shakespeare leads us to infer this. He rarely leaves what seems against nature without suggesting some reason for it. Just imagine what those two haughty, high-tempered, hard-hearted, icy-minded, very intelligent women, who were now about forty years of age, had suffered from their overbearing, hot-tempered father. They had inherited their father's temperament, but had been forced to keep it down for all these years, and to suffer in the repression. It is not difficult to conceive what a huge heap of silently borne insults, abuse, violent discourtesies, was piled up with in their memories; how long they had nursed their wrath; how the hypocrisy with which they had borne their slavery irritated that wrath daily, and how long their souls desired revenge. There is some reason—I had almost said excuse—for their conduct. It was the result not only of their wicked, merciless nature—it was also caused by the long oppression which claimed to be just and loving when it was only selfish—and it grew into a steady hatred of their father.

It is hate that speaks in their icy words, long-cherished hate, infinite boredom, years of silent, smouldering irritation. Fathers who believe that their children are bound by natural law—even after they are grown up—to endure anything from them and their tempers; who think, because of their fatherhood, that they may treat their children as they dare not treat their acquaintances; who claim every submission from them as a right, and are furious or sulky if the claim is not allowed, are terrible plagues; as dangerous to the small society in which they live as ferocious tyrants are to a nation. They often make such hatred in their children as Lear made in Goneril and Regan. Such hatred is common enough, but the cases are few where the children, like Goneril and Regan, get the power to work their retaliation. When then we think of what they did, of their relentless driving of the old man into the black storm, into despair and madness—when the cold devilry of their savage carelessness appals the sense—let us remember that it was not without a cause.

Even Cordelia must have suffered from her father. But Cordelia was born good, and suffering only educated her goodness into greater goodness. Yet when Lear is so unworthy as to measure his gifts by the love outwardly professed to him before witnesses; when she sees that he is blind to the inner wickedness of Goneril and Regan, and to her own devotion, she is almost tried too much. She is a little short with her father. She lets her scorn of the whole affair appear in her silence. 'What have you to say, my daughter?' 'Nothing, my Lord.' Her long-tried love is indeed not lessened. But it cannot stand the hypocrisy of the whole scene. Nor is she gentle to her sisters, whose savage heart she knows; nor does she hesitate to let her scorn fall on Burgundy who will not have her as wife when she has no dowry. She is not quite the unimpassioned angel so many represent her to be—and let us be thankful for that. Her exquisite gentleness, her unspeakable tenderness and pity, her human love, would miss something of their perfection had she no anger against cruelty, no scorn of meanness and hypocrisy.

There is a drawing by Ford Madox Brown of Lear in this first scene. He is represented as a huge old man, half-sunk in his great chair, unable to move, a ruin of a man. I have seen Irving represent Lear, and all through this first scene he shook like a man who had suffered from palsy. Irving pictured a broken man. But Shakespeare did not mean Lear to resemble either of these impersonations. Lear was one of an early race of men, strong even in old age. All his life he had lived in the open. Age had not weakened his body any more than his mind. There is no physical feebleness suggested in this first scene; and when we meet him again he comes home from a hunting with his hundred knights, vigorous, and ready for feasting and drinking. 'Let me not stay,' he shouts, ' a jot for dinner; go, get it ready.' And this hunting and feasting has been going on for a fortnight. This was the Lear of Shakespeare, and that he made him a hale, strong old man deepens the tragedy of his breaking-up, accounts for the protracted struggle he makes against his sorrows, for the awful agony he undergoes in the struggle, and afterwards for the fury and strength, as of a wounded Titan, with which he outfaces and outdoes the rage. of the storm. It is no half-paralysed old man, but a giant smitten to the heart, who is finally broken down. This, I think, is what the actor should embody.

His agony begins at the house of Goneril. Lear has

struck one of her gentlemen for chiding of his fool. And her revenge is started. Put on, she cries to Oswald, what negligence you please—I will get rid of him.

> Idle old man !
> That still would manage those authorities
> That he hath given away.

To torture him is pleasant to her. The fool, who sees clearly Lear's folly because folly knows folly, presages that which Lear does not imagine. His gibes shake the confidence of the King, and when Goneril comes in he is prepared a little for her vicious use of the power he gave her—for her sharp lecture on him and his insolent retinue. Still, he is taken aback. 'Are you our daughter?' This is not Goneril—and am I Lear?—and the solid earth seems to dissolve into illusion with this change of his habitual life. Never before has he met with a check. No wonder his very personality seems to desert him. 'Is this Lear?' 'Who is it can tell me what I am?' 'Lear's shadow!' answers the bitter fool —and Lear uses the impression he has received to pretend, in scorn, that he does not know Goneril, meets her with impotent sarcasm—

> Your name, fair gentlewoman !

At this scorn Goneril's savage rage, ice cold, pours down upon his head. 'His retinue makes her court like a riotous inn. The life he leads is a shame for an old man, who should be reverend. Disquantity your train. Let them be fifty, not a hundred, and know yourself.'

At which the fierce temper of the King breaks out, and with it the agony which ingratitude awakes. There is no moderation in his words.

> Darkness and devils !
> Saddle my horses ; call my train together.
> Degenerate bastard ! . . .
> Woe, that too late repents.
>
> .   .   .   .   .   .
>
> Detested kite ! thou liest.

He thinks of Cordelia. Shakespeare, with one touch, marks how Lear has sorrowed in grim silence for his loss of her. When Lear hears that his fool has pined away after her departure, he cries

> No more of that : I have noted it well.

This inward sorrow for Cordelia adds itself to the first agony he suffers from Goneril, and both together beat him into fury. Then comes that appalling curse—primeval in its antique simplicity, terrible on a father's lips, coming home to that which is deepest in a woman—appealing to great Nature herself, one of whose first laws Goneril had injured.

> Hear, nature, hear ; dear goddess, hear !
> Suspend thy purpose, if thou didst intend
> To make this creature fruitful :
> Into her womb convey sterility :
> Dry up in her the organs of increase,
> And from her derogate body never spring
> A babe to honour her ! If she must teem,
> Create her child of spleen ; that it may live
> And be a thwart disnatured torment to her.
> Let it stamp wrinkles in her brow of youth ;
> With cadent tears fret channels in her cheeks ;
> Turn all her mother's pains and benefits
> To laughter and contempt ; that she may feel
> How sharper than a serpent's tooth it is
> To have a thankless child !—Away, away !

Higher and higher, passion rising over passion, climbs the storm within; his tears break forth. They terrify him and shame him, and his curses redouble.

> Blasts and fogs upon thee !
> Th' untented woundings of a father's curse
> Pierce every sense about thee !

And all the time Goneril stands by, cool, rigid, relentless, enjoying her father's pain, happy in the thought that Regan will carry out to the full that which she has begun, beating down the weak interference of Albany with politic reasons. 'He is dangerous; he will try to resume his

power. I know his heart,' she says, thinking of all she
has suffered in the past.

The agony of Lear has begun. We meet him next at
Gloucester's castle, where he has gone to throw himself
on the kindness of Regan. She is of even harder granite
than her sister. Yet Lear, though he has lived with her
for many years, knows nothing of her character. He
speaks of her 'tender-hefted nature,' of her comfortable
eyes. What sort of a father has this man been? He has
lived wholly in himself!

Regan is cruel for cruelty's pleasure; Goneril is cruel
more for policy than pleasure. Both are cruel from a
settled hate. When Cornwall says that Kent shall sit in
the stocks till noon, Regan cries, 'Till noon! till night, my
lord, and all night too.' When Gloucester is brought in
as a traitor, her cruelty is savage. She makes them bind
him 'hard, hard, the filthy traitor!' She plucks his beard
and tears out his hair. When Cornwall plucks out one of
Gloucester's eyes, her fury of cruelty calls for the other.

> One side will mock another; the other too.

She tells him, to double his physical pain, that his son
has betrayed him to them, and rejoices to add to his
physical pain the sorrows of the heart. Her last words
are incarnate cruelty—

> Go thrust him out of gates, and let him smell
> His way to Dover.

This is the creature to whom Lear flies for refuge from
Goneril. It is flying from the tigress' to the shark; and
Lear is driven out into the storm and the unsheltered
hill. It is Regan who says to Gloucester asking pity
for her father—

> O, sir, to wilful men
> The injuries that they themselves procure
> Must be their schoolmasters. Shut up your doors.
> CORN. Shut up your doors, my lord; 'tis a wild night;
> My Regan counsels well; come out o' the storm.

The frigid ruthlessness of this lifts our indignation into that excited temper to which the immensity of passion in the scene of Lear in the storm brings no surprise. By slow degrees, by many careful touches, step by step, we arrive to the central scene on the wild heath of outward storm and inward passion.

All through this scene between Regan and Lear, Lear is trying, fearful of his brains, to restrain himself, to keep his head. He excuses Cornwall for not coming to meet him. 'He may be ill; and then we are not ourselves; I will forbear.' Suddenly he looks at Kent in the stocks, and his passion breaks loose.

> Death on my state! wherefore
> Should he sit here?

And he swears he will beat the drum at Regan's doors till she come forth. Then he feels he is losing self-command.

> O me, my heart, my rising heart! But down!

When Cornwall and Regan appear, he is quiet and scornful, but when it dawns on him that Regan is perhaps one with Goneril, his fury cannot be repressed. He curses Goneril; calls, like Caliban, on the plagues of the morbid earth to infect her bones. Then he falls back again into piteous appeal to Regan, who, grim as death, bids him hear the trumpet that announces the arrival of Goneril. The sight of her maddens Lear; and he calls on the heavens, who themselves are old, to take his part—a splendid imagination, which links his sorrow to the sorrow of the universe.

I will not go through the rest. Lear changes, as before, from bursts of passion to quiet entreaty. Beaten to and fro from the weather of fury to the weather of self-control, and in the contest fearing to be mad—repelled at every point with icy severity, patient in vain—till at last he knows that all is useless and that his mind is

breaking. 'O fool! I shall go mad!' he cries, and rushes
out into the tempest.

He is not really mad all through this scene, nor is he
physically broken down. His strength of mind and body
is gigantic. He has made a desperate fight for self-
control. When we meet him again, on the moor and in
the storm, he is not yet mad, nor weak of body. He is
fighting, like Prometheus, against the gods, who like his
daughters are his foes. Nor is his intellect less strong
than his body. The tempest in his heart has heightened
for the moment all his powers; and the insight, extent,
and word-shaping of his intellect are greater than they
have ever been. He sees not only himself, but the fate
and sorrow and crime of the whole world. This passes,
like a vision, in full realism, before his mind. And he
concentrates the vision into speech. No madness as yet—
but the intellect at its highest range and the emotions at
their tensest strain. One touch—and they will slip over
the border into madness, into that region where the will
commands and forbids no more. That touch is given by
the entrance of Edgar who plays the madman. Lear,
surprised, lets loose his self-command—becomes a spirit-
brother of Edgar; and being no longer tortured by his
efforts to retain his self-control, slides into real madness,
and is at once gentle, kindly, and scarcely troubled. Only
now and then, little touches of sanity bring him back for
a moment to the torture he has mercifully forgotten.

No words can tell the imaginative greatness of the
scene on the black and lonely moor and in Lear's black
and lonely heart. To conceive it as it is conceived was
a splendid imagination. To shape it then, and fix it in
the evasive element of words; to grip the heart of every
moment of it, and to heighten and make it eternal in a
poetry equal in thought and passion, was yet more
splendid. Nor is a lower element neglected. It is

pictorial as few scenes are in literature. We see the landscape, the night, the lightnings and the rain, Lear among them with his white hair upon the wind, the fool, Kent, the hovel, Edgar—not by set description, but by the flying words which glance across the passions and thoughts of the men.

The tempestuous splendour is doubled and redoubled, flash on flash of lightning, crash on crash of thunder, amid the roaring wind. They are the fitting elements for Lear's passion which, louder and fiercer than the material storm, rains and thunders and lightnings, adding its intellectual tempest to the wind and rain. The fool's wild jesting gives a fresh wildness to the raging elements, and to Lear. When their wildness is at its height, Edgar's imitative madness awakes and deepens the growing madness of Lear, and is itself in tune with the demoniac darkness, the biting wind, and the wicked rain. And, at last, Gloucester slips in (when Lear is wholly mad), to add his own half-insane sorrow to the dreadful night.

At first, Lear is the master of the furious elements. Their rage is but the soulless reflection of his rage. He calls on them to blow and crack their cheeks, to drown the churches to the steeple-top, to rumble their bellyful. They can never reach the height of his passion. Then, with a swift turn of imagination, he sees the elements as the destroyers, and bids them, executors of all-annihilating Thought, singe his white head; nay more, blot out of existence' book the base and cruel universe, nay, its very seeds of life—all germinating Nature herself—which could give birth to universal ingratitude.

> You sulphurous and thought-executing fires,
> Vaunt-couriers to oak-cleaving thunder-bolts,
> Singe my white head! And thou, all-shaking thunder,
> Smite flat the thick rotundity o' the world!
> Crack nature's moulds, all germens spill at once
> That make ingrateful man!

No madness breathes there, but imagination, winged by
sorrow and wrath, soaring to heights beyond our knowledge. Then, with another nimble turn of impassioned
intellect, he cries that he does not tax the elements with
original unkindness to him—

> Nor rain, wind, thunder, fire, are my daughters.

They owe me nothing, as my daughters do; but yet Goneril
and Regan have made them slaves to beat him down—vile
things,

> That have with two pernicious daughters join'd
> Your high engender'd battles 'gainst a head
> So old and white as this. O, O, 'tis foul !

But he will still be patient, for again he dreads the
shattering of his brain. And out of this momentary
quiet (and his soul enlightened by all that he has
suffered), he thinks, perhaps for the first time in his life, of
the dreadful state of the world rather than of himself. But
his thought is coloured by the hypocrisy he has met
with. This too he links now with the elemental war. He
pierces deep into the hidden blackness of mankind—down
to its shameful roots—

> Let the great gods,
> That keep this dreadful pother o'er our heads,
> Find out their enemies now.   Tremble, thou wretch,
> That hast within thee undivulged crimes,
> Unwhipp'd of justice : hide thee, thou bloody hand ;
> Thou perjured, and thou simular man of virtue
> That art incestuous : caitiff, to pieces shake,
> That under covert and convenient seeming
> Hast practised on man's life :—close pent-up guilts,
> Rive your concealing continents, and cry
> These dreadful summoners grace.—I am a man
> More sinu'd against than sinning.

The passage is dark with the unlighted, hopeless vision
of life that sets this play apart. Then for the first time,
he feels that the fierce strain is more than the will can
bear. 'My wits,' he says, 'begin to turn.' But they have

not yet left him.   His argument with Kent is as clear as high intellect can make it.

> Thou think'st 'tis much that this contentious storm
> Invades us to the skin ; so 'tis to thee ;
> But where the greater malady is fix'd,
> The lesser is scarce felt.   Thou 'ldst shun a bear ;
> But if thy flight lay toward the roaring sea,
> Thou 'ldst meet the bear i' the mouth.   When the mind 's free,
> The body 's delicate : the tempest in my mind
> Doth from my senses take all feeling else,
> Save what beats there.   Filial ingratitude !
> Is it not as this mouth should tear this hand
> For lifting food to 't ?   But I will punish home.
> No, I will weep no more.   In such a night
> To shut me out !   Pour on ; I will endure.
> In such a night as this !   O Regan, Goneril !
> Your old kind father, whose frank heart gave all—
> O, that way madness lies ; let me shun that ;
> No more of that.

All this is clear intelligence, and what follows is born of a higher intelligence.   For, when he thinks of his own anger and pain, he is brought, as never before, to think of the pains of others — and out of a ruined King's mouth is heard the plainest judgment, since Langland, in English literature of the thoughtlessness of the great, and the misery of the poor—the first condemnation of the black villainy of the Social State—when Shakespeare, in his dark brooding over the guilt of man to man, and with a pitiful fury in his heart, puts these words into the mouth of Lear—

> Poor naked wretches, wheresoe'er you are,
> That bide the pelting of this pitiless storm,
> How shall your houseless heads, and unfed sides,
> Your loop'd and window'd raggedness, defend you
> From seasons such as these ?   O, I have ta'en
> Too little care of this !   Take physic, pomp ;
> Expose thyself to feel what wretches feel,
> That thou mayst shake the superflux to them,
> And show the heavens more just.

There is no madness there—but at this instant Edgar's cry is heard—

> Fathom and half, fathom and half!
> Poor Tom!

The imitative madness wakes the latent madness in Lear. His wits fly instantly. And it is curious how all his rage almost immediately departs, and only at short intervals revives. He ceases to think; ceases to argue. He is quieted by Edgar's companionship. He takes to him at once. He pities him because he has been ruined by his daughters. All his thoughts wander astray. He calls Edgar his learned Theban, his Athenian, his philosopher. Only once, his reason seems to return when he asks, looking at Edgar's nakedness—

> Is man no more than this? Consider him well. Thou owest the worm no silk, the beast no hide, the sheep no wool, the cat no perfume. . . . Thou art the thing itself! Unaccommodated man is no more but such a poor, bare, forked animal as thou art.

But this is only momentary, the last flare of expiring reason. Is this man? this only? Then I will be as he—

> Off, off, you lendings! Come, unbutton here!

and he tears off his clothes as madmen do. In all the rest, in the hovel, in the farmhouse, Lear is mad and wanders like a madman. His arraignment of Goneril before the Fool and Edgar is terrible. His arraignment of Regan is more terrible, and the vision of her escaping is an absolute madman's cry—

> And here's another, whose warp'd looks proclaim
> What store her heart is made on.—Stop her there!
> Arms, arms, sword, fire! Corruption in the place!
> False justicer, why hast thou let her 'scape?

With what care, with what finish, with what pains of thought this slow advance of madness is built up! No one can closely read it without laughing to scorn the view that Shakespeare was an artist who wrote without thought, who had no care for finish, who never blotted a line. Even if we did not know that he rewrote his *Hamlet*, and worked it for his own honour and posterity into twice the thing it was, these scenes in Lear would be enough to prove his intense persistency in finish.

At this point of the play we lose sight of the Fool; nor do we hear of him any more till Lear, in his last frenzy, mixes him up for a moment with Cordelia. The two creatures who loved him most, and who were from the beginning of his agony always linked together in his mind, become for an instant of madness one when he bears Cordelia's dead body in his arms, crying aloud—

> And my poor fool is hang'd.

When first we meet the fool, Lear has not seen him for two days, and he wonders why, for they have loved one another. At last he knows in his heart that his fool is angry with him for his exiling of Cordelia, and he feels with that wrath and sorrow. He has reproached himself as deeply as the fool reproaches him; and when he sends for his 'boy,' he knows what all his bitter sayings mean. They are the anger of love unjustly injured.' But 'Lear's love for Cordelia has now returned in full flood. The fool feels its deep regret and pain, and forgives his master, but cannot help being bitter. Lear understands; and their common love binds them together in the deep hiding-places of the soul. This is their mutual secret, and they give it no words. No one knows it but they alone. Therefore the old, the giant king, and the young, the delicate jester, cling together, in pathetic contrast, through all the furies of the battle between Lear and his daughters, through the terrible wild night on the pitiless moor. Nothing but death will part those who both love the lost, the mourned Cordelia. This is the atmosphere, the 'aura' which Shakespeare has created around them; and it makes the mysterious attraction which every one has felt steal into them from this 'poor fool's' heart in touch with the heart of Lear.

The fool's love for Lear does not appear in words, for he loves Lear through his love for Cordelia. But Lear's love for the fool is expressed. It is something more than a king's light sentiment for a jester, and it develops into a deeper feeling during his agony. He calls him 'my pretty knave.' 'Poor fool,' he says,

> I have one part in my heart
> That's sorry yet for thee.

With his new thoughtfulness for others, begot of his suffering, Lear turns in the storm to feel with his fool. 'Come on, my boy, art cold?'—and he leads him into the shelter. What he has felt for the whole world of the poor, he feels for his delicate jester. As to the fool himself, he differs, with a world of difference, from all the other fools in Shakespeare's work. He seems more of a spirit than a man; elusive, evasive; the outlines of his thought, of his personality, continually changing like the images in a revolving kaleidoscope; only one thought constant—the folly of Lear who banished Cordelia and gave all to those who hated him and her. Then he is half-witted, and the half which has no wit sings snatches of old songs, and his mind whirls, like a dancing marsh-fire, among shreds of thought and images; but the other half which has wit remembers his past experience of men when he was saner than now. Half of what he says is close to the point, and he says it so bitterly that we know he has suffered from the heartlessness of the world. There is a stored up, half-cynical wisdom in the song he sings—

> Have more than thou showest,
> Speak less than thou knowest,
> Lend less than thou owest,
> Ride more than thou goest,

Learn more than thou trowest,
Set less than thou throwest ;
Leave thy drink and thy whore,
And keep in-a-door,
And thou shalt have more
Than two tens to a score.

And the rest of his wild talk in this scene is so sharp to the matter that Kent says

This is not altogether fool, my lord.

This mixture of sense and non-sense, of sanity and insanity running in and out of one another, adds to the mystery of his nature, to the feeling we have that he belongs in part to another world than ours. He has something of the attractiveness of an elf. And indeed he seems to come into the play out of the unknown, like a spirit, and he passes out of it like a spirit. He lives through the great agony of Lear, and dies when it is at its height. For he is delicate of body, sensitive as a child, and fearful. He trembles before the darkening frown of Goneril. When he finds Edgar in the hovel, he cries out in terror—'Help me, help me'; and the cold night and bitter wind are more than he can bear. When he says in the farmhouse, to close the scene,

I 'll go sleep at noon,

he knows that his love and his life are over. He dies, and Lear is left alone.

When we meet Lear again, he is safe in Dover, mad, but with intervals of sanity. I have no time to speak of the further picture of his madness when he meets Gloucester and Edgar. It is worthy of close study. He is partly personal, partly impersonal. Nor does he repeat one image or thought of the previous outburst — save for an addition to his attack on the social state—an even bitterer cry against its blindness, carelessness, but chiefly its hypocrisy. What Goneril and Regan seemed to be, but were not, is at the bottom of his mind. In his better time he refuses, shamed, to see Cordelia. And then arrives Cordelia. And having been in the cold hell of hatred, the regions of thick ribbed frost where Goneril and Regan live, we find ourselves in heaven—in Cordelia's heart, warm with love, minute and exquisite in tenderness, where sweetness and beauty are enthroned. There are no words to tell the loveliness of her soothing voice, the golden beauty of her pity and her love.

'All blest secrets,' she cries to the Doctor—

> All you unpublish'd virtues of the earth
> Spring with my tears! be aidant and remediate
> In the good man's distress.—

Shakespeare himself sketches her, as if he loved her beyond expression, in the words of one who saw her when she heard of the fate of her father. I must quote this matchless poetry.

KENT. Did your letters pierce the queen to any demonstration of grief?
GENT. Ay, sir; she took them, read them in my presence,
And now and then an ample tear trill'd down
Her delicate cheek: it seem'd she was a queen
Over her passion, who most rebel-like
Sought to be king o'er her.
KENT. O, then, it moved her.
GENT. Not to a rage: patience and sorrow strove
Who should express her goodliest. You have seen
Sunshine and rain at once: her smiles and tears
Were like a better way: those happy smilets
That play'd on her ripe lip seem'd not to know
What guests were in her eyes; which parted thence
As pearls from diamonds dropp'd. In brief
Sorrow would be a rarity most beloved
If all could so become it.

At last she finds him, and Lear, comforted, recovers his senses. And then Cordelia sees him as he sleeps. Lovely and lovelier are her words, but loveliest when he wakes. Yet they are as brief as her passion is deep. Her heart is too full for speech—sobbing breaks her voice, but every sentence is a world of feeling and of thought.

O, look upon me, sir,
And hold your hands in benediction o'er me :
No, sir, you must not kneel.

LEAR.　　　Pray do not mock me :
I am a very foolish fond old man,
Fourscore and upward, not an hour more nor less ;
And, to deal plainly,
I fear I am not in my perfect mind.

.　　　.　　.　　.　　.

Do not laugh at me ;
For, as I am a man, I think this lady
To be my child Cordelia.

CORD.　　　And so I am, I am !

LEAR.　Be your tears wet ?　Yes, 'faith.　I pray, weep not :
If you have poison for me, I will drink it.
I know you do not love me ; for your sisters
Have, as I do remember, done me wrong :
You have some cause, they have not.

CORD.　　　No cause, no cause.

Not even in Imogen did Shakespeare ever reach the divine simplicity of passion that these words reveal and conceal. 'And so I am, I am.' 'No cause, no cause.' Out of the Eternal Love in a man these things come.

The pity is so great that unthinking persons have wished for a happy ending to this play. There have been such remakings put upon the stage by audacious persons who did not know themselves or Shakespeare. He was in no mood for this. In the dark unbelief in any just gods which now, as I think, possessed him, he slays the guiltless, after in fierce justice he has slain the guilty. Goneril, Regan, Cornwall, Edmund have died violently. Cordelia and Lear meet as violent a death. Cordelia is hanged, ignobly hanged by one as merciless as Regan. Nor is she alone in her fate. The course of affairs is cruel not only here, but everywhere. So Shakespeare thought in these sunless days. So thought Cordelia when they took her to prison.

We are not the first
Who with best meaning have incurred the worst.

Yet, the indelible sweetness of Shakespeare's nature re-asserts itself in the redemption of the soul of Lear. Cordelia has breathed upon him and he has received the Spirit. In the last sane things he says as he is led away to prison, his violence, love of luxury, hatred of the world, are far behind him, gone for ever. Love is best and the simple life. Prison and pain are nothing to love. Even the mystery of the world is solved by it. He is like a happy child.

> Come, let's away to prison;
> We two alone will sing like birds i' the cage:
> When thou dost ask me blessing, I'll kneel down
> And ask of thee forgiveness: so we'll live,
> And pray, and sing, and tell old tales, and laugh
> At gilded butterflies, and hear poor rogues
> Talk of court news; and we'll talk with them too,
> Who loses, and who wins; who's in, who's out;
> And take upon's the mystery of things,
> As if we were God's spies: and we'll wear out,
> In a wall'd prison, packs and sects of great ones
> That ebb and flow by the moon.

It is his last hour of happiness. When we next see him he comes in, seized again by frenzy, with Cordelia dead in his arms. All the world knows that heart-cracking scene, where in the face of Lear's Titan grief, all the rest speak only broken words. At last his heart breaks asunder:

> Thou'lt come no more,
> Never, never, never, never, never!
> Pray you, undo this button: thank you, sir,
> Do you see this? Look on her, look, her lips,
> Look there, look there!—　　　　　(*Dies.*)

And Kent to Edgar who lifts the King, crying,

> Look up, my Lord,

says the last word that thousands and thousands of men, in this wild world, have said to such a sorrow—

> Vex not his ghost: O, let him pass! he hates him
> That would upon the rack of this tough world
> Stretch him out longer.

HISTORICAL PLAYS

VIII

KING JOHN

THE play of *The Life and Death of King John* was written in the years which saw the production of the historical dramas of *Henry VI.*, *Richard II.*, and *Richard III.*, and its proper date is 1594. About the same date *The Merchant of Venice* was written in which Shakespeare turned from history to romance. The source of *King John* is not to be found in any of the Chronicles, but in another play on the same subject, written 1589 by some mere playwright, and printed in 1591, *The Troublesome Raigne of King John*. Shakespeare clung so closely to the framework and to the patriotic and anti-papal spirit of *The Troublesome Raigne*, that his own play may be called a recast of it, rather than an original play. Yet it is altogether a new thing.

Its patriotism is as vivid, but less violent, and its opposition to the Papacy is not ferociously insisted on, but diffused through the substance of the play. The writer of *The Troublesome Raigne* used or misused the events of history as its writer pleased, and Shakespeare in his play took a similar licence. Why, being quite able, as in his other historical dramas, to follow history almost accurately, he chose in this drama to play pranks with facts, and in some cases without dramatic necessity, I can only conjecture, and indeed it does not make much matter. The real matter is the play itself, its presentation of human passions, and the probable insight it gives us into the personal patriotism of Shakespeare.

It may be amusing to find out Shakespeare's deliberate errors, and we can discover them in every text-book on this drama, but when we read or see the play, it is best, for the time, to assume that Shakespeare was right in his variations from the truth.   History is one thing, and it is good, of course, to know the facts.   But Art is another thing, and, however she may choose to manipulate the facts, she is excused if her deviation from fact enables her to create new images of humanity, and varied pictures of our life.   If Shakespeare, for example, had followed historical fact, we should never have had the scene between Arthur and Hubert, or the wild magnificence of the grief of Constance, or Faulconbridge's steady loyalty to England when all seemed lost; and even one of these representations is more important in its truth to human nature, and in its influence on humanity, than any accurate knowledge of the facts about King John.

I should like to have seen Shakespeare at work on *The Troublesome Raigne*, which he took as his original.   It is not quite a bad play, but his humorous rage at its weakness, false passion, and blundering execution, could only have been matched by the delight he had in reconceiving, re-forming, re-charactering the whole of it. It is told of Michael Angelo that his friends brought to him a huge block of marble, ten feet high, which some futile sculptor had begun to shape, and then, in despair, had the grace to surrender.   The great artist saw beneath the rude block the noble statue of David which stood for so long in front of the palace of the Signoria at Florence.   He sprang upon it with chisel and mallet, in a fiery energy, and out of the formless marble emerged, as if at the voice of a God, the young conqueror of the Philistine.   With a like fire and fury of creative energy, we may imagine Shakespeare hewing out his *King John* from the formless mass of the *Troublesome Raigne.* What joy was his as he felt, rising into speaking life beneath his hand, the terrible motherhood of Constance, the piteous childhood of Arthur, the growing manhood of Faulconbridge, the dignified statesmanship of Salisbury, and the strange figure, mingled of vile clay and gold, of the King whom he slew on so burning a couch because he had wronged England. There is no joy in the wide world to be for one moment compared to the joy of creation; and all men of creative genius know and have loved that lonely rapture.

'Slain, because he had wronged England!' That is part of the spirit which underlies this play. The patriotic emotion of the time, which the overthrow of the Armada had lifted into a passionate belief in the glory and honour of England, was deep in Shakespeare when he wrote this play. It breathes through all its Acts like flame. It has here a steadfastness of belief in itself which England has never lost. It is firmly based, in the character of Faulconbridge, on the will and feeling of the whole people. It conceives by his voice England as unassailable, or, if assailed, as secure of conquest while Englishmen still love their land.

> This England never did, nor never shall,
> Lie at the proud foot of a conqueror,
> But when it first did help to wound itself.
> Now these her princes are come home again,
> Come the three corners of the world in arms,
> And we shall shock them : nought shall make us rue,
> If England to itself do rest but true.

The Bastard is Shakespeare's incarnation of the patriotic pride of the England of Elizabeth. And this is all the more remarkable because the King of whom Shakespeare writes was in his mind a bad representative of England. He paints one side of John as mean, greedy of power, a reptile in craft for selfish ends, a shrinking murderer, an ungrateful King. Yet he is at the head of England, and because he represents her by his position, he is to be supported; not for his own sake, but for the sake of the country. The lords who, angry with John's murder of Arthur, join themselves to France are, in the eyes of Faulconbridge, degenerate and ingrate revolts, who like Nero rip up the womb of their dear mother England, and who should blush for shame. The very women, he says, will trip after the drum, and turn their thimbles into gauntlets, rather than yield England to the foreigner. Nor does Salisbury, joined to France, feel his position happy, even though he hates the murdering King—

> Is 't not pity, O my grieved friends,
> That we, the sons and children of this isle,
> Were born to see so sad an hour as this :
> Wherein we step after a stranger, march
> Upon her gentle bosom, and fill up
> Her enemies' ranks, (I must withdraw and weep
> Upon the spot of this enforced cause),
> To grace the gentry of a land remote,
> And follow unacquainted colours here ?

John was, historically, a Frenchman ruling over England. Of that Shakespeare knows nothing in the play. He feels to France as Elizabeth's England felt. The army of France in England is the army of a foreign invader, without a shred of right to meddle in the question of the heirship to the throne. And the island wrath of the soil of England 'heaves itself against' the steps of an alien foe. Nothing lay deeper than that spirit in the England of Shakespeare, and he gave it voice.

Another element pervades this drama, and belongs to the time at which it was written. It was resentment at the pretensions of the Church of Rome to assume an authority over England independent of the Crown. I have no doubt that Shakespeare expressed his own views and those of his audience on Papal interference in the answers

John gives to the Legate, Pandulph. 'Tell the Pope this tale—

> and from the mouth of England
> Add thus much more,—That no Italian priest
> Shall tithe or toll in our dominions ;
> But as we, under heaven, are supreme head,
> So under Him that great supremacy,
> Where we do reign, we will alone uphold,
> Without the assistance of a mortal hand :
> So tell the pope, all reverence set apart
> To him and his usurp'd authority.'

Pandulph, the Legate, answers by the excommunication which dissolved all human ties between the nation and the sovereign, blest those who revolted, and canonised as a saint him who took away by secret course the life of the King.

> And meritorious shall that hand be call'd,
> Canonizèd, and worshipp'd as a saint,
> That takes away by any secret course
> Thy hateful life.

Imagine what Shakespeare's audience felt when they heard that anathema of death. It went home to the heart of the audience. There was not a man in the pit who had not heard that Rome had treacherously played for the assassination of Elizabeth, had openly attacked her legitimacy, and urged the Roman Catholics of England to throw off their allegiance. I should like to have been in the theatre and heard the roar which saluted this dialogue between John and Pandulph. Then again, as the Cardinal speaks, Shakespeare paints the Roman Church as putting aside the most solemn vows, the conscience and honour and faith of men, if those were against her interests and power. King Philip appeals to the Legate to consider the new-made treaty which has put an end to a bloody war, which has been knit together

> With all religious strength of sacred vows.

Shall we play 'loose with faith,' he cries, 'so jest with heaven, stain with blood the marriage-bed of peace' ?

> O, holy sir, . . .
> Out of your grace, devise, ordain, impose
> Some gentle order.

This appeal to natural morality, to Christianity, conscience, honour, and for peace, Rome flings away.

> PAND. All form is formless, order orderless,
> Save what is opposite to England's love.
> Therefore, to arms! be champion of our church,
> Or let the church, our mother, breathe her curse,
> A mother's curse, on her revolting son.

And the audience heard in the words the answer of Rome to Philip II. to let loose the Armada on the shores of England.

Then follows, when the French King again appeals to the faith he has pledged to John, a speech by the Legate of the finest-woven casuistry, which is worth study as an example of Shakespeare's intellectual power throwing itself into the brain of a Roman Casuist labouring, for the sake of the Church, to dissolve all the bonds of honourable faith between man and man. And Pandulph ends, as usual, with Rome's reiterated threat of spiritual doom, bearing with it national ruin.

As if this were not enough to blacken the character of Rome before the audience, there is placed a long conversation between the Dauphin and the Legate, in which he comforts Lewis for his transient loss of Blanch by assuming, with cynical coolness, the certain death of Arthur, now in the hands of John, and the Dauphin's heirship to the throne of England as the husband of Blanch whom he will now marry. Not a ray of pity for the fate of the child crosses the mind of the Churchman. There is nothing in his mind but the supremacy of Rome. 'Come, noble Dauphin, John and England are in your hands. I will whet on the King.' He is just as dead to all human suffering when he hears Constance crying out her woe for her lost son. Philip is sorry for her. 'O fair affliction, peace!' Pandulph is as hard as a stone.

Lady, you utter madness, and not sorrow.

And when, in words which might move the flint, she cries she shall not know her son in the court of heaven he will be so changed by suffering, this priest gives comfort thus—

You hold too heinous a respect of grief.

Oh, cries Constance in reply—seeing his frozen heart—

He talks to me that never had a son.

Not only public morality, but the tenderest ties of humanity, are thus represented as despised by the Church, when her interests are endangered. Fancy how Englishmen followed all this—men who had heard of the pitiless massacre of St. Bartholomew's Day, of the cruelties of Spain in the Low Countries, of the blessing the Pope had given to the ravishing soldiery of the Armada, of the treacherous work in England. No play of Shakespeare appealed more strongly than this to the national heart and honour, and the national wrath with Rome. As I read it, I seem to hear Shakespeare's own passion beating in its verse. It may even be that it was owing to his personal sympathy with England's wrath with Roman pretension and treachery, that he chose, in the case of this play, not to follow the Chronicles, but to adopt as his source a play in which the facts of history could be manipulated as he pleased. He had thus a free hand so to modify and change events that they should be used to express his opinions and those of his hearers on the questions of his own day. Some explanation, at least resembling this, must be given of his reckless, apparently unnecessary, violation of historical fact.

The character of King John is perhaps nearer to historical truth than anything else in the play. Only he is not quite so bad a man in it as he actually was.

'Foul as hell is, hell is made more foul by the presence of John,' was the judgment of his contemporaries. This tradition has so influenced the critics of this play, that they have made the John of Shakespeare much more wicked and vile than the dramatist represented him. They have searched into every line for badness and have found it. But the King in Shakespeare's hands is no such unredeemed a villain. He is, as he really was, an able politician, a wise war-leader, a bold and ready pursuer of his aim. He stands up for England, and when he does submit to the Legate (changing apparently his steadfast mind) it is not so much to bow to Rome, as to overthrow—as he does—the whole of the conspiracy of his foes against the English Crown. He gains his end; his revolting nobles are brought back to his dying bed, and the invaders are forced, raging, to leave the shores of England. Nor is he represented as a coward, as some have said. He is quite as physically though not so morally brave as Faulconbridge.

On the moral side Shakespeare joins with his accusers. On that side he is represented as he is, the ruthless politician, the murderer of Arthur. But even that villainy does not turn Faulconbridge against him ; Faulconbridge who stands for England against the whole world ! John is a wicked king, but, wicked or no, he represents to Faulconbridge England and her fates. As such he clings to him, supports him when the rest leave him, cheers him in his dismay, reports him to the French as the gallant and victorious king, denounces the revolting lords,—and idealising him thus as the embodiment of England—comes even to love him, when he is ill fortuned, and finally to mourn his death.

> Art thou gone so ? I do but stay behind
> To do the office for thee of revenge :
> And then my soul shall wait on thee to heaven,
> As it on earth hath been thy servant still.

And this double aspect of John—bad and good—under which the Bastard views his master is also Shakespeare's representation of him. It was not his cue, at a time when England stood alone against the envious Continent, to lower the monarchy of England. The case of Richard III. was different. To lower him was to exalt the Tudors, the true heirs of England in the eyes of an Elizabethan. Here King John was against France. He must not then be represented as infamous, even though he slew the rightful heir. The King stands for England.

Therefore John, except as the murderer of Arthur, is not completely blackened in this play. No one, not even Henry V., can speak more kingly, more concisely, than King John to the ambassador of France; nor did Henry V. act as rapidly, more like a great commander-in-chief, than John against France. He is on Philip's back before Philip thinks he has left England. In war, John is pictured as prompt to act, subtle to plan, making victory a certainty; and when, out of a difficult position in which France and the Church are both against him, he has wrung victory, the French confess his genius in war and policy—

> Lew. What he hath won that hath he fortified ;
> So hot a speed with such advice disposed,
> Such temperate order in so fierce a cause,
> Doth want example : who hath read, or heard,
> Of any kindred action like to this ?

It is the description of a great general.

Before the first fifty lines are over, we meet the two matters on which the whole of the play is to turn. First, we understand from Elinor's speech that Arthur's claim to the throne is just, that John holds it against him by force: 'Your strong possession much more than your right' is your title to the crown. The working out of that is half the play. The second point is that John and the Church are in ruthless opposition. And this is marked by John's cynical phrase—

> Our abbeys and our priories shall pay
> This expedition's charge.

This quarrel rules the other half of the drama. These two points made in the first fifty lines are another illustration of Shakespeare's careful preparation for all that is to follow.

Close upon this, following up John's denial of Arthur's claim to England, is the arrival on the stage of Faulconbridge, John's great supporter, who towers above all the rest, the natural not the legitimate cousin of the King. The scene is a curious one, and John appears in it, not as the rude, truculent villain he was, but as the grave dispenser of law, one who knows a man when he sees him, and welcomes him with frank and ready friendship.

Nor is Shakespeare's King John less dignified, less regal in speech and act when he meets King Philip before Angiers. His defiance of France is grave and courteous, and when war is inevitable, what he says is thoughtful in its sorrow for war, even Christian in its feeling.

> Then God forgive the sin of all those souls
> That to their everlasting residence,
> Before the dew of evening fall, shall fleet,
> In dreadful trial of our kingdom's king !

This is not the speech of the foul king that history has drawn in the colours of hell.

But now, and with a touch, he changes from this high mood into that evil temper which blackens all the good in him. His dominant passion is to keep the crown he has unjustly taken. Any wrong done for that seems right, and the doing away of Arthur is now the first necessity. Murder sits in his heart, ruthless, politic murder. France supports Arthur, and to divide France from Arthur, John agrees to marry Blanch, his niece, to the Dauphin—

> John, to stop Arthur's title to the whole
> Hath willingly departed with a part.

This peace leaves Arthur unsupported; he is no longer a danger to John; but it earns and develops that maternal rage of Constance, which Shakespeare uses so magnificently.

When the Pope's Legate appears, the second element of the drama takes form. The Church is against John, for he has offended its supremacy. John answers him as Elizabeth's England would have answered. Shakespeare in this lifts high the figure of John. The Legate breaks up the peace. Philip is forced again to support Arthur against John, because John is against the Church. Arthur becomes again a danger; he is taken prisoner in the battle. And then—murder, long debated in alternating thoughts, determines itself for act. The good in John is drowned by the evil. Spite of conscience, of pity, of justice, and of honour, he will make his crown safe. But he is ashamed of the deed, or rather of entrusting it to another. Richard III. has no shame for his murders; Macbeth performs his own, and it is a soldier's honour, and a host's, rather than conscience, which disturbs him. John shrinks from the murder, recoils from innocent blood; conscience touches him, but no pity; policy overtops conscience; 'he has a mighty cause to wish the death of Arthur.' But he fears his own design, fears to place it in words—wishes for the night to hide his soul from itself; wavers round the telling his desire to Hubert—dreads to hear it in words, for then it is irrevocably shaped. It is a wonderful passage, and it is worth while to compare it—with all its subtle differentiations—with the soliloquy of Macbeth before the slaying of Duncan.

I had a thing to say, but let it go :
The sun is in the heaven, and the proud day,
Attended with the pleasures of the world,
Is all too wanton and too full of gawds
To give me audience : if the midnight bell

Did, with his iron tongue and brazen mouth,
Sound on into the drowsy ear of night;
If this same were a churchyard where we stand,
And thou possessed with a thousand wrongs;
Or if that surly spirit, melancholy,
Had baked thy blood and made it heavy-thick,
Which else runs tickling up and down the veins,
Making that idiot, laughter, keep men's eyes
And strain their cheeks to idle merriment,
A passion hateful to my purposes;
Or if that thou couldst see me without eyes,
Hear me without thine ears, and make reply
Without a tongue, using conceit alone,
Without eyes, ears and harmful sound of words;
Then, in despite of brooded watchful day,
I would into thy bosom pour my thoughts:
But, ah, I will not! yet I love thee well.

HUBERT.   So well, that what you bid me undertake,
Though that my death were adjunct to my act,
By heaven, I would do it.

KING JOHN.   Do not I know thou wouldst?
Good Hubert, Hubert, Hubert, throw thine eye
On yon young boy: I 'll tell thee what, my friend,
He is a very serpent in my way;
And wheresoe'er this foot of mine doth tread,
He lies before me: dost thou understand me?
Thou art his keeper.

HUBERT.   And I 'll keep him so,
That he shall not offend your majesty.

KING JOHN.   Death.
HUBERT.   My Lord?
KING JOHN.   A grave.
HUBERT.   He shall not live.
KING JOHN.   Enough.

What can be more dramatic than those five whispered
sentences? They are like the heavy strokes of a death-bell.

Then, free from this fear, John has no remorse till his
lords, hearing of the murder, leave him in burning indignation, and join the French invaders. Then he repents,
not of the murder, but of the mistake he made. And
he turns all his ill temper upon Hubert. His talk is a
mingled skein. Now he thinks of his own danger; now
his conscience seems to trouble him.

> It is the curse of kings to be attended
> By slaves that take their humours for a warrant
> To break within the bloody house of life.

There speaks the politician fearing for his crown.

> O, when the last account 'twixt heaven and earth
> Is to be made, then shall this hand and seal
> Witness against us to damnation !

And there speaks Conscience. Nothing can be more subtle than the interchanging play of these two motives in the talk of the King with Hubert, while as yet he does not know that Arthur is alive; and that Shakespeare meant to represent this to and fro of policy and conscience in the soul of John, is plain from the last words where John says of the kingdom of his soul that in

> this confine of blood and breath,
> Hostility and civil tumult reigns
> Between my conscience and my cousin's death.

This view of John, which makes him capable (unlike Macbeth and Richard) of feeling the call and sting of conscience, and therefore not altogether bad, is again insisted on by Shakespeare. When the lords see him conferring with Hubert, and suspect him of the murder of Arthur, Salisbury says

> The colour of the king doth come and go
> Between his purpose and his conscience,
> Like heralds 'twixt two dreadful battles set :
> His passion is so ripe, it needs must break.

And John, ending the scene, cries out—

> I repent :
> There is no sure foundation set on blood,
> No certain life achieved by others' death.

This is not the picture of a villain lost to all sense of shame, of an utterly ruthless character.

He has been also accused of cowardice, but Shakespeare gives no hint of that. On the contrary, John answers quickly to the Bastard's cry—

> Be great in act as you have been in thought.

It is only when the burning of the poison gnaws his heart, that his courage yields a little to mortal agony.

This is Shakespeare's presentation of John—not altogether wicked, good and ill mingled in him; swept into crime by policy, but sometimes repentant; wise in action and thought; brave in battle; not overwhelmed by misfortune; a murderer against his conscience; a king who, because he stood against France and the Papacy for England, is half forgiven by Shakespeare who thinks of him as the Bastard thinks, and for the same reasons.

I do not speak of the minor characters, of Philip, the Dauphin, of Salisbury and Hubert, even of Arthur. That high pathetic scene between him and Hubert, in which boyhood is so tenderly drawn, with such loveliness of poetry that it would awake the soul of pity had she slept for a thousand years, is so well known and loved that it needs no description, and is above analysis. I turn to Constance and to Faulconbridge.

Faulconbridge is intended by Shakespeare to be, amidst a crowd of selfish kings, princes, and nobles, all pressing to their own advantage, an incarnation of the honest Englishman who loves his country, abjures the foreigner, clings to his king at all hazards because the king represents England; is not indifferent to his own interests; is bluff, outspoken, and brave as a lion, yet has a clear eye to see beyond the follies of the world into the serious heart of affairs. He can philosophise on the mad world, because he really stands apart from all the rest. Amid all the changes of politics, the quarrels which are knit and unknit around him, he is steadily consistent. The principles he lives by remain at the end what they were at the beginning; they change only by development. Nor is he without natural and simple affection, the faithfulness of which is always to be relied on. He loves the King; I have already quoted his passionate farewell to his dead master. He heartens and consoles the King when misfortune lies heavy on him. He is faithful to the last, even when he disapproves the King. Yet when he sees the dead body of Arthur, and thinks that the King is guilty of the murder, his natural pity and indignation break out of his heart—'Sir Richard, what think you?' cries Salisbury, and Faulconbridge replies—

> It is a damned and a bloody work ;
> The graceless action of a heavy hand.

This is the man who, when we first meet him, has come to the court from the country to defend his claim to his father's property—denied to him because he is not his father's son, but a bastard got on his mother by Richard Cœur de Lion. But he loved fame more than property, and when he is recognised by the King as the son of Richard, when Elinor asks him to follow her fortunes and receive knighthood, he flings away his claim, and will live to make his own fortune and his own fame. He rejoices in his sonship to the great warrior; he tells his mother, whom his affection consoles, that she was justified in yielding to the conqueror of the lion, that he is for ever grateful to her; and he leaves her happy and at ease. Brave, ambitious, rough and frank, he has yet a kind heart, and a wise mind in affairs because his heart is kind.

Shakespeare lifts him in this scene out of the country-man into the courtier without lowering his character. No sooner is he in his natural element as a king's son, no sooner does he realise that here, in war and policy, he can fulfil all the dreams he must have had when lost in the solitude of the country, than he flings his old life away for ever with a laugh. He sees the varied movement of the great world open before him like a fan, and his spirit burns to join the mellay. John and Elinor watch his soul rise to his eyes; they see the man emerge from the chrysalis; and they knit him to their side. This is, cries Elinor—

> The very spirit of Plantagenet!
> I am thy grandam, Richard; call me so.

Nevertheless, he is not carried away out of good sense by his new honours. I am, he says, with his good-natured cynicism—

> A foot of honour better than I was;
> But many a many foot of land the worse.

He laughs at the conventions of society which is chiefly made up of fools, but for that very reason suits a ' mounting spirit ' like himself—one who observes, and will make of his observation means to grow—one who will soothe the world with deceit's sweet poison when it is necessary, yet will, on the whole, be true. This first of his soliloquies paints him as less noble than he becomes.

Shakespeare slowly develops Faulconbridge into a great nobility of character. Great affairs, in which he plays a serious part, lift him into greatness. There is that in him—his honest truthfulness, his unbroken faith —which makes him equal to arduous events, and above them. His large conception of England and of his duty to her and to the King as the image of England, enlarges his mind, strengthens him in difficulty, opens his soul and sets him apart, in dignified separation, from all these kings and nobles who are struggling, without any high idea of country and duty, for their own ends alone. He grows steadily from the brave and self-seeking man of the first Act, from the vainglorious soldier of the third, to the serious patriot and the honourable statesman of the last.

Only one personal matter is at his heart. It is the avenging of his father on Austria, his enemy. To give his anger

full reason, Shakespeare makes Austria guilty of Cœur de
Lion's death, which he was not; and to enable his personal
revenge, keeps Austria alive who had been really dead for
some years. Faulconbridge mocks his enemy before the
assembled princes, and in the battle slays him. When
that is done, he has no more personal aims. He is for
England only.

At first, however, he is only the bold, boastful soldier
who rejoices in the fight, and whose exultation expresses
itself in an unbridled eloquence. He mouths his swelling
words, as if Shakespeare were Marlowe.

> Ha, majesty! how high thy glory towers,
> When the rich blood of kings is set on fire!
> O, now doth Death line his dead chaps with steel;
> The swords of soldiers are his teeth, his fangs;
> And now he feasts, mousing the flesh of men,
> In undetermined differences of kings.

'Tis a pleasant vanity! And so he goes through the
whole debate, laughing and blustering, his manhood
shouldering through the press, mocking the wordy citizens
of Angiers—

> Here's a stay,
> That shakes the rotten carcase of old Death
> Out of his rags!

He mocks even more at the Dauphin's sentimental love-
making—no reverence in him for a French prince—and
finally is contemptuous of them all; and of himself, who
would, if he could, join in their pursuit of gain. But
there is a difference. They think their ends are worthy,
and sacrifice honour, faith, and truth to win them. He
knows that the means they use degrade their ends, and
despises them for that; and despises himself when he
follows their example. This is his soliloquy—

> Mad world! mad kings! mad composition!
> John, to stop Arthur's title in the whole,
> Hath willingly departed with a part:
> And France, whose armour conscience buckled on,

Whom zeal and charity brought to the field
As God's own soldier, rounded in the ear
With that same purpose-changer, that sly devil,
.   .   .   .   .   .
That smoothed-faced gentleman, tickling Commodity
Commodity, the bias of the world . . .
This bawd, this broker, this all-changing word,
Clapp'd on the outward eye of fickle France,
Hath drawn him from his own determined aid,
From a resolved and honourable war,
To a most base and vile-concluded peace.
But why rail I on this Commodity ?
Not for because he hath not woo'd me yet :
Not that I have the power to clutch my hand,
When his fair angels would salute my palm ;
But for my hand, as unattempted yet,
Like a poor beggar, raileth on the rich.
Well, whiles I am a beggar, I will rail
And say there is no sin but to be rich ;
And being rich, my virtue then shall be
To say there is no vice but beggary.
Since kings break faith upon commodity,
Gain, be my lord, for I will worship thee.

Such was his temper then—a warrior only and a self-pushing man of the world.   But when Arthur is slain, and his master is in mortal danger, and England is invaded—these terrible events shake him out of himself into a graver, wiser, and nobler man.   He speaks his mind about Arthur's death to the King with faithfulness, but he does not, like the rest, abandon the King.   Even in the murder of Arthur, he feels how fierce was John's temptation. Moreover the King to him is England, and England now is the only mistress of the Bastard's soul.   He becomes from henceforth the protagonist of the drama—the real king of events, the centre round which all the action revolves.   And his character, purged of its half-cynic selfishness, rises to the level of his position.   He speeds to the support of the King.   He takes a lofty tone of reproof to the disloyal nobles who are false to their country.   When the French land in England, he alone stands against them for England, gathers and arrays the forces of the kingdom. He lifts the despondent King with noble words into courage, bids him contend to the death, make no compromise, let no Cardinal make peace but make it with our own arms. These are his high-hearted words—

> But wherefore do you droop? why look you sad?
> Be great in act, as you have been in thought.

He outfaces the Dauphin and the French lords with swelling words. He bids them hear, in his defiance of them, the voice of England's King.

> For thus his royalty doth speak in me.

He leads the battle and supports it—

> That misbegotten devil, Faulconbridge,
> In spite of spite alone upholds the day.

He does not despair even when half his power is lost in the Lincoln Washes; and, when the King is dead, his wisdom takes precedence and governs the action of the lords of the kingdom. He incarnates the constancy of England in the play.

And now for Constance. Amid all this hurly-burly of wars, contending kings, selfish interests, walks like a spirit the awful figure of Constance—worn and wasted mother-hood maddened by loss and grief; primeval motherhood isolated from everything else in its own passion.

> Look, who comes here! a grave unto a soul;
> Holding the eternal spirit, against her will,
> In the vile prison of afflicted breath.

When she is present, all the others recede into the background—are only scenery for her wild figure, with disordered garments and hair unbound, and the sound of death in her voice. The actress who should undertake her part is scarcely born in a century. It needs a majestic woman whose soul has lived in the depths; it needs a man's strength to keep up so continuous a frenzy of passion. It needs a self-control, most rarely found in any artist, to prevent the fury of the part, its total abandonment, from carrying away the actress beyond the self-mastery she must hold over her emotion, lest her execution of the part should break down into feebleness, into mere rant and shouting. Moreover, she must have a noble intellect as well as a pitiful heart to act the part adequately; and added to that—a spirit of imagination to feel the poetic passion in the speech of Constance. All she says, in her grief, is steeped in the waters of poetry; the penetrating pity of imagination pierces through her words into the secret recesses of sorrow.

As to the intellect required, the part needs to be conceived on large and simple lines, so as not to lose its grandeur; and yet, within that simplicity, the part is so variously and finely conceived and wrought, that she who acts it must have a hair-dividing, subtle intellect to wind in and out among its changes. Constance is not mad; she is only frenzied with grief, and the frenzy seems sometimes to rise into insanity. But she never loses the clear sequences of thought, and never (as a madwoman would do, as Ophelia does) gambols from the sense. Even her wildest cry, when she apostrophises Death, when she gets nearest to madness, is in intellectual order! Instead of becoming (as a madwoman in excitement would certainly become) more incoherent, she becomes quieter and quieter to the end of the scene, more clear and simple. The changes are as subtle, as delicate as the changes of a cloud; and their infinite interchange of feeling and thought needs a great intellect to conceive them, a passionate heart to follow their intricacy of emotion, and a great, grave, and self-mastering artist to represent them.

When we meet her first, she has no grief, but eager wrath that her son is kept out of his heritage; and keen desire, because she loves him, that he should have it. She does not care, because of any politic reason or desire of power, to make him king, but does care because he is her son, and she his mother. It is her love that is the motive. The motive of Elinor, her opponent, is love of power. Even in their first quarrel these motives are plainly disclosed: Elinor's violence is cool; her policy and not her heart speaks. Every word of Constance is charged with the physical passion of motherhood. Motherhood, universal motherhood, the deep agony of the female in animals and in humanity;—her defence of her young, her desire, her hope for them; her fury at their loss, her rapture at their recovery; motherhood unmodified by civilisation—it was that which rose into Shakespeare's soul and before his imagination, when he pictured Constance. Only, here he did not picture the happy motherhood of Hermione, or the proud joy of Volumnia in her son, but the misery of a mother's loss; the tigress robbed of her whelps.

For, indeed, Constance is a tigress. We do not understand the terrible frenzy into which her sorrow passes till we understand that she has a naturally violent temper. Her attack on Elinor is savage, and Elinor answers her in kind. These fine ladies have foul tongues, but Constance is the most furious. So loud is the battle between these two, and so much more fierce is Constance, that Arthur, the innocent cause, the little peaceful island in these stormy seas, is weary of the noise;—weary, the delicate child, almost of life. 'Good my mother, peace!' he cries.

> I would that I were low laid in my grave ;
> I am not worth this coil that's made for me.

And the French King, though on Constance's side, yet thinks she is too violent.

> Peace, lady, peace, or be more temperate.

Her violence redoubles when the peace is made between England and France, and Arthur's cause is overthrown.

The third Act begins with her indignant entrance on
the scene—

> Gone to be married ! gone to swear a peace !
> False blood to false blood join'd.   Gone to be friends !
>
> .   .   .   .   .   .
>
> Lewis marry Blanch !   O boy, then where art thou ?
> France friend with England, what becomes of me ?

In all this scene the unregulated violence of her speech is
flashing with imagination.   The poetry never fails, never
weakens.   There is not a word out of place ; scarcely a
word too much.   There is no fading into feebleness of
the similes.   They are crisp and short, and illuminate the
passion of the woman.   Thought runs to overtake the
previous thought before the first has fully shaped itself—
a mark of emotion at its height.   When we think that
she can say no more, she says something more rich and
beautiful than she has yet said.

'Pardon me,' says Salisbury—

> > Pardon me, madam,
> > I may not go without you to the Kings.
> Const.   Thou mayst, thou shalt ; I will not go with thee :
> I will instruct my sorrows to be proud ;
> For grief is proud, and makes his owner stoop.
> To me, and to the state of my great grief
> Let kings assemble ; for my grief's so great
> That no supporter but the huge firm earth
> Can hold it up : here I and sorrows sit ;
> Here is my throne, bid kings come bow to it.

The Kings enter.   She rises from her throne on the ground
like a queen of immortal wrath (like Margaret before the
Tower), to curse the day when France has beguiled her,
'this day of shame, oppression, perjury,' and cries to the
heavens in a splendid invocation.

> Arm, arm, you heavens, against these perjured kings !
> A widow cries ; be husband to me, heavens !
> Let not the hours of this ungodly day
> Wear out the day in peace ; but, ere sunset,
> Set armèd discord 'twixt these perjured kings !
> Hear me, O, hear me !

Her wish is fulfilled. The Legate separates the peace, and
there is war between France and England. But in the
fight Arthur is taken, and the boy knows well what will
happen. He loves his mother, and he cries—

> O, this will make my mother die of grief.

And then, we see the grief of Constance. She sees him
dead already in his captivity to John. She is dead in his
death. Sorrow, only sorrow, passes by, as Constance
crosses the stage; and she calls on death,

> Misery's love,
> O, come to me.

Was ever a sadder thing said in this sad world! The full
apostrophe to death may be said to be too fantastical—

> O amiable lovely death!
> Thou odoriferous stench! sound rottenness!

It has the sound of madness, but it is only frenzy at its
height playing with images. Were it madness, it would
not at once be followed by those magnificent lines, charged
with imaginative thought, invoking death—

> Arise forth from the couch of lasting night,
> Thou hate and terror to prosperity,

nor by her close argument that she is not mad in answer
to the Legate's accusation, nor by her clear consciousness
that her wit is somewhat disordered, nor by the soft and
piteous picture of her sorrow to the Cardinal and the
King. On the verge of frenzy, she has as yet a clear
mind. There is no madness in this speech, where sorrow
and beauty live together—

> And, father Cardinal, I have heard you say
> That we shall see and know our friends in heaven :
> If that be true, I shall see my boy again ;
> For, since the birth of Cain, the first male child,
> To him that did but yesterday suspire,
> There was not such a gracious creature born.
> But now will canker sorrow eat my bud,
> And chase the native beauty from his cheek,

And he will look as hollow as a ghost,
As dim and meagre as an ague's fit,
And so he 'll die ; and, rising so again,
When I shall meet him in the court of heaven
I shall not know him : therefore never, never
Must I behold my pretty Arthur more.

PAND.   You hold too heinous a respect of grief.
CONST.   He talks to me that never had a son.
K. PHIL.   You are as fond of grief as of your child.
CONST.   Grief fills the room up of my absent child,
Lies in his bed, walks up and down with me,
Puts on his pretty looks, repeats his words,
Remembers me of all his gracious parts,
Stuffs out his vacant garments with his form ;
Then, have I reason to be fond of grief.
Fare you well : had you such a loss as I,
I could give better comfort than you do.
I will not keep this form upon my head,
When there is such disorder in my wit.
O Lord ! my boy, my Arthur, my fair son !
My life, my joy, my food, my all the world !
My widow-comfort, and my sorrows' cure !

With that in her heart, she could not live. She broke
her heart and in a frenzy died. But before she dies,
Shakespeare, by the words of King Philip, has adorned
her image with beauty, and veiled it with pity.

Bind up those tresses. O, what love I note
In the fair multitude of those her hairs !

Then, finally, judgment falls on John. The misfortune
of his realm is doubled to him by the burning poison of
which he dies. The last words he hears are of the ruin of
his kingdom. He does not live to hear of its salvation.
No words of death, of violent death, are more terrible,
more poetic, more wild with imagination, than those of
John in dying.

P. HENRY.   How fares your majesty ?
K. JOHN.   Poison'd,—ill fare—dead, forsook, cast off ;
And none of you will bid the winter come
To thrust his icy fingers in my maw,
Nor let my kingdom's rivers take their course

Through my buru'd bosom, nor entreat the north
To make his bleak winds kiss my parched lips
And comfort me with cold. I do not ask you much,
I beg cold comfort ; and you are so strait
And so ingrateful, you deny me that.

IX

HENRY IV

PART I

Henry IV., which must be considered as a single play, was divided by Shakespeare into two parts owing to its great length; and the first part forms our subject. It and *Henry V.* are the completion of that great dramatic representation (as it were in one drama) of more than ninety years of English history, which, taking in all the civil wars of the Houses of York and Lancaster, was brought to its conclusion and catastrophe in *Richard III.*

Richard II. and *III.* were written in 1592-3; *Henry IV.* and *V.* in 1596-7-8. Five years of constant work, practice, and development lay between them. It is easy to feel, as one compares the earlier with the later work, how much greater an artist Shakespeare was now than when he wrote the two Richard plays. The versification is fuller, almost rhymeless, weightier in sound, less unequal, more carefully wrought, better poised, less barking than it is in *Richard III.*, less femininely fluent than in *Richard II.* In all the more dignified parts of the play it is as great in movement, music, pause and beat, as it is at any period of Shakespeare's life. He has now grasped and uses all the capabilities of his blank verse.

Not only is the verse developed, but the matter. The poetry is charged with thought, both human on life, and philosophic by intuition. There is scarcely a line in the graver scenes which does not give us pause for thinking, for questioning; which does not lift the veil from some

252

movement of the soul, represent some turn of passion, or some scene of transient or continuous meditation in the secret chambers of the spirit. And this is done not only for a few characters, but for a host of various men, whose thoughts, whose turns and moods of feeling, whose circumstances, have been first observed with the keenest interest and pleasure, and then recorded with an imagination, intelligence, and fineness of execution which is a constant and stimulating surprise. The execution is as fine as the observation is accurate. And there is added to all this that which great genius gives to its work—the personal spirit of the artist, which—proceeding from his silent conception and its attendant passion, and then from the outward form he has given to it—awakens and sets on fire the thought, imagination, and passion of the reader; and continues to do this from generation to generation, as if it belonged to eternity, and was itself of an eternal power. As long as the human race endures will the great poet thus impress himself upon men, and teach them to understand and to love one another. Shakespeare had now reached the fulness of that power. But it was not till he came to write the three lovely comedies, which followed *Henry IV.* and *V.*, and the mighty tragedies which followed those comedies, that he disclosed all that he could do with the fulness of that power.

There was a further development which regards the historical plays alone. Shakespeare in *Richard III.* followed his Chronicles step by step. He did not reorganise the events for the sake of his drama with any artistic purpose. He bound himself down to the history, and shackled, so far, his imagination. Nor, save in one little scene in the streets (where he brought three London citizens together to talk of politics), did he pass in these Richard plays out of the circle of king and nobles, queens and princes, into other and lower scenes of human life. Nor does his work touch the common people, save in the garden scene in *Richard II.* He does not go outside of his Chronicle.

But in *Richard II.* there is a change. In the development of Richard's character he does pass out of fact into bold invention. We know nothing from history of Richard emerging from the weakness and folly of a luxurious and light-minded King into a quiet steadiness and courage as he drew near to death; nor have we any knowledge of his change into one whom we may call a wildered poet. The addition of impassioned poetic utterance to Richard the Second is a pure invention of Shakespeare's, and was done out of his own soul placing itself with poetic passion into Richard's character and circumstance. And the result is that this little King in whom the Muse of History takes but small interest, is made one of the most attractive characters in the history of England; attractive not so much in himself, as in the problems of human nature which from his development by Shakespeare arise for explanation.

Shakespeare had then begun to shake off the fetters of history. In *King John*, the next historical play, Shakespeare went further in this self-emancipation. He makes events and persons bow to his dramatic conception. He treats historical facts just as it pleases him as an artist to treat them. He makes persons alive who were dead, and those who were alive dead. He changes the age of Arthur. He laughs at the limits of time and place. What I wish, he seems to say, things to be for my artistic purpose, they shall be,—and they are. Nevertheless, in *King John*, we are still wholly involved in the upper ranges of society and its many varieties. In only one scene does he break away for a few moments from the 'nobility.' The tale of Falconbridge, of his mother and brother, before he joins the court, touches the country life of England.

Then comes *Henry IV*. In that play he is no longer, as in *King John*, reckless about historical fact. He clings quite fairly to the truth, though for the sake of his artistic contrast he makes Hotspur and the Prince of the same age. He emancipates himself from ' annalism ' in a different way. The slight touches we have had of men other than kings, barons, and legates, now develop into the creation of human life as it exists in the country, in the town, and in the camp. We are brought from the council chamber, where great princes, barons, bishops, and kings arrange affairs of State, to the Boar's Head Tavern, where Falstaff swills his sack with his train of drunken followers ; among ostlers and drawers and travelling chapmen, and thieves and harlots and discharged soldiers and watchmen. We are at home with the foolish and tender Hostess of the Inn, and we take pleasure, for the sake of Falstaff's wit, in scenes of low frolic and brawling. We are transferred from Gadshill to the wild north-country, where the rebels set their forces in array and the Welshmen join the conspiracy. We touch the Scot in the Douglas, and the Celt in Glendower. We walk among the common soldiers, and hear their views of war and kings. We move among the captains and lieutenants. We are carried into the rustic life of the hamlets. We see the country magistrates and their sports and their foolish ways; the ploughman, the cobbler, and the tradesman of the village; the starving beggars in rags whom Falstaff enlists. A host of names, not represented as characters in the play, are on the lips of the waiters and ostlers in London, in the talk of the squires and peasants of the village, and each of them is so touched in description that we seem to know them. The range over human life is indefinitely extended. Shakespeare uses all the experience of his early days in the streets of London, and of his earlier life in the country about Stratford, to animate his play, to vary its representation of life, and to amuse his audience. He crowds this common life with incident, with characters, with thought set in action—and over all Falstaff presides, as much the king of this low whirl of humanity as Henry is of the court and the battlefield.

It must have given Shakespeare the greatest pleasure when he threw off all the solemn restraints of history, and betook himself to pure invention ; when there opened out before his eager imagination the streets of the city, the plains and villages of the country, filled with the daily life of England. With what eagerness he used his power we may see in the creation of Falstaff, that triumph of imaginative and executive genius. The artist who made him was swimming on the wave-crest of good-humour.

What Shakespeare (in thus adding common life to history) did for the ideal of true history was not realised by historians for some centuries. History continued to be for a long time only a narration of what courts and governments and policy did in war and peace. Only lately have some historians begun to realise that the doings, thoughts, and daily life of the burgher and the working-classes and of the poor of the country itself; of their ways and speech; above all, what the literature of England was and made, were also history, and not rarely more important history than the doings of states-men and armies. They might have learnt that lesson long before if they had only considered what Shakespeare has done in *Henry IV.* and *Henry V.*

The play can scarcely be called a regular drama. It is, but not so plainly as *Henry V.*, a dramatic representation in tableaux of a continuous series of events, taken from the latter years of Henry IV.'s life and ending with his death and the accession of his son to the throne. It has no plot, no central action, no invented complication

towards a determined end. The representations on the one
hand, of the political life of the realm, and, on the other, of
the low life of Windsor, Rochester, and London—of the
court and of the people—are not welded together, as they
should be in a regular drama. They are kept too separate
for that. The many unconnected scenes would leave the
drama without any unity, were it not for Prince Henry.
His figure, his character, moving through both these
representations of two kinds of life far apart from one
another, and moving through both with an equal ease,
links them and the play into a sort of unity. In all the
scenes the one figure of the Prince is seen dominant. In
a lesser way, Falstaff does the same kind of uniting work.
He is fallen into base living with thieves and good-for-
nothing fellows, drunkards, and ill-women, but he has been
page to John of Gaunt at the court; he is still admitted
to Windsor, to the company of the great earls at war; he
is still a captain of the common soldiery. He too, even in
his ruin, brings the separate parts of the drama together.
Otherwise there is no union between the classes and the
masses. We are not in a democratic country. In spite
of Shakespeare's effort, we are not. But we are, in the
play, in a country of Shakespeare's making, which is very
likely to become democratic. The people, even the lowest
of them, have got into history. This vague, half-realised
position of Shakespeare's mind towards the people is the
same in *Julius Cæsar* and in *Coriolanus*.

The play begins; the first person who speaks is the
King, and we understand in a moment what his life has
been since we left him in *Richard II.*

> So shaken as we are, so wan with care,
> Find we a time for frighted peace to pant.

England has been daubed with her own children's blood:
acquaintance, kindred and allies, in civil butchery, have

been opposed each to each. A pause at last has come, and the King is not now the quick, eager, ambitious, stirring Bolingbroke we knew in the play of *Richard II.*—untiring in ardour and craft, bearing into his manhood the strength and energy of youth. He is worn with war, troubled, longing for rest, doubtful of his right, scalded with thoughts of all that he has done against his conscience for ambition, sore with the thought of the slaughter he has brought on England.

What is his remedy? It is to join the crusade! A strange remedy! to heal the curse of war by joining a new war! These kings can never be quiet; they do not think of letting the land rest, of letting their soldiers beat their swords into ploughshares. When they think at all of the people, they think of them as fodder—the burgher for cash, the peasant for battle. The nobles think the same—anything to have fighting, to pursue their only profession. When the great barons were not at war with the foreigner, they went to war with the king or with one another. They had nothing else to do. Even civil war was better than rusting in their castles, bored to death. Therefore, it was the policy of kings to make enemies abroad, and to employ their nobles, under them, in war outside the kingdom. And if Henry could not make a fighting claim on France, he hurried his earls to the Crusades. And he hid, in this latter case, his policy under the mask of religion.

Henry makes his motive religious in words which have been quoted a thousand times—

> To chase these pagans in those holy fields
> Over whose acres walk'd those blessèd feet,
> Which fourteen hundred years ago were nail'd
> For our advantage on the bitter cross.

But his real motive was to employ his turbulent barons far from England—to make weak the elements of rebellion.

Weary he was, but Shakespeare knows that his politic craft is as active as it had been of old. However— and with this the drama begins—he was not to have his crusading consolation. News comes that in the north Percy has conquered the Douglas; but that he refuses to give up his prisoners to the King. That is, he and his father Northumberland attack the royal prerogative. Their message is almost a message of rebellion. Civil war is again at hand; there is no peace for the King. And on the top of this, the evil life of his son is brought home to him by the contrast between the riot and disorder of the Prince and the noble report of Hotspur's fame. The ✓ heart of the King and of the father is broken with sorrow.

On these two motives, his relation to the rebellion of the northern faction, and his relation to his son, the character of the King is developed by Shakespeare in this first part of the play. But, in order to complete the representation and to link the play back to that of *Richard II.*, the past character of Henry while he was yet Bolingbroke is carefully inserted into the drama by Shakespeare; and first, by the raging comment which Hotspur makes upon him. He is a king by murder, unjust, a canker in the state, a subtle, proud, vile poli- tician, a king of smiles, a fawning greyhound; one who has fooled, discarded, and shook off with jeering and disdained contempt those who sacrificed their honour to place him on the throne.

This is an enemy's view of his character. Hotspur backs it up, Act iv. Sc. 3, by a résumé of Bolingbroke's first arrival in England after his exile, in which again the subtle craft of the King is insisted on, his slow crawling into more and more of power. He seemed to weep

Over his country's wrongs ; and by this face,
This seeming brow of justice, did he win
The hearts of all that he did angle for ;

and then he turned on those who had uplifted him, broke oath on oath, and drove them from the court. Worcester adds to the picture, and speaks straight to the King's face. He has broken his oaths, treated them as the cuckoo treats the sparrow, till

> By unkind usage, dangerous countenance,
> And violation of all faith and troth

they have been forced into rebellion.

Craft and soft words to win his goal, hardness of heart to keep what he has won, are part of Shakespeare's character of the King; and now, in many a suggesting phrase, he adds to these elements a steady control of temper, which brings the King victory in the end, but which is an intense irritation to those enemies who, like Hotspur, cannot keep their temper. Then when the day is won, Henry is sketched as one who abandons with coolness those friends of the past who, even in small matters, now oppose his will. Moreover, he is as firm-fixed as a rock to keep what he has won, by craft if possible, if not, by fearless battle. Then he is made liable, in spite of his calm subtlety, to sudden impolitic rages, such as we have marked in the Bolingbroke of *Richard II.*, at any infringement of his privileges or his will. Yet, when the fury has broken out, he is able to repress his anger for the sake of policy, and now, in his old age, for the sake of bringing peace to his distracted and world-worn life. He turns to Worcester before the battle of Shrewsbury, and offers full forgiveness. This is a character much mingled, but which never wants for a firm and self-mastering will, driving all the King's powers to his chosen goal. Such is Henry painted by Shakespeare in the colours of his enemies.

But we are not left with that picture only. Shakespeare, with his infinite care to complete his drawing, makes Henry himself paint for his son his past career, and at the same time connect this play with that of *Richard II.*

' I was not, as you, my son, have made yourself, common-
hackneyed in the eyes of men, stale and cheap to vulgar
company ':

> But like a comet I was wonder'd at ;
> That men would tell their children 'This is he !'

He praises himself in contrast with Richard, but Shakespeare makes plain the contrast between the dissembling
of the King and the open boldness of the Prince. The
contrast is vivid; and there is something of the irony, of
Shakespeare in the King pressing upon his son the
imitation of that part of his character which was the chief
cause of his quarrels with the nobles, and in afterwards
advising him to be like Hotspur, whose character was the
very opposite at all points of that of the King. It really
reads as if, in his despair of his son, Henry did not know
what to say or to do. Then, in that interview of the third
Act, alone with his son, the King's craft fails him, or is
forgotten in his fatherhood. Shakespeare, in his love of
natural piety, brings into clearness the common emotions
of a father's heart, and we see the subtle King no more.
We forget, as we listen, the baseness of his politic play to
win and keep the crown, even while the words in which he
recommends such subtlety to his son are still in our ears.
That his tenderness should be foolish and bring tears to
his eyes, uplifts his character. Nor in the second part of
the play does Shakespeare cease to dwell on this. We
part in peace from Henry, because he loves. Then too,
and this adds dignity to his affection, he is jealous for his
son's honour. 'Think of what Percy has done, of the
fame he has already won. Think how I feel when I
hear of your low and fameless life, you who are my
dearest enemy and ought to be my dearest friend.' The
Prince answers he will so deal with Percy, if the King
will forgive, that all his honours shall be his; and Henry
in a burst of trust and joy, as natural then, as it is

generally apart from his cautious character, forgives, forgets, and is happy

> A hundred thousand rebels die in this :—
> Thou shalt have charge, and sovereign trust herein.

The whole scene is a piece of pure and subtilised nature— the very utterance of a king and a father.

Henry, dealing with the rebels, is quite different from this vision of himself as a father moved, below the crafty surface, by natural affection. He is bold, rough, peremptory, to Worcester, Hotspur, and Northumberland, dismisses them abruptly, will not even hear them; a king determined to be a king. In patience he has been smooth as oil. Now, wearied, patience has passed into impatient pride.

> Worcester, get thee gone ; for I do see
> Danger and disobedience in thine eye :
> O, sir, your presence is too bold and peremptory,
> And majesty might never yet endure
> The moody frontier of a servant brow.

This is his hot temper, jealous of his rights and privilege, and it lasts all through his interview in the first Act with Northumberland. He will not give a farthing to ransom Mortimer. 'Let him starve upon the barren mountains. He has revolted, let him die. You tell me he fought valiantly with Glendower. You belie him, Percy; he never fought; he durst as well have met the devil. Speak of him no more, and

> Send me your prisoners with the speediest means,
> Or you shall hear in such a kind from me
> As will displease you.'

A strong king—resolute to defy his barons, to open the gates of war; as fearless as he was crafty. Yet, when the battle is set in array, he offers the gentlest terms, unconditional pardon, kind consideration of their griefs. But his craft, and half-lying, and disloyalty to his word have been so great in the past that Worcester and Vernon cannot believe in his kindness or his truth. Wherefore, he is one of those men who, good on one side, and ill on another, finds his good rendered incapable by his ill, and his ill strengthened by his good. All his life is a weary war for want of resolving plainly to be all open-hearted or all crafty. Though he has won his power by solid will, and keeps it by the same solidity of will, the subtlety of the man, mixing itself with his will, enters into his policy and his conscience, and makes him waver at times in action; and this wavering prevents him from being understood. Men think they will get round his will, think that he is afraid, think that he does not know his own mind—and to rebel against him, and to conquer him, seems easy. It only seems so; Henry can always unsubtilise himself into resolute action.

Prince Henry is as finely delineated as his father, and is, perhaps, more interesting. The difference between them is so radical, that it is only at intervals that they meet in peace. The son separates himself from his father because he understands his father's character and is out of harmony with it. The father feels apart from the son because he does not understand his son's character. Then the King is old before his time, mustering his forces with difficulty to face his trouble, longing for peace; but the Prince is passionately young, unwearied as an eagle, and to rest seems to him to die. There is too great a space of feeling between him and his father for them to live together, save in time of war when in action they are united.

Such a young fellow would be bored by a court full of ceremony, alive with intrigue, with solemn persons about him like Westmoreland and Blunt. He might be driven into riot and folly—anything in which he might employ his surplus force, expend the torrent of his blood,

which, checked, would make him ill. And this is what
Shakespeare meant. If the Prince could not find legitimate means for this overflow of youthful blood in war,
he would disperse it by illegitimate means; and he
found these means in a life so low for a prince that all
the world wondered. But then the world did not know
the attractiveness of Falstaff to one who, like Prince
Henry, loved intelligence and wit, and loved them all the
more because they were so surprisingly bound up with
sensuality, drunkenness, and folly. This was just the
combination which would please a young man like
Henry, greedy of sensation in his youth. The high
ceremonial life of the court sickened his energies, and
wearied him to the marrow.

Some say he had no craft in the play, that nothing of
his father was in him. But that is unlikely. There
ought to be a shade at least of heredity in him; and
Shakespeare, who is often an hereditarian, does not forget
this. He marks it in the Prince's first soliloquy. Falstaff
has no sooner left him, Poins has no sooner induced him
to join in robbing the merchants, he has no sooner played
completely up to their rascality, than he speaks to himself:

> I know you all, and will awhile uphold
> The unyoked humour of your idleness ;
> Yet herein will I imitate the sun,
> Who doth permit the base contagious clouds
> To smother up his beauty from the world,
> That, when he please again to be himself,
> Being wanted, he may be more wonder'd at,
> By breaking through the foul and ugly mists
> Of vapours that did seem to strangle him.
> If all the year were playing holidays,
> To sport would be as tedious as to work ;
> But when they seldom come, they wish'd for come,
> And nothing pleaseth but rare accidents.
> So when this loose behaviour I throw off
> And pay the debt I never promised,
> By how much better than my word I am,
> By so much shall I falsify men's hopes ;

And like bright metal on a sullen ground,
My reformation, glittering o'er my fault,
Shall show more goodly and attract more eyes
Than that which have no foil to set it off.
I 'll so offend, to make offence a skill ;
Redeeming time when men think least I will.

This is crafty enough. He has already settled his aim in
life beyond these follies, and with all the cool deliberation
of his father. He wears disorder on the surface; below,
all is planned. Meanwhile he will have his amusement—
the 'rare accidents of life' which please and satisfy his
youthful blood. He takes that amusement strangely, and
in a society so far removed from that of his rank and
breeding, that it seems as if he desired to wash every
memory of them out of his mind. And he does this well,
with his native eagerness, quite as if he enjoyed it greatly.
He makes himself at home with Mrs. Quickly and Poins
and the servants of the Inn. Put him anywhere and he
flings himself into the heart of the situation—a drinking
bout with Falstaff, or the battlefield at Shrewsbury. This
pliant activity of youth is matched with an intelligence
as quick and pliant. He can speak on the cares of the
kingdom with his father, in counsel with his fellow-nobles
concerning the war, and with equal ease and mastery in
a low public-house among riotous thieves and drunkards.
He loves to match himself in a battle of wits with
Falstaff, and he is often as quick and witty as Falstaff.
His intelligence is flashing, and he companies with Falstaff
for the sake of his intelligence.

But this was only half the man. When legitimate
means for the using of youthful energy were afforded him
by war, Shakespeare sends him into it like a fire into a
dry wood. All his folly is as if it had never been. The
companion of Falstaff gives way to Prince Henry; and it
is the real Henry whom we meet, the chivalric, courteous,
quick-fighting, resolute, intelligent, grave-considering

young knight, from plume to spur one star of battle, the
victor of Agincourt in the flush of his youth. Shakespeare marks this by the vividness of his description—

> I saw young Harry, with his beaver on,
> His cuisses on his thighs, gallantly arm'd,
> Rise from the ground like feather'd Mercury,
> And vaulted with such ease into his seat,
> As if an angel dropp'd down from the clouds,
> To turn and wind a fiery Pegasus,
> And witch the world with noble horsemanship.

He rescues his father in the battle and slays his rival
Percy. Who is more gallant, more at home in war? His
courtesy, as a chivalrous knight, is as great as his courage
and skill in arms; and his courage and skill are as
strange and wonderful to his foes and friends as
his riotous life had been. His challenge to Percy
is couched in words so gracious, modest, honourable,
so full of his enemy's praise, that Vernon who heard it
told Percy that England did never wear so sweet a hope
as it had in Harry, Prince of Wales. To read the challenge,
Act v. Sc. 2, and to read Vernon's report of the challenge,
is to understand what Shakespeare meant Henry to be
below his mask. Nor does he yet—in this first part—
leave his picture without a further touch. When we hear
him, over the corpse of his foe, bid him farewell, we are
made to feel how much serious observation of life, how
grave a consideration of it, lay underneath the outside of
the man who rioted with Falstaff and his crew.[1]

> Fare thee well, great heart!
> Ill-weaved ambition, how much art thou shrunk!
> When that this body did contain a spirit,
> A kingdom for it was too small a bound;
> But now two paces of the vilest earth
> Is room enough: this earth that bears thee dead
> Bears not alive so stout a gentleman.

---

[1] This impression is deepened by his farewell to Falstaff, whom he
supposes to be dead on the battlefield.

This is the picture, and it is hard to match it with the other Prince who plays the highwayman at Rochester.

At the root of both aspects of the man, and explaining both, is the effervescence of youth. In peace, when there is nothing to do, he will fling himself into folly that he may feel his life; in war, his name is chivalry. He is an outsider in folly, he is an insider in war. Nor does he ever forget, even in his worse rioting, much less in the wars, his kingship near at hand. He knows exactly what he will do. Within the wild youth there is a steady, determined, almost an icy will; a cool prudence, an experience of men stored up for use, a self-knowledge and self-control, which are at all points so strangely different from the qualities he has shown to the world, that, when they emerge, they surprise all men of his own class into admiration and delight.

This is Shakespeare's conception of the man, whom he will complete in *Henry V.*, and from point to point of this play he marks it carefully, till the hour when the transformation takes place, and the play is ended. With what judgment, with what an equal pencil, he draws this picture, I need not describe.

It is with some pleasure that we turn from Henry to Hotspur. They are set in knightly contrast. At the beginning the King compares the warlike fame of Percy with the unwarlike riot of the Prince. But the Prince proves that he is a better warrior than Percy, and that comparison ends. The real contrast is in character. We turn, I have said, with some pleasure from Henry to Percy, because, conscious of the cold prudence of the Prince hidden under his imprudent life, we are glad to company with a bold, frank, hot-tempered, reckless, true-speaking creature like Hotspur, who has no craft in him at all. For a time we are pleased, but, when we have been Percy's comrade for a little, and find no foresight in him, no self-control, no thought, no use of experience, no judgment; only animal courage, passion for fame, chivalrous joy in battle, little thought for others, even for his wife; small respect for his elders, the intelligence of a fighting-cock alone, a courtesy which is lost at once when he is bored, as he is with Glendower—we begin to lose something of our pleasure. He is not much more than a great-couraged, warm-blooded noble, with a furious temper, and an inordinate self-consideration; wholly incapable of leading men or keeping them together. Had he come to England's throne as the King wished, he had never united the barons, or won the field at Agincourt. There are only a few men like the Prince in an army, who have equal intelligence and bravery, craft and frankness. There are hundreds of men like Percy; men of the greatest use in battle when they are well led, and forced to be obedient to leaders; but who, when they lead, destroy armies, irritate their men, and lose campaigns. That is the real contrast Shakespeare made; and I think he deliberately exaggerated a little his picture of Hotspur. It is just as well that the character should be, as it were, idealised. Its faults will then be clear, as well as its excellences.

Hotspur first appears in that famous speech where he describes his irritation at meeting a court fop on the field of battle; but we have heard before of his warrior-fame. His defence of Mortimer is full of a soldier's passion, and a soldier's friendship, audacious in its contradiction of the King. And he lashes even the quietude of the King into anger. When the King leaves the room, having demanded Hotspur's prisoners—

> An if the devil come and roar for them,
> I will not send them : I will after straight
> And tell him so ; for I will ease my heart,
> Albeit I make a hazard of my head.

NORTH. What ! drunk with choler ? stay and pause a while :
Here comes your uncle.

Neither his uncle nor his father can bring prudence to lower his anger. He mocks and scorns the King. He will have vengeance on him. Then his uncle speaks of a plot with danger in it. The word danger changes his swift mood. 'Danger! danger! that is mine—danger brings honour with it; all for honour!' And he is as wild in speech for honour as he has been for anger—

> By heaven, methinks, it were an easy leap,
> To pluck bright honour from the pale-faced moon,
> Or dive into the bottom of the deep,
> Where fathom-line could never touch the ground,
> And pluck up drowned honour by the locks;

An instant passes and he leaves that cry, and shouts a new defiance to the King. Absorbed in his fighting wrath, he listens to nothing his elders say, nothing

> Save how to gall and pinch this Bolingbroke.

Northumberland, his father, is puffed away by him, but marks his folly with some scorn—

> Imagination of some great exploit
> Drives him beyond the bounds of patience.

Worcester bids him farewell till he can control himself and listen. His father cries out upon him—

> Why, what a wasp-stung and impatient fool
> Art thou to break into this woman's mood,
> Tying thine ear to no tongue but thine own!

At last, he listens, but as he hears of the conspiracy, he imagines it is already brought to its close. Before the game's afoot, he lets slip the hounds upon it. This is not the man to match himself with the cool and foreseeing King, with the concealed wisdom of the Prince.

All for war, nothing for policy, is Hotspur. He dreams of battle till the sweat stands on his brow. He starts when he sits alone. He murmurs tales of iron war. His wife speaks to him; he does not listen, but calls his servants to bring his horse. She asks him if he love her.

' Away,' he cries, ' away, you trifler!—Love ? I love thee not.
When I'm on horseback I'll swear I love thee infinitely.'
He mocks her, but with good humour—

> constant you are,
> But yet a woman : and for secrecy,
> No lady closer ; for I well believe
> Thou wilt not utter what thou dost not know ;
> And so far will I trust thee, gentle Kate.

Then he is brought face to face with Glendower, the
wizard Welshman. He is infinitely bored with his
pretensions to magic, with his poetic phraseology, with
his music. He meets the magical business as Huxley
would have met a spiritualist. When Glendower says he
framed to the harp many an English ditty lovely well,
and that Hotspur never had this virtue ; he answers, as
good scorners of poetry answer—

> And I am glad of it with all my heart :
> I had rather be a kitten and cry mew
> Than one of these same metre ballad-mongers.

Nothing sets my teeth on edge so much as mincing
poetry. As to the skimble-skamble stuff Glendower talks
for hours about Merlin and the prophecies, dragons and
griffins, couching lions and rampant cats, and all the
devils' names that were his lackeys—I mark him not a
word.

> I had rather live
> With cheese and garlic in a windmill, far,
> Than feed on cates and have him talk to me
> In any summer-house in Christendom.

He puts Glendower, by this scornfulness and impatience,
past patience. Yet Glendower is a chief limb of his
enterprise, whom Prince Henry would have soothed and
flattered and made his own. And Worcester blames him
heavily for this ; and sums him up—

> You must needs learn, lord, to amend this fault ;
> Though sometimes it show greatness, courage, blood,—
> And that's the dearest grace it renders you,—
> Yet oftentimes it doth present harsh rage,

> Defect of manners, want of government,
> Pride, haughtiness, opinion, and disdain :
> The least of which haunting a nobleman
> Loseth men's hearts, and leaves behind a stain
> Upon the beauty of all parts besides,
> Beguiling them of commendation.
>
> HOT. Well, I am school'd : good manners be your speed !

Fit for fighting, fit for nothing else; yet he is lovable enough. When we meet him on the day of the fight, he is in his true element. War quiets him, and he speaks well and statelily.

> O gentlemen, the time of life is short !
> To spend that shortness basely were too long,
> If life did ride upon a dial's point,
> Still ending at the arrival of an hour.
> An if we live, we live to tread on kings ;
> If die, brave death, when princes die with us !

It is sorrow when this bold youthfulness meets death, and at the hand of his rival. Yet he leaves the world nobly, and a moment's thoughtfulness irradiates his unthinking soul in death.

> O, Harry, thou hast robb'd me of my youth !
> I better brook the loss of brittle life
> Than those proud titles thou hast won of me ;
> They wound my thoughts worse than thy sword my flesh :
> But thought's the slave of life, and life time's fool ;
> And time, that takes survey of all the world,
> Must have a stop. O, I could prophesy,
> But that the earthy and cold hand of death
> Lies on my tongue.

Only in death to look forward, to have only then the gift of prophecy, only then to live beyond the present, only then to feel that thought should master life, and life be not the fool of time—that was very pitiful. I wish he had fought at Agincourt.

At least, he had the courage of his opinions. Not so Northumberland, his father. He is another of Shakespeare's delineations of one who lets 'I dare not wait upon I would.' Perhaps the constant presence with him

of such a firebrand of impetuosity as his son slowly
drove him back into a cautiousness which bordered on
fear; and in this he is quite unlike his character in
Richard II. He was then strong, or seemed to be strong;
now he has grown into weakness. He goes to bed, sick
he says, and sends a sort of medical certificate, when he
ought to be in the rebel camp. 'He could not get his
friends together, the thing was dangerous, but do you,
my son, go on, and make the attempt.' This is the plea
of a man half-drugged with the fears of age. Percy is
indignant with his father, but it is a piece of his chivalry
that he defends his father before the world. But his
father's defection dismays the rebellion, and is its defeat.
This sketch of Shakespeare's, as we shall see, is worked
out afterwards into a complete picture.

Then there is Glendower. It is curious to read Shakespeare's little study of the Celt. I do not know whence he
derived his materials, but the representation is so remark-
ably apart from the English character, and so sharply
contrasted with Hotspur—the sturdy and contemptuous
Englishman of the North—that I imagine he amused
himself by clashing them together in Hotspur and
Glendower; exaggerating the dividing qualities of both,
or rather, making them exaggerate each his own national
qualities. Every word Glendower says irritates Hotspur
into scornful speech. Every word Hotspur says makes
Glendower feel that this Englishman thinks him a man
self-deceived, a fool to believe in himself, and—if not a
conscious, yet an unconscious liar. This apposition of
two national characters, each driven by the other into
angry opposition, is a curious thing to find. It is, as it
were, a picture-prophecy of English and Irish in contact
—each in extreme—even to the present day.

Glendower is full of pride, derived from his magic
power. He believes in his own magic. The heaven was

full of fiery shapes when he was born. Extraordinary signs have marked him from mankind. He can call spirits from the vasty deep. Then he has the Celtic eloquence concerning Nature. His talk is full of sounding adjectives, of phrases more fanciful than imaginative.

> The hour before the heavenly-harnessed team
> Begins his golden progress in the east.

He is a poet and a harpist; makes English ditties quite 'lovely and sleep-inducing.' He calls for music, and the musicians hang in the air a thousand leagues away, and come at his powerful word to please his guests. As I read, I seem to company with some Celtic persons I have known. And as I read Hotspur's answers I seem to company with rough squires, or scornful scientific English persons, whom also I have known. Shakespeare, in this dialogue, has brought into clash two temperaments which exist everywhere in opposition; and he has exaggerated both, I fancy, for his own amusement, and for ours.

HENRY IV

PART II

THE second part of *Henry IV.* (written 1598-9) opens at Warkworth Castle, 'this worm-eaten hold of ragged stone,' where the Earl of Northumberland is waiting for news of the battle of Shrewsbury. He, saving his skin, has deserted his brothers in rebellion, and been false to his son—'crafty-sick,' when he should have been sick of craft. It is curious how the whole set of those who of old accompanied Henry IV. are represented by Shakespeare as attracted by the King's example into craft as the guard and guide of life and policy. Northumberland practises it even on his own son who is the very antithesis of craft. Hotspur hates it, specially in his father.

Henry IV. combines a strong will with craft—a powerful combination; but Northumberland combines it with weakness of will, and ruins the rebellion by his vacillating fear. A flux of words charged with poetic sentiment is, in Shakespeare, one proof of weakness of character. He added it to Richard II., he adds it here to Northumberland. News comes to the Earl that his side has won the battle; then a vague report that it may be lost; and finally a clear report that his son is dead, Douglas taken, and his fellow-rebels executed. All through the scene, which is most dramatically managed, Northumberland unpacks his senile soul with words full of poetic illustrations. He is a master of metaphors.

> The times are wild ; contention, like a horse
> Full of high feeding, madly hath broke loose
> And bears down all before him.

When the messenger with bad news comes in, he is content with two metaphors—

> Yea, this man's brow, like to a title-leaf,
> Foretells the nature of a tragic volume :
> So looks the strond whereon the imperious flood
> Hath left a witness'd usurpation.

Again—

> Even such a man, so faint, so spiritless,
> So dull, so dead in look, so woe-begone,
> Drew Priam's curtain in the dead of night,
> And would have told him half his Troy was burn'd,
> But Priam found the fire ere he his tongue,
> And I my Percy's death ere thou report'st it.

Again—

> the first bringer of unwelcome news
> Hath but a losing office, and his tongue
> Sounds ever after as a sullen bell,
> Remember'd tolling a departed friend.

Then, when Northumberland hears the whole tale of ruin, he says he is like a fevered man who, impatient of his feeble fit, breaks like a fire out of his keeper's arms, and ' weakened with grief, is now enraged with grief.' Then his issue of words turns to violence of words. He shouts and cries; calls on Nature to upturn itself in sympathy with his sorrows. Feeble bluster is in every word. It is senility run riot.

> Let heaven kiss earth ! now let not Nature's hand
> Keep the wild flood confined ! let order die !
> And let this world no longer be a stage
> To feed contention in a lingering act ;
> But let one spirit of the first-born Cain
> Reign in all bosoms, that, each heart being set
> On bloody courses, the rude scene may end,
> And darkness be the burier of the dead !

No wonder Travers said when he heard this—

> This strained passion doth you wrong, my lord.

No wonder, after the exhaustion of this fruitless blether, Northumberland calmed down—and began to think of running away into safety.

His interview with Lady Percy, in the second Act, underlines all these weaknesses. He will go to the war he says; his honour drives him. But his son's wife, full of scorn, tells him he has already forfeited his honour when his son looked northward in vain for his father, and when he, the father, broke his word to his son. And when she says, 'Save yourself and us, there is no need to trouble about honour now,' he is at once persuaded and flies to Scotland—but he does not leave without his metaphor:

> 'Tis with my mind,
> As with the tide swell'd up unto his height,
> That makes a still-stand, running neither way.

When we hear this and all the other empty phrases made when acts were needed, we are ready to say with Hotspur

Nothing sets my teeth on edge so much as mincing poetry.

At last, this admirable sketch is closed by the contempt of the Archbishop of York acquainting the rebel lords that he has received letters from the Earl of Northumberland.

> Their cold intent, tenour and substance, thus:
> Here doth he wish his person, with such powers
> As might hold sortance with his quality,
> The which he could not levy; whereupon
> He is retired, to ripe his growing fortunes,
> To Scotland: and concludes in hearty prayers,
> That your attempts may overlive the hazard
> And fearful meeting of their opposite.

'Twere better he had died then than touched so deep a dishonour.

I turn to the King and the Prince. When we meet them again they are no longer at one as they were in the activities of war. The Prince, weary of the dull court, has again gone back to riot with Falstaff—and to his study of men; and the King is left without his eldest son to help his sorrows or share his care for England.

In the fifth scene, when he comes on the stage in his nightgown, we are shown his heart by Shakespeare. In a famous passage we hear his apostrophe to Sleep. 'Why dost thou fly the eyelids of a king and close the beggar's and the ship-boy's eyes?' It is too long to quote, but beauty and nobility meet in its poetry. As we read it we think with pity how tired the strong man has become; how changed from the Bolingbroke of old! He is like his father Gaunt, when Gaunt, worn with life, laid himself down to die. Did he think, as he spoke, of the days when he met his father's cool philosophy with a young man's passion? Did he picture himself and his son, who was now as fiery as he had been of old? All that he asks now of life is rest; and rest he cannot have, save the rest of death. And then his thoughts turn from himself to his kingdom, and to its fate when he is dead and his wild son succeeds him. He speaks of this to Warwick and Surrey; he recalls the far-off days, and Richard's unhappy fall, and the civil fates that followed, and the prophecy Richard made of old that Northumberland would break up his league with him and divide the kingdom into war. 'O God!' he cries, 'had I but known then all the peril, all the trouble, all the blows of conscience, all the friendships broken, I had sooner died.' He puts this into words, full of his grave intelligence, full of that observation of natural law which one traces so often in Shakespeare. A geologist might use the words:

> O God! that one might read the book of fate,
> And see the revolution of the times
> Make mountains level, and the continent,
> Weary of solid firmness, melt itself
> Into the sea! and, other times, to see
> The beachy girdle of the ocean
> Too wide for Neptune's hips; how chances mock,
> And changes fill the cup of alteration
> With divers liquors. O, if this were seen,
> The happiest youth, viewing his progress through,
> What perils past, what crosses to ensue,
> Would shut the book, and sit him down and die.

Warwick does not answer this despondency. But he does answer the King's wonder at Richard's prophecy being true; and the answer reveals the philosophic atmosphere of the court which Prince Henry was bored with; and the philosophic thought which Shakespeare himself had begun to cherish in his work.

> There is a history in all men's lives,
> Figuring the nature of the times deceased ;
> The which observed, a man may prophesy,
> With a near aim, of the main chance of things
> As yet not come to life ; which in their seeds
> And weak beginnings lie intreasured.
> Such things become the hatch and brood of time.

The King does not care for the explanation, but something in the words rouses his brave spirit. The weakness of age and disease slips from him. His soul is, in its recesses, always strong. He is like his father Gaunt and his son in that. 'Are these things, then,' he cries, 'necessities? Then let us meet them like necessities'; and he turns to present war.

When we next meet the King, in this careful and delicate picture of him, the rebellion is at an end, and his thoughts are now wrapt round his son, and what will become of the kingdom when his son succeeds. He loves the boy who fought so well at Shrewsbury. And, moved by this inward love, he paints the Prince in brighter colours; he is gracious, says the King, if he be observed—

> He hath a tear for pity, and a hand
> Open as day for melting charity :
> Yet, notwithstanding, being incensed, he's flint ;
> As humorous as winter, and as sudden
> As flaws congealèd in the spring of day.
> His temper, therefore, must be well observed :
> Chide him for faults, and do it reverently,
> When you perceive his blood inclined to mirth ;
> But, being moody, give him line and scope,
> Till that his passions, like a whale on ground,
> Confound themselves with working.

Could any lines show clearer understanding of what was
on the surface of the Prince, and clearer misunderstanding
of the depths of his character? Yet, he has little hope.
O what, he thinks, will not England suffer from my son!
Warwick sees more clearly. The Prince, he says, is
studying humanity. He is like a man who, learning a
strange tongue, must needs learn the grossest words as
well as the best, that he may know the whole of the
language; but, having known them, he will not use
them; he will even hate them.

> So, like gross terms,
> The prince will in the perfectness of time
> Cast off his followers;

but he will know mankind, its evil as well as its good;
and will love the good the more, measuring it by the
evil he has seen. This excuse then is invented by
Shakespeare for the riotous life of the Prince. He is
studying—for use as a king—all sides of human nature.
And if Shakespeare himself had been accused, as he was,
of having lived as riotous a life as the Prince, that is the
excuse he would have made: 'I have studied man.'

While the King and Warwick thus speak, Westmoreland enters with the news that peace is full in England.
It is too late a boon to save the King; the hand of death
is at his heart. The phrase in which he tells his friends
that good news is too late for him is so poetic on the lips
of this grave King, that it seems as if coming death had
changed the practical into the imaginative man. When
the soul is close to departure, its imaginative powers
break through the crust and begin to show what they
will be. These words are strange in the mouth of the
King, as strange as his apostrophe to Sleep—

> O Westmoreland, thou art a summer bird,
> Which ever in the haunch of winter sings
> The lifting up of day.

The King faints, and Clarence cries—

> The incessant care and labour of his mind
> Hath wrought the mure, that should confine it in,
> So thin, that life looks through and will break out.

And now Shakespeare brings the father and son to understand one another. In life they never could have seen each the other's heart. Their two temperaments were like flint and steel; when they met sparks flew and fire blazed. But when death took all the fire from the flint, and these two knew they could never meet again, the lovingness in both brought them together. It is a famous scene, and the mingling in it of their personal lovingness and of their political craft—so natural to both of them—is done with a delightful skill by Shakespeare. They are quite affectionate, and quite worldly minded. And indeed they were bound to be men of the world. Their kingdom was in mortal danger. Their path needed the wariest, the craftiest walking. And whatever their differences were—one thing was first with both of them—they were determined, at all costs, to secure their crown. On the means for that aim, the end of their last talk turns exclusively. They see one another clearly, in this last lonely converse; and it marks Shakespeare's careful art that even in the pity and pathos of this scene he is not led away by the sentiment of the moment to ignore the worldly craft in which their characters are at one.

At another point also he brings them together. Both are sorely troubled by the cares, the demands, the unrest of Kingship. This underlies the King's life; it kills him in the end. The Prince's apostrophe to the crown in this scene, his accusation of it as the murderer of his father, dwell on the same thought. He is full of it in *Henry V.* before the battle of Agincourt. The Prince, however, is able for the strife, and assumes, with steadfast resolution, the crown and all its troubles. The King puts by the crown, unable for its cares. He is old, the Prince is young. Nevertheless—for all the fire of youth—the Prince feels the burden of imperial duties. He is not the character to fling them to the dogs of riot, as Falstaff thinks he is. They press him into action, but when the image of the long stress and pain of kingship steals in this quiet hour on his imagination, the desire of rest, the comfort of sleep, steal also into his thoughts. What his father feels in reality, he feels in prophetic fancy. Hence it is that Shakespeare has brought them both together very graciously in a common invocation to sleep, in the contrast they both make between the sleeplessness of a King and the unbroken rest of the peasant. I quote the Prince's soliloquy as he sits by the bed of the dying King. It repeats the motive of the King's soliloquy in the previous Act; and, at the same time, Shakespeare develops in it not only the tenderness but also the royal pride of the Prince's character—

> Why doth the crown lie there upon his pillow,
> Being so troublesome a bedfellow ?
> O polish'd perturbation ! golden care !
> That keep'st the ports of slumber open wide
> To many a watchful night ! Sleep with it now !
> Yet not so sound and half so deeply sweet
> As he whose brow with homely biggen bound
> Snores out the watch of night. O majesty !
> When thou dost pinch thy bearer, thou dost sit
> Like a rich armour worn in heat of day,
> That scalds with safety. By his gates of breath
> There lies a downy feather which stirs not :
> Did he suspire, that light and weightless down
> Perforce must move.
>   My gracious lord ! my father !
> This sleep is sound indeed ; this is a sleep,
> That from this golden rigol hath divorced
> So many English kings.
>   Thy due from me
> Is tears and heavy sorrows of the blood,
> Which nature, love, and filial tenderness,
> Shall, O dear father, pay thee plenteously :

My due from thee is this imperial crown,
Which, as immediate from thy place and blood,
Derives itself to me.   Lo, here it sits,
Which God shall guard : and put the whole world's strength
Into one giant arm, it shall not force
This lineal honour from me ; this from thee
Will I to mine leave, as 'tis left to me.

[*Exit with the crown.*

The King wakes, asks for the crown, and thinks the
Prince has, in his greed for it, not waited for his father's
death—

I stay too long for thee, I weary thee.

It is a difficult conversation to invent, and it is wonderful
with what ease Shakespeare invents it.   The things said
are worthy of kings and men.   From point to point the
harmonising explanation slips with ease.

It satisfies the soul that the King and Prince are brought
together in natural affection.   It satisfies the civic feeling
in us that they are both anxious for the welfare of the
kingdom.   Then, his mind at rest about his son—so far at
peace—the old King dies ; and we part from Henry IV. as
we part from most of Shakespeare's characters, forgiving
all, seeing his good rather than his wrong, content that he
should pass away in quiet.

Meanwhile, away in Gloucestershire, far from these
high arguments of royalties, our great magician opens the
doors of the country life and of its rustic indwellers.   We
see the village among the low hills, and the sloping fields
where the sower is flinging the red wheat, Shallow's
orchard and the arbour, the pigeons in the air, the hens
in the meadow, the smith at his forge, Hinckley Fair and
the carrier, honest Clement Perkes o' the hill, and that
knave Visor whom Davy, Shallow's servant, supports
against the honest man.

And there is Justice Shallow and Justice Silence, and
Falstaff is their guest.   And the servants have absorbed

their masters' foolish ways, and the masters have grown like their servants; all are fools together. The atmosphere and traditions of the village, centuries old; the juice of the common earth and its slow ways, have soaked into their characters, and they all think and feel in a similar way; but each with a difference. Shallow is a hospitable fool, with a flash or two of wisdom. His talk is all repetition, a bustling, self-important fool, but so good-natured that we do not regret his company. As to Justice Silence, he violates his name with babble. But then we only see him when he and Shallow, Bardolph, the Page, Davy and the servants are all drunk together; and Silence is jovial with songs, and he and Shallow are as merry as grigs. It is excellently well done and very harmonious.

We have seen them all before, and they are then sober. But they are more agreeable drunk than sober. These two Justices, both of them near seventy years old, talk of little else than their riotous dissipation when they were young in London and as foolish as they are now. Falstaff knew them then, and heartily despises them. Yet he is far worse than they. He was once a decent gentleman. And it is piteous to think of the page of the Duke of Gaunt and now of the drunken satyr planning to cheat his host, and fleecing the villagers pricked for the King's service. 'Tis a vivid, rustic episode, a picture flung into the midst of grave affairs. Shakespeare was remembering his Stratford days.

We pass from it to the great interests of London, to the transformation of Henry v. Once the Prince is King— having full room to develop himself—he carries out the plan, sketched in that first soliloquy, which, in his wildest pranks, he has never for a moment forgotten. All the trouble his brothers, his great lords, expect from his reign, he happily disappoints. He groups all the features of his change in his treatment of the Chief Justice whom he had struck on the bench and who committed him to prison; and the speeches of both these high gentlemen are worthy of them and of the occasion.

The speech of the King does not shirk the riotous past, but makes us conscious that he has always been the Prince. We feel, beneath his stately words, the self-knowledge, the self-command, the long thoughtfulness, the individual genius, the steadfastness of aim, which underlaid his wildest follies.

> And, princes all, believe me, I beseech you ;
> My father is gone wild into his grave,
> For in his tomb lie my affections ;
> And with his spirit sadly I survive,
> To mock the expectation of the world,
> To frustrate prophecies, and to raze out
> Rotten opinion, who hath writ me down
> After my seeming. The tide of blood in me
> Hath proudly flow'd in vanity till now :
> Now doth it turn, and ebb back to the sea,
> Where it shall mingle with the state of floods,
> And flow henceforth in formal majesty.

It seems hard that at his coronation he should publicly abandon Falstaff, and I wish the parting had been otherwise done. But Shakespeare's Henry was never soft-hearted; and it was amazingly insolent of Falstaff to meet the King before all his people at the solemnity of the coronation with 'God save thy Grace, King Hal; God save thee, my sweet boy.' No King could bear that impertinence! Yet, while he banished his old comrade, he provided him with a competence.

Who is not sorry for Falstaff? Yet Shakespeare has so lowered him of late by making him a mere cheat, the heartless robber of Shallow, that we look on his fall as justice. Yet, it is pitiful. 'The King has killed his heart' —and the grief of it, piling itself on his diseases, is the last stroke which kills the old rascal we have borne with and loved so long.

Falstaff is a pure invention of Shakespeare's, and from beginning to end he is never below, and often above, the high level of intelligence, wit, and clear self-consciousness on which he begins to live before us. In the most varied circumstances, at the Eastcheap inn, before the Chief Justice, in the London street, on the battlefield, at Shallow's house in Gloucestershire, with princes, thieves, great earls and harlots, with London street boys and with country justices, he is always the same brilliant naughtiness; the same observant, and self-observant human soul; the clear critic of humanity and the critic of himself; using all the weaknesses of mankind to minister to his own advantage, yet without doing any real injury, save by his example, to those he laughs with and plays upon. There's no malice in the man, no envy, hatred, injuriousness, no real rudeness or unkindness. He backbites no one but himself. We feel kindly to him, he is himself so kindly. Till we meet him in the *Merry Wives of Windsor*, where he is not himself, where his character lives on altogether a lower level, he is harsh to none of his followers. And, even though they are well acquainted with all his sensual follies and tricks, they admire and even love him. Bardolph, whose pimpled face and flaming nose Falstaff had laughed at a hundred times, cried out when he heard he was dead, with all a rogue's passion for his master, ' Would I were with him, wheresome'er he is, either in heaven or in hell.' ' Aye sure,' answers Mrs. Quickly, whom he had fleeced and abused, ' he 's not in hell; he 's in Arthur's bosom, if ever man went to Arthur's bosom.' There are but few respectable men who would get epitaphs so affectionate from their friends, and so appreciative. Even the Prince, who knew his naughtiness, speaks of him with kindness when he thought him dead—

What ! old acquaintance ! could not all this flesh
Keep in a little life ?   Poor Jack, farewell !
I could have better spar'd a better man.
O ! I should have a heavy miss of thee
If I were much in love with vanity.

It is this absence of malice in Falstaff, and of all the foul
companions of malice, this presence of a good-humoured
pleasurableness, which do not so much excuse, as veil,
his rascality and sensuality.   He tolerates and is tolerated.
He is more than tolerated; he is enjoyed.   He ministers
to the gaiety of the world, and that is good, even when
the gaiety is of that low kind which pleased the frequent-
ers of the Boar's Head.   For the world is not only sad
with good reason, and loves to be relieved a little of that
sadness; but it is also sentimentally sad, and for no good
reason—making a great deal more of its sorrows than it
need—and that it should be laughed out of this, even
by rogues like Falstaff, is not bad for its morals and
its progress.   Shakespeare, as we see in Falstaff and
Autolycus, had no dislike of the rogue, provided the rogue
had wit enough, with kindliness, to amuse the world,
and to sting its stupidity into some intelligence.   Yet,
the right balance is kept; he never canonised or white-
washed the rogue.   We are not likely to sugar over the
faults either of Autolycus or Falstaff because we are
pleased with their wit, good-humour, and self-enjoyment.

There is one fault, however, if Shakespeare allotted it
to Falstaff, would have spoilt his representation of the
man, and made him as contemptible as Parolles.   The
fault is cowardice, the fault which earned for Parolles
absolute contempt.   After the betrayal of his friends
this boaster makes through fear, he is ignored by every
one; he does not exist.   No such contempt attaches
itself to Falstaff.   We never despise, never ignore him.
He is blamed, rebuked, laughed at and with, but not
despised.   When we have finished the play, it does not

seem natural that Falstaff should be the coward he has
been represented 'to be upon the stage. He was not
eminently brave, but he faced danger when he was forced
to do it with the ordinary physical courage of a man,
and Shakespeare meant that to be part of his character.
Twice he seems to have meant otherwise—first, when at
the highway robbery near Rochester, Falstaff runs away
roaring from the Prince and Poins; and again, when
faced by Douglas on the field of Shrewsbury, he feigns
to be dead; and in both these cases the tradition of the
stage represents him as a trembling coward. In the first
instance, it is no wonder that he ran away. He was old,
enormously fat, and quite unable to face two young and
vigorous highwaymen. It was the best thing he could
do; and ordinary courage, which is all we can expect
from Falstaff, who is no hero, does not ask a man to be
fool enough to face overwhelming odds. And to back up
this view, neither the Prince nor Poins, when they discover
themselves and expose Falstaff's amusing boasts, mock at
him as a coward, but as an inconceivably audacious liar;
and once, when the Prince does touch on cowardice,
Falstaff, for the moment serious, answers, 'I'm not John
of Gaunt, your grandfather, but no coward, Hal!'

Then, when matched with 'that fiend Douglas,' he
feigns death, we must remember that again he was over-
matched, and that he was not such a hero as to love his
honour more than his life. He chose life before certain
death. It is not heroic, but it does not prove him to be
a coward, and all the more because he had no honour
to support. His honour he has laid by, when he fell into
bad living. He is frank enough about that; arguing out
the matter like the witty rascal he is.

Can honour set to a leg? No. Or an arm? No. Or take away the
grief of a wound? No. Honour hath no skill in surgery, then? No.
What is honour? A word. What is that word honour? Air. A trim

reckoning! Who hath it? he that died o' Wednesday. Doth he feel it? No. Doth he hear it? No. It is insensible then? Yea, to the dead. But will it not live with the living? No. Why? Detraction will not suffer it. Therefore I'll none of it: honour is a mere scutcheon: —And so ends my catechism.

Having then lost this reason for standing up to Douglas, we can scarcely call him a coward for living up to his principle, and preferring life to death. Yet, if he always did so, if he always shirked the fight, one might fairly call him coward. But Shakespeare does not make him shirk. He is appointed by the Prince captain of a charge of foot. One would not place a coward there. He takes his men into the thick of the battle where all are slain but three. Sir Richard Coleville, a brave knight, yields to him at once. None of the princes or knights after the battle charge him with cowardice. The Chief Justice speaks of the good service he did at Shrewsbury. On the whole, Shakespeare meant him to love life, to think discretion the better part of valour, but not to represent him as a coward.[1]

We must remember if we wish to think of Falstaff (as Shakespeare drew him), that he was originally a knight of good repute, known even on the Continent to fame, a man of birth, bred up at the court, a page to John of

---

[1] What I have said above concerning the alleged cowardice of Falstaff is partly taken from an *Essay on the Dramatic Character of Sir John Falstaff*, by Maurice Morgann. It was published in 1777. Its aim is to prove that Falstaff was not meant by Shakespeare to be a coward, but it also treats of his whole character, and incidentally and with great penetration of the genius of Shakespeare. There is not a better piece of Shakespearian criticism. The book is scarce, but is, I hear, to be reprinted. But when it was published, so strong was the opinion that Falstaff was meant by Shakespeare to be a coward, that every one laughed at it. Johnson, when he heard of it, said, 'I suppose the next thing will be to prove that Iago was a pattern of virtue.' The book proves that Falstaff was not the coward of the stage. It ends by proving its point too much. Falstaff had the common courage of the common man, but not of the honourable man. His degraded life had taken the impulse of honour out of his courage. A foul life he preferred to a noble death. He had no honour left to lose.

Gaunt, with whom he was allowed to joke; with an ability which would have fitted him for good service to the state, witty, and a gentleman. This ancient quality and honour of Falstaff now and again emerge in the play, to touch us with the pity of their loss. They emerge badly in his singular insolence to the Chief Justice, which the Chief would not have endured at all had Falstaff not once been of his society, and which Falstaff (had he been of the same rank as Bardolph) would not have dared to exercise. The same thing may be said of his gross familiarity with the Prince and with John of Lancaster. He is —though he is fallen—allowed the privilege of a. gentleman. That is a part of Shakespeare's presentation of him.

But he is a fallen gentleman. He has given way at every point to a sensual habit—a drunkard, a glutton, a liar, a licentious profligate; and, for means to indulge these coarse pleasures, a cheat and a robber. He is gross of body, diseased by vice, dependent on what he can get from others by flattery and dishonest practice. No means of getting money are dishonourable to him. It seems incredible that we should endure, much less like, the man. Yet, like the Prince, we enjoy him, at times we are fond of him. And we heartily forgive him all his faults—or rather we forget them. Why? Well, first, we only meet him on the stage; and underneath any disapproval of him lies our enjoyment of his pleasantry, his good humour, his good nature, his mellow wit, his gay way of taking life, his agility and cheerfulness of mind, his wild exaggeration of lying, the intense enjoyment he feels in his own wit, and in his power of twisting out of difficulties; his profound understanding of himself, his honest appreciation of all the faults of his character, even though he persuades himself, when he has confessed them in a soliloquy, that they are or resemble virtues. All this is quite delightful on the stage with the deceiving veil of representation thrown over it, 'and we give him,' as Morgann says, ' when the laugh is over, undeserved credit for the pleasure we enjoyed.'

Secondly, he has the courage of his situation. Most men would be ashamed of his condition, both of body and mind and purse: huge of body and diseased, sensual of mind, beggared of money. Most men would have sunk down into apathy or despondency or into a debtor's prison. But he is curiously active of body, always gay, and so persuasive and attractive that his creditors lend him money to pay themselves. When they do not, he cheats or steals, and enjoys this war against society. He defrauds in every direction. The government does not escape, nor the silly magistrates, any more than Mrs. Quickly or the travelling merchant. Such a man we are not bound to like in real life, but on the stage he amuses us. But the real thing we like in this naughty person is his courage; the way he uses all that is against him so that it is for him; the bold face with which he meets life; the long fight his gaiety makes against the drag down-ward of his vices and disease, till, at last, he can fight no more. We look back on him when he dies, and say with the Prince—

> Poor Jack, farewell !
> I could have better spar'd a better man.

Then, thirdly (no matter in how rude or immoral an envelope it is), we enjoy, provided it be not cruel or malicious, intellectual power, wit, quickness in fence; the power of changing front against an unsuspected difficulty, and, when driven into a corner, of eluding, evading, and escaping. Falstaff's brain is quicker than a fine fencer's sword. And with the quickness is a brilliancy which charms with its surprising turns of fancy, even of thought. When we contrast in our mind's eye this agility of mind with his enormous body, larding the earth, a new excite-

ment of dramatic pleasure is added to our sight and
hearing of Falstaff.

Then, lastly, Falstaff, when alone, commenting on himself and on the world, full of self-knowledge and of self-
excuse, exaggerating into excellences his vices for his
private amusement (as in his glorification of drinking
sherris), discussing with himself how much honour is
worth, and how much more worth is life in comparison
with it; chuckling over his cheating of the government,
and exaggerating its iniquity that he may laugh at his
own trickery and hug himself in his own pleasure, is as
amusing and attractive as he is when he is the penetrating commentator on persons like John of Lancaster and
Justice Shallow. He sees with keen insight into what is
foolish in them; he does not see their good; and he uses
whatever is foolish for his own purposes. It is well to read
these soliloquies together. He is his own painter, and his
brush is realistic. He has, like Iago, this habit of lonely
self-appreciation. But it is not always appreciation.
When he remembers the past when his life was worthy,
he is self-contemptuous, and his self-contempt makes
him despise others. Then when he has cried down all
the world and himself into a general scorn, and made
goodness and badness of equal importance, he gets back
into full satisfaction with himself. Any little pricks of
conscience or honour which may have disturbed him he
has got rid of by talking them out to himself; and he
drifts easily into thinking of himself as part of the
stream of things. 'I can't be otherwise. I am a part of
Nature, let Nature have her way. There are fools like
Shallow, and there are clever dogs like me, and if the
young dace be a bait for the old pike, I see no reason in the
law of nature but I may snap at him. But why argue
about these things? Let time shape, and there's an end.'

Thus, giving up any strife of the old goodness in him

against his sensual nature, he is wholly lost in his appetites; but he gets the advantage of his bold unrepentance. He does and says what he likes without shame. All he wants is gold that he may live his life of indulgence, and for that he lies unblushingly, and plumes himself on his lying so well. The real wonder of the man is that all his drink and lust have not injured his wits. He not only knows himself, but he knows men and women, and uses them when they are fools, or of his own degraded type. But the good or the honourable he cannot use; and the one person in the society he has made around him whom he never comprehends is the Prince. The deep-set, steadfast aims of Henry, the seriousness below the riotous exuberance, the certainty of being able to change when he comes to be King, never cross the mind of Falstaff. He thinks he will be first favourite of the new King; and this is the point where his wit—at last spoilt by his life—fails to see clearly. There is something pitiful in the assurance with which he carries Shallow away to London, crying out that the 'King is sick for his company, that the laws of England are at his commandment.' It is more pitiful still, when the King turns on his boon-companion, and will not know him—

I know thee not, old man, fall to thy prayers;

and sends him to the Fleet, and then to banishment on pain of death ten miles from his presence. This slays the old man who, in his kindly heart, loved the young Prince with whom he had for so long played the fool. He cannot bear the blow. He dies as the King leaves for France. It was like Shakespeare to gather pity round the dying man whom he had created; and in one word of Falstaff's old friend, Mrs. Quickly, he enshrines a crowd of piteous thoughts for our memory of Falstaff—

The King has killed his heart.

Nor did he leave him on his death-bed without images of innocent life, of childhood and the country life when he was a boy—so that we might feel, perhaps, that he would be pure and fresh again—

> 'A made a fiuer end, and went away, an it had been any christom child ; 'a parted even just between twelve and one, even at the turning o' the tide ; for after I saw him fumble with the sheets, and play with flowers, and smile upon his fiugers' ends, I knew there was but one way ; for his nose was as sharp as a pen, and 'a babbled of green fields.

Well, there are green fields, I trust, where he is gone, for surely he lives ; and he and his like, in those sweet pastures, are children again.

HENRY V

Henry V. is the natural conclusion of *Henry IV.*, and yet its spirit is quite different from that of its predecessor. We feel that Shakespeare was glad to emerge in it from English questions of statecraft, from civil wars and dissensions among the nobility, into one plain issue— a war with France, with which, as he wrote, he could sympathise more than he could with civil war; by which, though in an unjust war, the various parties in England (when Scroop, Cambridge, and Grey were executed) were united in one aim under one King. It had been difficult to give a full swing to his patriotic feeling, when he had to feel blame for both sides in the civil wars of Henry IV. It was not difficult now, but joyful, to let himself loose on the honour and greatness of England; and he has done it in this play. The play is a song, with trumpets, to the glory of England, and it is full to the brim not only with the exultation of the patriot, but also with the spirit of joy in the artist. This side of the play I state fully; but it was tempered and modified by thoughts of the immoral side of war.

Every one has said that it can scarcely be called a legitimate drama. It tries to be one, but it does not succeed. It begins dramatically; it introduces the low life of the town which Shakespeare had represented in *Henry IV.* in contrast with the grave council of the King, the Church and the nobles. But he drops this contrast after the first Act, and we are wholly involved in the

events of the war, told one after another in a series of
tableaux; the manner of which the elder Dumas imitated
for the stage in certain dramas about Napoleon and the
Revolution. Dramatic tableaux might be a fair definition
of *Henry V.*; and the insertion of a Chorus at the beginning of each Act, in which the history of what we are to
see is sketched, seems to support this definition.

The writer's aim is rather to describe action than to
present the souls of men in dialogue. He, being Shakespeare, does open to us the hearts of the speakers, but that
is not here his main object. His main object is to tell the
tale of a glorious hour in the history of England, of a great
battle won against gigantic odds by the heroism of his
people, and of a great War-Leader who in this hour of
terrible danger showed himself a hero; a great Englishman who redeemed the faults of his character by unyield-
ing courage in mortal danger, by trust in himself and in
his soldiers, and by intellectual war—the Clive of the
Middle Age of England.

In the first Chorus, where Shakespeare draws that flashing picture of the Monarch of War, in poetic menace and
splendour,

> Then should the warlike Harry, like himself,
> Assume the port of Mars ; and at his heels,
> Leash'd in like hounds, should famine, sword, and fire
> Crouch for employment,

he appeals to the audience to help him out with their
imagination. If you see one horseman, see a squadron; if
you look round on this cockpit, behold the vasty fields of
France; when you see the walls of this theatre, see England on one side, France on the other, and roll between
them the perilous narrow seas. When you listen, hear
kings speaking, soldiers chatting round the watchfires,
arrows hissing through the air, horses trampling in the
charge, the shouting of beleaguered towns, the noise of

defeat, the thanksgiving of the victors, the quietude of Peace.

What confidence Shakespeare, when he demanded this for his naked stage, had in his power to stir the creative imagination of his audience, to be the poet who bodies forth the shape of things not seen, who places the listener now in London, now in Paris, under the walls of Harfleur, on the field of Agincourt—in the space of a single hour ! And, indeed, what confidence also he had in his audience; what a full belief in their imaging power ! Everything that scenery can tell is now told to us. We call for 'spectacle' to help our jaded creativeness. But no scenery save a few boards was needed to make an Elizabethan audience see the dreadful fight at Agincourt.

I have said that Shakespeare, leaving with pleasure behind him the civil broils of the last reign, came with eagerness to tell of a King whom, at least in a great portion of the play, and in contrast with Henry iv., he represents as an open-hearted, bluff, plain-spoken, fighting King; and of a victory, not over brother Englishmen, but over a foreign foe. It is plain that he enjoyed this part of his task. He was not a fighter himself, but he who had lived with Essex, Raleigh, Sidney, Drake and Howard could not avoid the thrill of war, the leaping of his blood when he heard of the great deeds of England in past wars, against heavy odds; when, among the shouting crowd, he welcomed the news of the singeing of Philip's beard in Spain, or saw the ships of Drake and the adventurers come up the Thames with their bellies filled with the ill-got gold of Spain. This temper runs through all his historical plays, and rings on them like steel on steel. It is a temper which has never been otherwise than powerful, chiefly for good, sometimes for evil, in this realm of England.

It is mixed up with the temper of patriotism—that is,

the love of our country as our Mother and our Home;
our love of her Honour in the past; our faith in her as
the refuge of our children and of liberty in the future.
Our duty, indeed our passion, is to keep her national
traditions free for noble development, her indwellers free
from oppression, and her coasts free from the invader.
War for these duties and this love, war in defence of all
we hold dear, is part of a just patriotism; and all Shakespeare's set outbursts of patriotic feeling in the historical
plays, on the lips of Gaunt, Faulconbridge, Hereford, and
others, are directed to this aspect of patriotism—defence
of England against the foreigner—a view of love of
country which the attempt of the Armada must have
driven home to the heart of Shakespeare and of every
Englishman.

Nothing of this special emotion of patriotism could
have filled the soul of Shakespeare as he wrote this
play, for in it England was not invaded, but the invader.
She was, in war, doing the very thing to another nation,
which it was part of her high patriotism not to permit
being done to her. The war was a wicked because an
aggressive war; and its only result was to sow the dragon
seed of the wars in France, and of the renewed civil wars
in England, when punishment of it fell on the House of
Lancaster in direful ruin, and then on the House of York.
Shakespeare knew this well. He never forgets this woeful
aspect of the war he pictures.

In what way then could patriotism speak? How could
Shakespeare, in this play, exalt the glory of England,
when the war was, he knew, first unjust, and then
fatal?

Well, the natural, the inevitable feeling of the mass of
any people is to wish passionately that its folk may have
the better of its opponents. One might as well try to
push back the tidal wave as the swell of this national

emotion. It has the force of a natural law. Now and then, men to whom Justice is dearer than this desire for the victory of their people rise so far above nature as to wish that their countrymen should be beaten in battle. They are brushed away by the national passion of which I speak. Shakespeare shared in that passion. Whatever origin the war had, he wished his people to win. And *Henry V.* is full of that common excitement. It is not a lofty element in patriotism, but it is a natural and inevitable part of it.

Again, patriotism, when it is ill-married to the weakness of national vanity, gives birth to national contempts. Each nation, while extolling itself, laughs the other to scorn. This is natural enough, but it is a fruitful source of wrong and folly. It has been thought for centuries in England to be a part of patriotism. The spirit of Nelson's sailors was the spirit of Englishmen towards the French, from the days of Creçi almost to the present day. Shakespeare himself is guilty of it in his picture of the French Dauphin and nobles before the battle. He enhances the glory of England when he sets the boastful splashing of the French over against the modest steadfastness of the English. It is a piece of his patriotism, but not a wise or useful one.

The third element in this patriotism of war was the most natural, the most useful to the nation, and the most noble. It was founded on admiration and affection for those qualities in the English which, in moments of tremendous trial, against overwhelming odds, enable them to win the victory. The French at Agincourt were five times more numerous than the English. They were well fed, their army was in good trim. The English were half-starved, ill-clad, and in retreat. But they had great steadfastness, unfaltering courage, belief in their leaders, unquestioning obedience, discipline, and the modesty of brave men. With these they won the battle. To praise and be proud of such a victory, to remember it for ever as a national encouragement, an inspiring tradition; to keep up in a people the honour and practice of the high qualities that won it; to scorn death rather than be false to its spirit—that would be part of a true patriotism, and of its praise from generation to generation, even if the war in which it was proved was in its origin unjust or in its aim unworthy. For these are qualities which exist in a people, independently of the follies and greed of the rulers who have caused the war.

And it is on these deep-set, noble qualities in the nature of his countrymen that Shakespeare most dwells in this patriotic poem. He embodies them all in the King before and after that battle-day; for he knew the weight of a single representative figure. But he does not neglect to show them in the great gentlemen of the kingdom—in York and Suffolk, Exeter and Sir Thomas Erpingham; in the captains and officers like Fluellen, in Welsh and Scotch and Irish, united in war, if divided in peace; and in the common soldiers like John Bates, Alexander Court, and Michael Williams. Each, in his several character, represents those typical elements of the English character which won, against enormous odds, the fight at Agincourt.

Nowhere in the historical plays is Shakespeare greater than in this representation. Its note is struck in the first words Henry says on the morning of the battle—

> Gloucester, 'tis true we are in great danger ;
> The greater therefore should our courage be.

And then with a light humour of moralising (as if death at hand kindled a smiling courage), he proves there is a 'soul of goodness in things evil' because their bad

neighbours and their evil case had made them rise
early,

> Which is both healthful, and good husbandry.

Then, as Henry goes through his camp disguised, he meets
Fluellen, who dwells on the wakeful discipline of the
English army in contrast with the noisy carelessness of
the French—

> Gow.   Why, the enemy is loud ; you hear him all night.
> Flu.   If the enemy is an ass and a fool, and a prating coxcomb, is it
> meet, think you, that we should also, look you, be an ass, and a fool,
> and a prating coxcomb,—in your own conscience now ?
> Gow.   I will speak lower.
>
> .   .   .   .   .   .   "
>
> K. Hen.   Though it appear a little out of fashion,
>   There is much care and valour in this Welshman.

Then the soldiery, Bates and Court and Williams, discuss,
quite quietly, the rights and wrongs of war as it affects
them, but it never occurs to them to abandon their ranks,
fail in obedience, or shirk a battle where they look for
certain death.   The King comes on them, disguised.
Bates tells him that the King (whatever outward courage
he wears) would wish to be anywhere else.   No, answers
Henry—nowhere else than here.   And the soldiers chime
in with the King and accept the battle.

The nobles also know the danger, but they face it with
joy—

> Salis.   God's arm strike with us ! 'tis a fearful odds.
>   God be wi' you, princes all ; I 'll to my charge ;
>   If we no more meet till we meet in heaven,
>   Then, joyfully, my noble Lord of Bedford,
>   My dear Lord Gloucester, and my good Lord Exeter,
>   And my kind kinsman,—warriors all, adieu !

This is the temper in which the nobles, as the soldiers,
go, they think, to death ; and the temper in which they
die is told by Shakespeare with a lovely grace and tender-

ness when Suffolk and York kiss one another into heaven—

EXETER. Suffolk first died; and York, all haggled over,
Comes to him, where in gore he lay insteep'd,
And takes him by the beard; kisses the gashes
That bloodily did yawn upon his face;
And cries aloud, 'Tarry, dear cousin Suffolk!
My soul shall thine keep company to heaven;
Tarry, sweet soul, for mine, then fly abreast,
As in this glorious and well-foughten field
We kept together in our chivalry!'
Upon these words I came and cheer'd him up:
He smiled me in the face, raught me his hand,
And with a feeble gripe, says, 'Dear my lord,
Commend my service to my sovereign.'
So did he turn, and over Suffolk's neck
He threw his wounded arm, and kiss'd his lips;
And so espoused to death, with blood he seal'd
A testament of noble-ending love.

They are lines which rob the battlefield of its horror and plant it with heartsease. And in a thousand stories of the private soldier, as well as of the officer and the gentleman, the tale of York and Suffolk has been repeated; for, indeed, nowhere does the divine greatness and beauty of human nature bloom with more eternal tenderness than in the crimson furrows of war.

The splendour and national inspiration of such steadfast valour break forth in the words of Henry before the battle; and their spirit is the spirit which makes nations great in peace as well as in war. It issues, as a bright stream, from days of heavy battle; but it is not the spirit of mere fighting; it is not born of the false glory of war. It is in the soul of men; and to praise it and urge it into act deserves the name of patriotism. Shakespeare put that spirit on the lips of Henry, and touched it with a grave humility; and the noble words arose out of the spiritual depth of a patriot King's emotion, rejoicing in his people's character. So far he is the patriot of war; so far Henry is his hero.

But he does not leave the other side of war unrepresented, nor is his hero free from its evils. The war Henry waged with France was an unjust and cruel war; base also in its origin. Shakespeare does not shirk that aspect of it. He seems to have had a steady but prudent hatred of all war which sacrificed the people to the advantage of kites and crows, of kings and nobles. At least, I hold that to be the underdrift of the historical plays and of *Coriolanus*.

He represents the Church, the King, and the Palace clique as the sources of the war, and each acting for his own advantage. The play opens with a conversation between the Bishop of Ely and the Archbishop of Canterbury. It seems the Commons had brought forward a bill which would strip the Church of half its temporal lands, and bring the proceeds to the State. 'What is to be done?' they ask. 'Why, get round the King. He is a true lover of holy Church; he is miraculously changed; he can even reason in divinity. With regard to the bill itself he is, alas! indifferent. But he is not indifferent to war. If we can prove he has some claim of descent to heirships in France, he will let this bill alone, and take our part; and we will offer him an immense sum for the expenses of the war. Let us then get up the war, and save the temporalities of the Church.' This is the remarkable conduct of the Church; and the whole representation of the ecclesiastical hypocrisy and trickery of these mitred rascals is a masterpiece of sugared scorn and indignation.

Then the Archbishop, in council, proves to the King's satisfaction, and on the flimsiest ground, that Henry is the rightful heir to France; and urges war, bloody war. He paints the Black Prince at Creçi, how he foraged in blood of French nobility; he blows the trumpet of English fame and bids the King awake his blood and

courage. The men of England, he cries, long for the
battle. Take them to France,

> With blood, and sword, and fire, to win your right :
> In aid whereof, we of the spiritual'ty
> Will raise your highness such a mighty sum
> As never did the clergy at one time
> Bring in to any of your ancestors.

A vile Christian, but a good politician! Without one
thought of pity for the miseries war will bring on the
French and English people, without one prophetic glance
into the future, the Archbishop of the Christian Church
of England unleashes, for the sake of gain, famine, sword,
and fire, the three dark hounds of war; and then, when
he has got his wicked way, assumes the philosopher,
wears the statesman's air, and delivers that famous speech
which compares the divers functions of men in a kingdom
to the ordered polity of the bees. Shakespeare displays a
master-hypocrite. How far the tale is historically true, I
do not know. But that is his picture of the matter, and a
splendid piece of irony it is.

And now, how is the King made by Shakespeare to
behave in this question of war ? He also starts this bloody
business for the sake of policy, not for any just cause. He
fears the nobility and all the feuds left behind by his
father's seizure of the crown. War will occupy their
minds; they love war, and they shall have it. His father,
dying, recommended that.

> Therefore, my Harry,
> Be it thy course to busy giddy minds
> With foreign quarrels ; that action, hence borne out,
> May waste the memory of the former days.

And the last words of the play of *Henry IV.* show that the
new King, to secure his power, had already resolved on war
with France. I will lay odds, says Lancaster,

> that, ere this year expire,
> We bear our civil swords and native fire
> As far as France.   I heard a bird so sing,
> Whose music, to my thinking, pleased the king.

So, as Shakespeare puts it, the Archbishop of Canterbury knew the King's mind before he made his solemn argument; and the King's speech, warning the Archbishop not to let loose the dogs of war unless on the gravest ground, was really a piece of hypocrisy, spoken to play the part of a temperate, just, and thoughtful monarch, while all the time his craft had resolved on war.   This is what Shakespeare represents, and he disapproved of it.   He makes that clear by the subtle address to the Archbishop with which the King opens the council.   While the King speaks, he knows the Archbishop wants war, and he himself is resolved on war.   The whole passage is steeped in irony, and the last lines (again remembering that war was already settled on between them) are really Shakespeare's gird with bitter scorn at the Archbishop—

> Under this conjuration speak, my lord ;
> For we will hear, note and believe in heart
> That what you speak is in your conscience wash'd
> As pure as sin with baptism.

Nevertheless, the King in the midst of his crafty policy is supposed by Shakespeare to have something of a conscience. The Church is represented as having none at all.

Many think that Shakespeare painted Henry as the perfect king; as almost the perfect man.   I am surprised when I read that view.   Shakespeare sat far too close to fact to represent Henry as entirely noble.   He painted him as he was: the crafty politician, the steadfast, masterly leader of men; England's hero-warrior; merciful in peace, ruthless and resolute in war, mild to his own, fierce to his foes as long as they fought against him.   His speech to the burghers of Harfleur is the speech of one who will not spare, to get his ends, one jot of the horrors of war to a conquered town.

His soldiers, if the town does not yield, shall have their full and savage way with women and children and old men. When, in the year after Agincourt, at the siege of Rouen, the town turned out twelve thousand men, women and children who would have weakened the defence, Henry would not let them pass through his lines. These innocent defenceless folk, down to the helpless children, died of starvation. It is well to remember that story when this English king is exalted into a perfect character; and it was well that Shakespeare should ask his imagination what lay beneath the glory of war. He replied by recording its horrors, and he puts them into the mouth of Henry at several points in the play; and with a certain irony, for Henry has made the war for his own purposes. He records them even more clearly when Burgundy, at the end of the play, describes what France had suffered from the curse of war—

> What rub or what impediment there is,
> Why that the naked, poor and mangled Peace,
> Dear nurse of arts, plenties and joyful births,
> Should not in this best garden of the world,
> Our fertile France, put up her lovely visage?
> Alas, she hath from France too long been chased,
> And all her husbandry doth lie on heaps,
> Corrupting in its own fertility.
> Her vine, the merry cheerer of the heart,
> Unpruned dies; her hedges even-pleach'd,
> Like prisoners wildly overgrown with hair,
> Put forth disorder'd twigs; her fallow leas
> The darnel, hemlock, and rank fumitory
> Doth root upon, while that the coulter rusts
> That should deracinate such savagery;
> The even mead, that erst brought sweetly forth
> The freckled cowslip, burnet and green clover,
> Wanting the scythe, all uncorrected, rank,
> Conceives by idleness, and nothing teems
> But hateful docks, rough thistles, kecksies, burs,
> Losing both beauty and utility.

And as our vineyards, fallows, meads and hedges,
Defective in their natures, grow to wildness,
Even so our houses and ourselves and children
Have lost, or do not learn for want of time,
The sciences that should become our country ;
But grow like savages,—as soldiers will
That nothing do but meditate on blood,—
To swearing and stern looks, diffused attire
And everything that seems unnatural.
Which to reduce into our former favour
You are assembled : and my speech entreats
That I may know the let, why gentle Peace
Should not expel these inconveniences
And bless us with her former qualities.

The picture is pitiful, but it does not move Henry in the least from his unjust demand. He will have his pound of flesh—

If, Duke of Burgundy, you would have peace,
. . . you must buy that peace
With full accord to all our just demands ;

and the just demand is that he should be acknowledged as heir to the kingdom of France. This is to be the mere conqueror, not the hero. Two years afterwards he was dead, dead at the height of his conquering glory.

Where Shakespeare does make the King heroic, is in his conduct before and after the battle. He enforces discipline on his soldiers. He insists that all goods taken shall be paid for. He hangs those followers of his who steal from the churches or the country-folk, and poor Nym and Bardolph perish in that fashion. He will have mercy shown to the captives. As long as he is not in actual battle, he is temperate in counsel. And when he is brought to bay, when, as the great war-leader, he is face to face with almost certain defeat and death, his attitude is indeed heroic. The desperate situation brings out all his manhood, fortitude, courage, and goodness. He is gentle, good-humoured, wearing a face of joy like a man inspired, full of trust in himself and his men, almost looking for victory! He will not ask another man from England. Proud of his brave soldiers, he is humble before God in whom he trusts. 'Not in our hands,' he cries, 'O Lord, lies victory, but in thine.' The way God is used by priests and kings in war is as irritating as it is impertinent, but still to confess Him as master of history (and not ourselves as Shakespeare represents France doing), has at least some grace, some humility, and therefore a nobler war-temper than to confess no power but our own. In all this Shakespeare does draw a hero.

But, again, he does not leave this splendid picture without painting another, of his own proper invention, to balance its effect. The King, going in disguise through the camp, meets three of the common soldiers who are in arms for his cause, and know nothing about it. They question his responsibility. 'We are,' they say, 'the King's subjects. We know not why he brings us into battle. If his cause be wrong, our obedience to the King wipes the crime of it out of us. If the cause be not good, the King has a heavy reckoning to make. All the slain will testify against him at the judgment day.' The soldier suffers in obedience to the warring King. Let the King look to it that his cause is just, else he makes every soldier sin— and that may be a black reckoning for the King. Henry's answer is so sophistical that I see in it another example of Shakespeare's irony. But the King has listened, and is left alone to think on what he has heard. And in an hour of revelation, when he is alone with God and his soul, Shakespeare makes the King see what he really is; and what difference there is between him and the peasant he has made his soldier. Policy has slipped from him, kingship has left him, the fiery fever of the great captain of war is dead in his heart. He is only a man among men. He shows the same temper as he shows in his speech to his father on his death-bed, so closely does Shakespeare keep the unity of his characters. He continues the thought with which he was full when he began his talk with Bates and Will—

I think the king is but a man, as I am : the violet smells to him as it doth to me : the element shows to him as it doth to me : all his senses have but human conditions : his ceremonies laid by, in his nakedness he appears but a man, and though his affections are higher mounted than ours, yet, when they stoop, they stoop with the like wing.

It is a noble, thoughtful temper, full of humanity, of apartness from his self, but it creeps back into self-consideration. The sense of kingship and the resolution to keep the powers of a king, which he has forgotten at the beginning, rise to the surface towards the end of the soliloquy. Conscience and kingcraft, as often before, meet at the end of it again. The soliloquy is a grave piece of thoughtful poetry. It is Shakespeare's vision of the finer nature of the man within the trappings of the king. But see how it ends—with a piece of self-deceit! 'The peasant,' Henry says, 'sleeps at ease, the king wakes; the peasant has the vantage of the king, but he little knows

What watch the king keeps to maintain the peace,
Whose hours the peasant most advantages.'

Yet, it was not peace that Henry had maintained, but war.

It is always a new wonder how close Shakespeare is to human nature. He knew that a man, after a shock of conscience, will, by the very confession of his wrong and weakness, induce forgetfulness of the weakness and the wrong, and even glide back into believing that his weakness has been strength, and his wrong right. It is another wonder that Shakespeare—seeing so clearly into the poor stuff of which we, and even heroes, are made,

realising the immense force of our self-deceit—should yet
have a great reverence left for human nature, should
forgive it so bounteously, and take in it such brave,
serious, and heartfelt pleasure. It is this sane, bright-
eyed, tolerant, almost divine way of seeing humanity
which gives him at least a fourth of his power over mankind. To say this is not here out of place, because it is in
this play that Shakespeare expresses (in a grave mirthful-
ness on the lips of the King) one of the roots of his own
thinking—

> There is some soul of goodness in things evil,
> Would men observingly distil it out.

I may say one word more on this representation of the
'for and against' of war. It was a habit, almost a trick,
of Shakespeare's to parody—sometimes for the sake of
humour, sometimes to strengthen a main issue of thought
or action—the doings of the great by the doings of the
common folk. He has done this, for example, in *Richard
III.*, in *Coriolanus*, and in the *Tempest*. Here, in the
ridiculous dialogue between Pistol and his French
prisoner, the action and the motives of Henry's invasion
of France are parodied. The greed of the King is echoed
by the greed of Pistol. The war is a bandit's war.
Pistol will have his ransom of two hundred crowns; if
not, death to his captive. Henry will have the whole of
France; if not, France shall perish.

Yet, while we have all these contrasted issues of the
war-question presented to us, one thing remains supreme
—the uplifting passion with which Shakespeare remembered and praised the mighty deed of Agincourt;
the spiritual glory of facing with hope and valiancy of
heart enormous odds, for the sake of the ideals and
memories of England. That rings through the whole
play, and it still rings in our hearts. The splendid war-
chorus at the beginning of the fourth Act tells us, with

uplifted passion, how Shakespeare felt when he looked back on the days of England's steadfastness and valour; how he felt when he heard the news of the great sea-fight in the narrow seas against the boasting odds of the Armada.

And now, as we look back on this treatment in art and by the artist-imagination of the question of war and the glory of war—not treated in a discussion, not from the point of view either of morality or philosophy or even of philanthropy, but embodied and explained by the art-creation of men of different types who, with no conscious reference to that question, nevertheless set it forth in different lights by speaking as their characters, their place in life, their interests and circumstances urge them —are we not amazed with the extraordinary balance of the poet's judgment? Some have seen nothing in this play but what we should vulgarly call Jingoism. They must be blind, or only read the Act in which Agincourt is fought. Yet, even in that Act, how much is said against the temper of the Jingo! The whole representation of war, by Shakespeare, is a miracle of quiet, temperate, austere judgment. A just and equal hand holds the balance.

Let me briefly repeat the representation. On one side, he reveals, with irony, the picture of a ruthless war waged for a cause not just, but unjust; set on foot, not for defence but for aggression; begun not even for glory, but for selfish policy; and the judgment is a condemnation. But, on the other side, he paints another picture. In the course of the war the King and his English are at death's door, devoid of all things but the courage of the soul, but love of the honour of England. Their King is great-minded, and so are they, in this overmastering hour, in which all that makes the heart of England great is tried to the uttermost. And Shakespeare, while he does not

forget the wrongs of the war, feels the magnificence and
magnanimity of this, records it in words which shall
never be forgotten, himself thrills with it, and thrills his
readers, and sends its glory down to us, to inspire our
valour, our steadfastness, and our love of the noble soul
of England.   For it was the soul which conquered at
Agincourt.

This manifold representation of the facts is marked by
just judgment, many-sidedness, penetrative imagination
of human nature, sanity of intellect, natural and healthy
passion; and its various phases are embodied in speech
which in every case arises, as it were inevitably, out of the
situation, and is fitted to the characters that speak it.
This is genius at work—the genius of a great dramatist.

And now, it is well to touch, briefly, the more poetic
or rhetorical passages in the play.   But, first, we are sometimes jarred by lines and phrases out of tune with the
situation, and out of tune with Shakespeare.   This is
owing to the playwrights who, seeing that money was to
be made out of a play which glorified England, pirated
and bedevilled it, adding to Shakespeare and subtracting;
decking him out with inserted plumes to please an excited
audience fond of war, and of the coarse thought which so
often attends on war.

Then again, in such a play, made up of a series of tableaux, pictorial poetry will be prominent; and the pictures
are extraordinarily vivid.   Their sharpness of drawing is
as great as their colouring.   The picture of the French
nobles in wild excitement before the battle, of the Dauphin
crying ' Ha, ha!' as he scents the victory, of his horse, the
Pegasus who bounds from the earth—

When I bestride him, I soar, I am a hawk ; he trots the air ; the
earth sings when he touches it ; the basest horn of his hoof is more
musical than the pipe of Hermes—

could scarcely be bettered.

The noble picture of York and Suffolk dying on the
field I have already mentioned. The picture in Chorus IV.
of the army before the battle, in the grey of the early
morning, and of Henry passing through their camp to
hearten them with the comfort of his courage and hope,
is alive in every word with the power of English poetry.
The second Chorus paints with imaginative exultation
England, that little body with a mighty heart, preparing
for war—

> Now all the youth of England are on fire,
> And silken dalliance in the wardrobe lies ;
> Now thrive the armourers, and honour's thought
> Reigns solely in the breast of every man.

The third Chorus is a masterpiece of descriptive poetry,
full of surprises of the imagination, of splendid, happy
words, and of resplendent pictures—

> Suppose that you have seen
> The well-appointed king at Hampton pier
> Embark his royalty ; and his brave fleet
> With silken streamers the young Phœbus fanning :
> Play with your fancies, and in them behold
> Upon the hempen tackle ship-boys climbing ;
> Hear the shrill whistle which doth order give
> To sounds confused : behold the threaden sails,
> Borne with the invisible and creeping wind,
> Draw the huge bottoms through the furrow'd sea,
> Breasting the lofty surge. O, do but think
> You stand upon the rivage, and behold
> A city on th' inconstant billows dancing ;
> For so appears this fleet majestical,
> Holding due course to Harfleur. Follow, follow !

Nor is the Chorus to Act V. less to be studied for descriptive power. It is not so vivid as the others, but in it
at least is contained that concentrated line which strikes
out into form the quintessence of London, and is more
true now than it was then—

> But now behold,
> In the quick forge and working-house of thought,
> How London doth pour forth her citizens !

These are splendid rhetoric in poetry, and the subject demands and excuses high rhetoric. Yet, when we think of the opportunity the glory of the great battle afforded for gorgeous rhetoric, we wonder with what a great artist's reticence Shakespeare has measured his words, and chastened the exuberance he might have been justified in using.

Finally, I draw attention to one of those dignified, grave, half-philosophical, half-political pieces of thoughtful poetry of which this play and *Henry IV.* are full. Weighty with intellect, they are inflamed throughout by imagination. I have quoted some of these already. I quote this in conclusion, well known as it is, that I may leave a solemn music in our ears. He is describing an ordered commonwealth, and compares it to the commonwealth of the bees—

> Therefore doth Heaven divide
> The state of man in divers functions,
> Setting endeavour in continual motion ;
> To which is fixed, as an aim or butt,
> Obedience : for so work the honey bees,
> Creatures that by a rule in nature teach
> The act of order to a peopled kingdom.
> They have a king, and officers of sorts ;
> Where some, like magistrates, correct at home,
> Others, like merchants, venture trade abroad ;
> Others, like soldiers, armed in their stings,
> Make boot upon the summer's velvet buds,
> Which pillage they with merry march bring home
> To the tent-royal of their emperor ;
> Who, busied in his majesty, surveys
> The singing masons building roofs of gold,
> The civil citizens kneading up the honey,
> The poor mechanic porters crowding in
> Their heavy burdens at his narrow gate,
> The sad-eyed justice, with his surly hum,
> Deliv'ring o'er to executors pale
> The lazy yawning drone.

O wonderful poet! Every hive in the world is alive in that description—and every city of men.

X

Printed by T. and A. Constable, Printers to His Majesty
at the Edinburgh University Press

Lightning Source UK Ltd.
Milton Keynes UK
UKHW021143100119
335177UK00006B/470/P